American Medical Association

Physicians dedicated to the health of America

Law for Physicians

An Overview of Medical Legal Issues

Carl Horn III

Donald H. Caldwell, Jr

D. Christopher Osborn

Law for Physicians: An Overview of Medical Legal Issues

Additional copies of this book may be ordered from the American Medical Association.
For order information, call toll-free 800 621-8335.
Mention product number OP317899.

ISBN 1-57947-007-6

BP38:99-758:2.5M:11/99

I dedicate this book with warm admiration to Eben Alexander III, MD; Anthony L. Asher, MD; Susan Chang, MD; Geoffrey S. Chapman, MD; Howard A. Fine, MD; Helen Bachvarov Gelly, MD; John A. Gelly, MD; Jay S. Loeffler, MD; and Patrick Y. Wen, MD.
Don Caldwell

I dedicate this book to the two finest physicians I know, A. Douglas Calhoun, MD, and L. Scott McGinnis, MD, and most of all to my wife, Wendy, and daughter, Savannah, without whose support I could not have written this book.
Chris Osborn

About the Authors

Carl Horn III is Chief US Magistrate Judge for the Western District of North Carolina and is a former First Assistant US Attorney. Judge Horn is the author of a number of books and articles on federal practice, including the *Fourth Circuit Criminal Handbook* (The Michie Company, 1994, revised annually) and *Federal Civil Practice in the Fourth Circuit* (Lexis Law Publishing, 1997) and, as his judicial duties allow, is a frequent speaker at seminars around the country.

Donald H. Caldwell, Jr, is an attorney in the private practice of corporate law in Charlotte, North Carolina. He received his AB in 1981 from Davidson College and his JD in 1987 from Vanderbilt University Law School, where he was editor-in-chief of the *Vanderbilt Journal of Transnational Law*. He is the author of *US Health and Policy 1999: A Guide to the Current Literature* (AHA Press). He is a member of the American Health Lawyers Association and the North Carolina Society of Health Care Attorneys.

D. Christopher Osborn is an attorney in the private practice of corporate and commercial litigation, professional liability defense, and insurance law in Charlotte, North Carolina. He received his BA with Highest Distinction in 1992 from the University of North Carolina at Chapel Hill and his JD in 1995 from the University of Virginia School of Law, where he was a Hardy Cross Dillard Scholar and a member of the *Virginia Law Review*.

Preface

Law for Physicians: An Overview of Medical Legal Issues is a general reference guide covering some of the most common legal issues encountered by today's physicians. Although the authors' intention is to provide timely and accurate information on current legal issues, no book can provide legal advice or serve as a substitute for personal consultation with an experienced attorney. Nevertheless, becoming familiar with these critical issues at the nexus of law and medicine will hopefully forewarn—and forearm—the alert reader.

As you read this book, or use it as a reference on issues of particular interest, you should keep in mind that some of the covered topics are in a state of rapid change and development, for example, the law governing health care fraud and abuse and physicians' unions. Other areas—medical malpractice, employment discrimination law, and taxation, to name a few—are relatively stable.

If further information is needed on the topics covered in this book, or on any other legal issues, American Medical Association (AMA) members are encouraged to contact an AMA health law attorney through the Member Service Center, 800 262-3211. However, because AMA legal counsel offers only general guidance, not personal legal advice, physicians should consult their own attorneys before relying on any information provided by AMA attorneys or in this book. For referral to a qualified attorney, you may contact AMA Solutions by phone at 800 366-6968, via e-mail at AMASolutions @ama-assn.org, or through the Internet at http://www.AMASolutions.com.

Acknowledgments

This book could not have been published without the contributions and assistance of many people. We wish to specifically acknowledge the following individuals.

Thanks to Karla L. Kinderman, JD, LLM, Senior Attorney, Health Law Division, AMA, for her thorough review of the entire manuscript and her helpful suggestions.

For their insightful and productive reviews of portions of the manuscript in process, thanks to Bruce Blehart, JD, Senior Counsel, Health Law Division, AMA (fraud and abuse); Leslie Miller, JD, Division Counsel, Corporate Law Division, AMA (income and estate taxes); and Helen Jameson, JD, Division Counsel, Private Sector Advocacy Group, AMA (physicians' unions).

Thanks also to Lorri Zipperer of the National Patient Safety Foundation and Doni Haas, RN, risk management specialist and board member of the National Patient Safety Foundation, who contributed their specialized expertise to the development of chapter 4.

Finally, thanks to Marsha Mildred, Acquisitions Editor; Jean Roberts, Managing Editor; Robert Miller, Marketing Manager; and Dawn Goldammer, Production Designer, all of the AMA, who shepherded the project through development, marketing, and production.

Contents

Section 2   Medical malpractice: Claim prevention, protection, and
             litigation

Introduction

The changing landscape of law and medicine

Barely a generation ago, the law as it then existed affected practicing physicians in only the most obvious and limited of ways. Medical malpractice law was at that time largely an undeveloped branch of common law, untouched by state legislative action. Hospitals operated under the umbrella of charitable tort immunity and almost invariably functioned as tax-exempt institutions. To the extent that health insurance existed, it did so overwhelmingly in the form of indemnity coverage supplied by Blue Cross and Blue Shield. Competition among hospitals or physicians' groups was viewed as being incompatible with the charitable aims of health care. Managed care existed only in embryonic form and in only a few communities on the West Coast. When attorneys, physicians, and administrators encountered each other, it was more likely to be on a golf course than in a boardroom hammering out acquisitions, in a courthouse litigating multimillion-dollar malpractice allegations, or at a state certificate-of-need hearing haggling over equipment purchases.

To the bewilderment and rage of large numbers of American physicians today, that idyllic age now seems long gone, perhaps forever. With regularity, insurance companies and government agencies such as Medicare and Medicaid arrogantly decree cuts in reimbursement. Following a decade of medical training, a physician may find herself arguing with unskilled bureaucrats at HMOs over whether she can admit patients for treatment. Service coding is a minefield in which a mistake can result in civil fines or even criminal indictment.

What spawned the enormous changes that we have seen over the past thirty-five years in the legal environment of health care, ones that have put insurance companies in the driver's seat in formulating health policy, substantially reduced physicians' compensation, and undercut the medical profession's historically strong sense of autonomy?

The first factor is simply the steady enactment of legislation, mainly at the federal level, aimed at broadening access to health care. Beginning with the passage of the Medicare and Medicaid acts in the mid-1960s up to and including the Health Insurance Portability and Accountability Act of 1996 (HIPAA) and the Balanced Budget Act of 1997 (BBA), Congress has responded to the public desire to expand the availability of health care services, although its efforts have stopped well short of guaranteeing universal coverage.

Once the camel of government reimbursement stuck its nose into the health care tent, it became inevitable that the rest of the beast would follow. The consequence has been increased federal oversight of both government and private dollars spent on health care and the imposition of both civil and criminal penalties on physicians who fail to comply with burdensome and often murky federal regulations. Sometimes, as with the enactment of the Employee Retirement Income Security Act of 1974 (ERISA), preemptive federal legislation targeted at protecting certain employee benefits has had the perverse effect of ultimately making private health insurance less accessible, at least for those with chronic illnesses. Additionally, wide-ranging environmental statutes such as CERCLA, RCRA, TSCA, the Clean Water Act, and the Emergency Planning and Community Right-to-Know Act have directly affected physicians by imposing new liabilities on health care facilities.

A second set of changes in the legal context of health care occurred during this period at the state level. Although there are periodic as well as regional variations, the number of overall malpractice claims has increased steadily. The Harvard Medical Malpractice Study reported that in New York State the frequency of claims rose from 1.9 paid claims per hundred insured physi-cians in 1955 to 8.4 in 1985.[1] A similar rise in claims has been experienced in all areas of practice and in every region of the country.[2] From 1955 to 1985, the size of malpractice awards and settlements in New York State increased by 7,400 percent.[3] The average successful claim for treatment rendered in 1955 was $6,000. For treatment rendered in 1985, the average was $500,000.[4] Since these statistics reflect only payments made under primary insurance policies, the real figure for 1985 may be closer to $1 million.[5] These are astonishing figures, even discounting for the high levels of inflation during this period.

Concerned with significant increases in malpractice premiums for physicians, a large number of states enacted a wide array of changes in their malpractice laws.[6] California's legislature passed the comprehensive Medical Injury Compensation Reform Act in 1975.[7] Several states, including Georgia and North Carolina, have recently enacted statutes requiring that professional malpractice claims be accompanied by a sworn statement by an expert substantiating the claim by attesting that some act or omission alleged in the claim was a negligent act or omission.[8] Also at the state level, legislatures have enacted certificate-of-need statutes that for the first time limited the ability of medical care organizations to add new equipment or facilities. Further, the states have implemented a range of new regulatory approaches to Medicaid in an effort to lower costs.

Third, evolving judicial doctrine in a number of areas has altered the legal landscape of health care over the past several decades. Reasoning that hospitals increasingly resembled commercial enterprises and that they could easily purchase malpractice insurance, courts across the country during the 1960s and 1970s, for example, struck down the doctrine of charitable immunity. Physicians' groups likewise encountered increasing governmental antitrust and tax scrutiny in the 1980s and 1990s as they became more complex and dynamic organizations.

Underlying all of these new statutory, regulatory, and judicial changes over the last three decades has been the explosion of new medical knowledge and related technology. Fueled by heavy federal and private financing, researchers have developed vaccines against a wide range of maladies, devised innovative therapies for cancer that have reduced its mortality, and refined CT, MRI, and PET diagnostic radioscopy, among other achievements. These advances have, in conjunction with the aging of the general population, raised health care costs to unprecedented levels.

This book seeks to illuminate—in a way that is simple without being simplistic—some of the legal issues that especially affect physicians in their professional lives. We have spent many hours discussing with physicians the issues that are foremost in their minds. We hope that this work will both allay unwarranted concerns and, at the same time, cast light on potential legal pitfalls for the unwary.

1. Report of the Harvard Medical Practice Study to the State of New York, *Patients, Doctors and Lawyers: Medical Injury, Malpractice Litigation and Patient Compensation in New York* 1–4 (Cambridge, Mass, 1990).

2. *Id.*

3. *Id.*

4. *Id.*

5. *Id.*

6. Donald H. Caldwell, Jr, *U.S. Health Law and Policy 1999: A Guide to the Current*
Literature, (Chicago: American Hospital Press, 1999), chap. 12. *See generally* Scott Becker, *Health Care Law: A Practical Guide,* 2d ed. (New York: Matthew Bender, 1998) at chap. 10; David W. Louisell & Harold Williams, *Medical Malpractice* (New York: Matthew Bender, 1997); Jennifer Begel, "Maine Physician Practice Guidelines: Implications for Medical Malpractice Litigation," 47 Maine Law Review 68 (1995); US Congress, General Accounting Office, *Medical Malpractice: Maine's Use of Practice Guidelines to Reduce Costs,* GAO/HRD-94-8 (Washington, DC: US Government Printing Office, 1993).

7. California Medical Association, *The MICRA Manual* (San Francisco: CMA, 1996).

8. *See, eg,* Robert D. Brussack, "Georgia's Professional Malpractice Affidavit Requirement," 31 Georgia Law Review 1,031–91 (1997); NC Gen Stat § 1A-1, rule 9(j) (West 1999).

Section 1

Big brother is watching:

Issues of fraud and taxation

Chapter 1

Health care fraud and abuse:

Enhanced civil and criminal penalties place honest physicians and providers at genuine risk

No honest physician or health care provider is in favor of fraud or abuse. Thus, the initial response by medical providers to stepped-up federal enforcement in this area may be approval ("I hope they catch all the abusers giving our profession a bad name") or indifference ("Since I don't lie or cheat, these new laws don't affect me").

Assuming a physician or provider is honest and conscientious—as, indeed, most health care providers are—there is some validity in either response. It is good to target the exceptional physician or provider who has chosen the low road, falsifying government forms, providing unnecessary medical services, or otherwise "cheating" the system to line his own pockets. It is also true that the great majority of good and honest providers are not intended targets of the recent federal crusade against health care fraud and abuse.

It does not follow, however, that ignorance is bliss. Indifference is not a responsible option. Unfortunately, there will be good and honest health care providers,

some of whom made careless mistakes or placed undue trust in employees to check the details, who will be investigated. Many will pay substantial fines, not to mention attorney's fees and related expenses. Others will be excluded from federally funded programs. A lesser number will be criminally prosecuted and, if convicted, will serve mandatory terms in federal prison.

Robert J. Milligan, an attorney specializing in this area, has suggested that a balanced approach to this subject depends on the attitude of the health care provider being counseled. On the one hand, we should alert the indifferent.[1] What they do not know can certainly hurt them—badly.

On the other hand, we can responsibly and properly "reassure the terrified."[2] Although there are good and substantial reasons for concern, specific steps also can be taken to minimize the possibility that a particular provider will be sued or prosecuted.

This, then, is the balance we seek. The irrefutable reality of stepped-up federal enforcement is a fact of life that should be sufficient to alert the indifferent. For those at the other end of the spectrum—the terrified—developing and implementing a comprehensive "compliance plan" should provide at least some reassurance. For those of you in between, it is hoped that being forewarned will significantly reduce the risk that the government's "grim reaper" will ever come knocking on your door.

Some Sobering Statistics

Although health care fraud and abuse were against the law before Congress adopted the Health Insurance Portability and Accountability Act of 1996 (HIPAA), HIPAA changed federal enforcement in two fundamental ways. First, it created new criminal offenses and broad civil remedies while strengthening existing ones. Second, and perhaps more significantly, HIPAA was part of a larger political initiative in which health care fraud and abuse became a top law-enforcement priority.

The results of these changes were apparent in the first *Annual Report of the Attorney General and the Secretary of Health and Human Services.* The attorney general heads the US Department of Justice, and the Department of Health and Human Services (HHS) administers Medicare and Medicaid. According to this report, published in January 1998, during the first full year the new laws were in effect (1997):

- Federal prosecutors opened a record number of civil investigations (4,010), a 61 percent increase over the preceding year.

- More than 2,700 individuals and organizations were excluded from federally funded health care programs in 1997, a 93 percent increase.

- There were a record 363 criminal fraud convictions, a 22 percent increase.

- The federal government collected a record $1.1 billion in criminal fines, civil penalties, and settlements from physicians and other health care providers—an amount expected to increase each year through at least 2005.

The Political Climate

According to US Department of Commerce statistics, annual health care expenditures have exceeded $1 trillion every year since 1994. With the federal government paying approximately 44 percent of all health care dollars, it is not surprising that legislators looking for ways to balance the budget would turn their attention to fraud and abuse in this very expensive area.

This is particularly true in light of the high fraud rate believed to exist in government-funded health care programs. In fiscal year 1996, for example, the Office of the Inspector General (OIG) of the US Department of Health and Human Services estimated $23.2 billion in fraud in what was then a $168.6 billion Medicare program—a fraud rate of almost 14 percent. With fraud rates in private health care estimated in the range of 3 percent to 5 percent, ever more expensive programs like Medicare and Medicaid become particularly attractive targets for budget-balancing politicians and regulators.

This was the political climate in 1996, the year Congress dramatically increased the arsenal available to detect and deter health care fraud and abuse. The results were the Health Insurance Portability and Accountability Act of 1996, then popularly known as the Kennedy-Kassebaum Act; new civil and criminal laws and enhanced penalties under existing ones; extension of the already far-reaching "money-laundering" and forfeiture statutes to cover health care fraud; authorization of an additional $548 million in multiyear funding for health care enforcement; and a broad initiative by the US Department of Justice to field and train federal prosecutors to specialize in health care enforcement in every district in the country.

Pamela H. Bucy, a former federal prosecutor and now Bainbridge Professor of Law at the University of Alabama, accurately summarizes the extent to which health care fraud and abuse have become a national law-enforcement priority:

The Department of Justice has designated health care fraud as its Number Two priority, [second only to] violent crime. The Attorney General has designated a special counsel to direct health care fraud efforts by all Department of Justice units. Health care fraud initiatives have been announced by the Antitrust Division, the Civil Division, the Criminal Division, the Tax Division, the Federal Trade Commission, and Inspectors General of a variety of agencies, including Railroad Retirement, Personnel Management, Amtrak, Defense, Labor, and the Food and Drug Administration. Nearly one third of the newly appointed United States Attorneys in the ninety-four Districts have announced health care fraud as a personal priority.[3]

Now that we have seen federal health care enforcement efforts for two full years following adoption of HIPAA, this much can be predicted with certainty: As substantial new resources continue to be allocated, the amount of fines and civil settlements, the number of physicians and providers excluded from federally funded programs, and the number of criminal prosecutions will all increase. Let me say it again: this much is certain.

What remains an open question is how the medical and legal communities will respond to this dramatically altered environment. Part of that response may ultimately include a political agenda—advocating, for example, certain "safe harbors" in the billing area, tighter definition of abuse, and reimbursement of physicians or providers wrongly accused of fraud or abuse. For now, however, the legal and political climate clearly runs in the other direction.

The current climate is reflected, for example, in the January 1998 annual report (of the US attorney general and secretary of HHS), which exuberantly hails "the most successful year ever in the nation's efforts to detect fraud and abuse against federal health care programs"; calls for "even greater participation in identifying and reporting fraudulent and abusive practices"; and solemnly announces "an attitude of *zero-tolerance* for fraud throughout our health care system."

The continuing results of federal enforcement marked by zero-tolerance were apparent a year later in the *Annual Report of the Departments of Health and Human Services and Justice,* issued in February 1999 and covering 1998 enforcement. According to the second annual report of the Attorney General and the Secretary of HHS:

• There was an additional 14 percent increase in criminal case filings in 1998, charging substantially more individual physicians with felony offenses than in any year in American history.

• A record 3,021 individuals and entities were excluded from federally funded health care programs, an 11 percent increase over the second highest year ever (which was 1997).

• There were another $480 million in judgments, settlements, and "administrative impositions" in health care fraud cases and proceedings—in addition to collection of judgments and settlements entered in previous years.

Clearly, as the report put it, "The detection and eradication of health care fraud and abuse [remains] a top priority of federal law enforcement." Whether this army of zealous investigators, regulators, and prosecutors can tell the difference between fraud and abuse—the proper object of their ire—and the legitimate practices of honest physicians and providers remains very much an open question.

Competent Representation

The most basic problem with the recent flurry of health care regulation is the increasingly broad definitions of fraud and abuse. Although these concepts may at first seem straightforward and even self-explanatory, Professor Bucy is correct that legislators and regulators intend to cover "a vast range of improper billing practices" and an undefined number of "acts inconsistent with acceptable business practices."[4] Of course, the precise definition of what is or is not fraud or abuse in this broad context will necessarily be left to attorneys and the courts—a prospect that leaves many health care providers distinctly uncomfortable.

Another reason health care fraud and abuse has become a complex, even befuddling, subject is the growing diversity of the legal arsenal available to investigators and prosecutors. Old laws and regulations and a host of new ones exist. There are civil and administrative rules, regulations, and remedies—some of which feel much like punishment to those on the receiving end—and a

growing number of criminal statutes. Further, criminal statutes carrying mandatory terms of imprisonment under inflexible sentencing guidelines are increasingly used to force civil settlement.

"Let's fight them in court" is a tough and expensive decision when the proceedings are entirely civil. When the calculation of downside risk includes the possibility of criminal indictment and prison, many find a way to pay the high dollars demanded in exchange for a global settlement.

Competent representation of a physician or health care provider in today's climate demands an understanding of both civil and administrative proceedings and the fine points of the criminal law. Not many attorneys are fully competent across this broad spectrum, so separate counsel will often be required to handle the civil and criminal aspects of a particular problem or investigation. Although this should not surprise medical professionals, for whom specialization has long been a reality, many still assume that "a lawyer is a lawyer is a lawyer" and may balk at having to hire separate counsel to handle what they perceive to be a single problem.

The bottom line here, however, is that competent representation of physicians and other health care providers requires attorneys, accountants, and perhaps other advisers who collectively *(a)* understand the civil and administrative laws and regulations governing health care; *(b)* understand how the complex health care delivery and reimbursement systems work, including the mountain of government forms and the complex accounting systems they employ; and *(c)* understand the criminal implications of a wide range of acts, omissions, and statements in general, and in health care in particular.

Criminal Statutes

[H]istorically health care fraud has been prosecuted under a variety of statutory offenses. Sixty-three percent of criminal prosecutions of health care providers for fraud [were] pursued in federal courts as violations of 30 different statutes. Thirty-seven percent of the reported prosecutions [were] pursued in state courts as violations of 20 different types of statutes.[5]

Although a larger number of statutes have been employed historically, the majority of federal prosecutions for health care offenses during the decade immediately preceding 1996 were under six statutes:

- 18 USC § 287 ("False, fictitious or fraudulent claims");

- 18 USC § 1001 (false statements);

- 18 USC § 1341 (mail fraud);

- 18 USC § 1343 (wire fraud);

- 42 USC § 1320a-7b(a)(1)(Medicare and Medicaid fraud); and

- 21 USC § 801 *et seq* (controlled substances offenses).

The Health Insurance Portability and Accountability Act of 1996 created four new criminal offenses, all aimed at health care fraud: (1) health care fraud; (2) theft or embezzlement in connection with health care; (3) false statements relating to health care matters; and (4) obstruction of criminal investigations of health care offenses. Congress also amended existing money-laundering and forfeiture statutes, making certain of a defendant's assets subject to forfeiture upon conviction under the new statutes.

Two definitions are key to understanding the stunning breadth of the new offenses created by HIPAA: "federal health care offense" and "health care benefit program." A federal health care offense is defined as:

a violation of or a criminal conspiracy to violate (1) section 669, 1035, 1347, or 1518 of [Title 18, United States Code]; [or] (2) section 287, 371, 664, 666, 1001, 1027, 1341, 1343, or 1954 of [Title 18, United States Code], if the violation or conspiracy relates to a health care benefit program.[6]

A "health care benefit program" is defined as:

any public or private plan or contract, affecting commerce, under which any medical benefit, item, or service is provided to any individual, and includes any individual or entity who is providing a medical benefit, item or service for which payment may be made under the plan or contract.[7]

Note that the definition of health care benefit program explicitly includes private as well as public health care plans, limited only by some "effect on commerce." Since virtually every health care plan affects commerce, the inclusion of these two words— *or private*—radically increases the scope of the new offenses over most of their federal and state predecessors, which typically governed only fraud involving public programs. Keep this broad scope in mind while reflecting on the statutory language of each of these new offenses.

Health Care Fraud (18 USC § 1347)

Perhaps the most significant of the new crimes created in HIPAA, Section 1347 provides:

Whoever knowingly and willfully executes, or attempts to execute, a scheme or artifice—

(1) to defraud any health care benefit program; or

(2) to obtain, by means of false or fraudulent pretenses, representations, or promises, any of the money or property owned by, or under the custody or control of, any health care benefit program, in connection with the delivery or payment of or payment for health care benefits, items, or services, shall be fined under this title [up to $250,000 per offense] or imprisoned not more than 10 years, or both. . . .

Again, the most significant feature of this new offense is its inclusion of private as well as public health care benefit programs. This means that the main limits on the potential reach of this statute are in the exercise of prosecutorial discretion in each federal district and in any constitutional limits that courts may impose under the commerce clause of the US Constitution.

Second, although it tracks earlier mail and wire fraud statutes, the Health Care Fraud statute doubles the maximum term of imprisonment under the earlier statutes from five to ten years. These more severe penalties have been incorporated into sentencing guidelines calculations. Boiled down, this means there will be mandatory terms of imprisonment for most of those convicted of health care fraud.

The third noteworthy point—and perhaps the one most likely to catch civil practitioners off guard—is that proof of the criminal violation does *not* require proof of any injury to the victim. Indeed, the victim need not even know of the fraud (or attempted fraud) as long as the *intended victim* falls within the broad definition of a health care benefit program.

Theft or Embezzlement in Connection with Health Care (18 USC § 669)

Section 669(a), the second criminal offense created by HIPAA, provides:

Whoever knowingly and willfully embezzles, steals, or otherwise without authority converts to the use of any person other than the rightful owner, or intentionally misapplies any of the moneys, funds, securities, premiums, credits, property, or other assets of a health care benefit program, shall be fined under this title or imprisoned not more than 10 years, or both; if the value of such property does not exceed the sum of $100 the defendant shall be fined under this title or imprisoned not more than one year, or both.

Again, this offense covers not only government-funded programs but also any private health care benefit program. Thus, the breadth of this statute in actual application will initially be determined by thousands of decisions of federal prosecutors. Eventually, these decisions may be limited somewhat by the courts. Given the broad commerce clause jurisprudence, it is unlikely that more than modest limits will ever be judicially imposed.

Note, too, that this statute includes a misdemeanor provision (if the amount of money involved is less than $100). Since most prosecutors would decline to prosecute any case involving less than $100, the most likely application of this provision is in plea negotiations. In other words, look in the future for global settlements and plea bargains around misdemeanor pleas and payment of substantial fines—a result that will allow the government to report a criminal conviction and collect substantial financial penalties but will allow a health care provider to avoid likely imprisonment and the stigma of a felony conviction.

False Statements Relating to Health Care Matters (18 USC § 1035)

Section 1035, the third crime created by HIPAA, provides:

Whoever, in any matter involving a health care benefit program, knowingly and willfully–

(1) falsifies, conceals, or covers up by any trick, scheme, or device a material fact; or

(2) makes any materially false, fictitious, or fraudulent statements or representations, or makes or uses any materially false writing or document knowing the same to contain any materially false, fictitious, or fraudulent statement or entry, in connection with the delivery of or payment for health care benefits, items, or services, shall be fined under this title or imprisoned not more than 5 years or both.

Note that this breathtakingly broad statute now makes it a federal crime to make any false statement—orally or in writing—on a material matter "in connection with the delivery of or payment for health care benefits, items, or services." Once again, in its rush to legislate, Congress has left any limits on the reach of this statute to the voluntary exercise of discretion by the prosecutor and/or whatever constitutional limits may be imposed by the courts.

Obstruction of Criminal Investigations of Health Care Offenses (18 USC § 1518)

Section 1518, the fourth offense created by HIPAA, provides:

(a) Whoever willfully prevents, obstructs, misleads, delays or attempts to prevent, obstruct, mislead, or delay the communication of information or records relating to a violation of a Federal health care offense to a criminal investigator shall be fined under this title and imprisoned for not more than 5 years, or both.

(b) As used in this section the term "criminal investigator" means any individual duly authorized by a department, agency, or armed force of the United States to conduct or engage in investigations for prosecutions for violations of health care offenses.

Modeled after existing obstruction-of-justice statutes, this new statute is arguably the broadest of them all. Note, for example, that to sustain an obstruction conviction, it is not necessary to prove that a crime has been committed by the health care provider under investigation. Rather, all that is necessary is that the defendant "delay[ed] or attempt[ed] to . . . delay the communication of information or records . . . to a criminal investigator." Therefore, an aggressive prosecutor might decide to charge the delay or attempted delay—a federal felony— even though no prosecution is warranted for the conduct initially under investigation.

Civil Remedies

Although there are other potential theories of liability, three main civil remedies are used in health care "fraud and abuse" today: (1) actions under the False Claims Act; (2) asset forfeiture proceedings; and

(3) exclusion from federal health care programs.

As has been noted, criminal charges are also increasingly threatened or actually brought in conjunction with civil proceedings. In fact, these criminal charges may be the catalyst for what only shows up in the statistics as a civil settlement.

The False Claims Act

The primary civil tool used to combat fraud against the government, including health care fraud, is the False Claims Act, 31 USC § 3729 *et seq* (FCA). It is a formidable weapon in the government's arsenal.

Initially adopted during the Civil War, the False Claims Act was amended and revised in 1986 in three significant ways. First, Congress made it clear that intent to defraud the government need not be proved. Rather, liability under the FCA only requires proof that the claim was false and an individual (or representative[s] of an organization) knew or should have known it was false. Liability based on what someone "should have known" is justified on the theory that one ought not to be allowed to engage in "willful blindness."

Second, in 1986 Congress dramatically increased the civil penalties under the False Claims Act, which are now $5,000 to $10,000 per false claim—in addition to treble damages. In health care fraud, which may involve hundreds or even thousands of smaller claims, this higher per-claim penalty can result in astronomical penalties. For example, the penalties for filing one hundred false claims would be $500,000 to $1 million—in addition to an amount three times actual damages suffered by the program or other "victim."

The third significant 1986 amendment was to the *qui tam* provisions, making it easier for a private citizen (known as a "relator") to bring a lawsuit under the False Claims Act. In a *qui tam* action, one or more private citizens file a complaint under seal. Instead of serving the complaint on the defendant, however, he serves it on the government. The government is then given an opportunity to investigate the allegations—often before the defendant discovers a lawsuit has been filed—and to decide whether to intervene in the case.

In the health care context, most *qui tam* actions are filed by employees, former employees, patients, or family members of patients. Those who litigate their claims successfully are entitled to substantial financial rewards, from 15 percent to 25 percent of any recovery if the government takes over the case, and up to 30 percent if the individual relator(s) successfully litigates the case without government assistance.

To reduce the risk that an employee will file a *qui tam* action under the FAC (or otherwise become a whistleblower), each health care provider should establish clear policies to receive and process employee concerns. Recognizing the increasing number of internal whistleblowers, Mark Pastin, president of the Council of Ethical Organizations, has suggested several strategies that each health care provider should consider.[8]

1.   Encourage, and never punish, internal reporting of any apparently unethical or illegal conduct. Based on a 1994 study, Pastin reports that "[e]mployees who felt they were punished for reporting a concern were much more likely to notify outside authorities."[9]

2.   Make it clear to all employees that unethical and illegal conduct will not be toler-

ated, and take active and visible steps to correct any improper conduct that is reported. More than written policies or lip service is necessary, however, to reduce the risk of an internal whistleblower. There must be a widely held perception that the company is sincerely interested in rooting out any violations brought to the attention of management.

3. Create, publicize, and properly staff a hotline for employees to air concerns and report apparent violations. Again, key to the success of a hotline is a broad-based perception that violations are taken seriously and promptly addressed. Assuming this is true, however, the rewards of a hotline are possibly the greatest of all. According to Pastin, "Companies with no internal reporting mechanism are *three times more likely* than similar-size companies with well-run hotlines to experience external whistleblowing in a given year."[10]

Asset Forfeiture

Another powerful tool in the government's civil arsenal is asset forfeiture. Traditionally used for "dirty" crimes like drug offenses and racketeering, more than one hundred state and federal statutes now allow forfeiture of *(a)* property used to facilitate covered crimes; *(b)* proceeds of covered crimes; and/or *(c)* property traceable to the proceeds of covered crimes.

When Congress adopted HIPAA in 1996 and extended the reach of the money-laundering statutes to cover health care fraud, it extended the reach of the civil forfeiture statutes as well. Pursuant to 18 USC § 982(a)(b), Congress also enacted authority to criminally forfeit gross proceeds—not just profits—of any health care fraud offense.

Civil practitioners and others encountering federal forfeiture laws for the first time are often surprised by their draconian flavor. Unlike most other legal proceedings, the government is initially required only to show probable cause, that is, that certain property was probably used to facilitate a covered crime or was probably purchased with the proceeds of such a crime. Further, this preliminary showing is made in documents filed with the court *ex parte,* that is, before the owner of the property has seen them and without giving the owner the right to respond to the allegations.

Once a federal judge (typically a magistrate judge, but sometimes a district judge) determines that the government has established probable cause, the burden of proof shifts to an owner opposing forfeiture. In other words, the government is entitled to keep the seized property unless an owner can prove that the government has its facts wrong.[11]

An owner of seized property, often accused of criminal wrongdoing in court documents filed in support of forfeiture, faces a classic "Hobson's choice." Unlike criminal proceedings—which may be ongoing or forthcoming at the time a forfeiture response is due—there is no presumption of innocence or the right to remain silent in defending against forfeiture of property. Indeed, if an owner asserts the right to remain silent or refuses to comply with the government's discovery requests, the claim is likely to be stricken and the property promptly forfeited.[12]

Owners of seized property who are also facing related criminal charges or who may face criminal charges in the future should ask the court to stay the forfeiture proceedings until after the related criminal proceedings are complete. Another alternative—not as satisfactory to the owner-defendant to be sure, but certainly better than losing both property and liberty—is to agree not to oppose the asset forfeiture in exchange for the government's agreement not to prosecute the related criminal charges.

Exclusion from Federal Health Care Programs

An excluded provider is ineligible to receive any payment under Medicare, Medicaid, or any other federally funded health care program. The latter includes exclusion from the Maternal and Child Health Block Grant Program and the Social Services Block Grant Program, both of which have health care components.

The history of exclusion as a civil remedy for health care fraud or abuse dates back to 1965, the year Medicare and Medicaid were created. Since that time, the power to exclude providers who fail to comply with the law or pertinent regulations has been steadily broadened. Professor Bucy traces the expansion of federal power to exclude providers from participation in government programs as follows:

The grounds for excluding providers were expanded in 1977 to require exclusion of practitioners "convicted of a criminal offense related to such individual's involvement in Medicare or Medicaid." In 1980, the grounds for exclusion were broadened further to include more health professionals such as administrators of health care facilities. In 1983, the Secretary of Health and Human Services delegated to the IG [Inspector General] the responsibility to detect, prosecute and punish fraudulent acts under Medicare and Medicaid. This gave the Inspector General authority to suspend and exclude

providers. . . . The exclusion remedy was expanded substantially in 1987 when the Medicare and Medicaid Patient and Program Protection Act (MMPPPA) was enacted. This Act mandated exclusion from Medicare and state health care programs of individuals who committed certain egregious acts, such as committing crimes of patient abuse or fraud. The MMPPPA also expanded grounds for exclusion.[13]

In HIPAA, adopted in 1996, Congress added additional mandatory grounds for exclusion, enhanced two existing permissive grounds for exclusion and added another, and created minimum periods of exclusion for seven of the fifteen permissive grounds. A year later, in the Balanced Budget Act of 1997, Congress again broadened the grounds for permanent exclusion, provided for a mandatory ten-year exclusion in certain circumstances, and expanded the exclusion remedy to cover certain entities controlled by family members of sanctioned individuals. The 1997 act also gave the Secretary of HHS greater authority to deny reinstatement of those who have been previously sanctioned or excluded.[14]

As indicated, exclusion falls in one of two categories, either mandatory or permissive. The secretary of HHS, through the inspector general, must exclude any provider who has committed any of the four grounds for mandatory exclusion. This mandatory exclusion may be permanent or for a period of up to ten years. As the name implies, there is no discretion in regard to a mandatory exclusion.

In contrast, the secretary of HHS is given broad discretion if a provider has engaged in any of the fifteen types of conduct for which permissive exclusion is allowed. The secretary's discretion includes whether to exclude at all and, if exclusion is ordered, its appropriate length.

The four grounds for mandatory exclusion are set out in 42 USC § 1320a-7(a) and implemented by regulations published in 42 CFR § 1001.101. They are:

1. conviction for a "criminal offense related to the delivery of an item or service under Medicare or a state health care program, including the performance of management or administrative services relating to the delivery of items or services under any such program";

2. conviction "under Federal or State law, of a criminal offense related to the neglect or abuse of a patient, in connection with the delivery of a health care item or service, including any offense that the [inspector general] concludes entailed, or resulted in, neglect or abuse of patients";

3. conviction "under Federal or State law, in connection with the delivery of a health care item or service or with respect to any act or omission in a health care program . . . operated by or financed in whole or part by any Federal, State or local government agency, of a criminal offense consisting of a felony relating to fraud, theft, embezzlement, breach of fiduciary responsibility, or other financial misconduct"; and

4. conviction "under Federal or State law, of a criminal offense consisting of a felony relating to the unlawful manufacture, distribution, prescription, or dispensing of a controlled substance."

Mandatory exclusions must be for at least five years and, if any of the aggravating factors set out in 42 CFR § 1001.102 are present, may be lengthened. Following the Balanced Budget Act of 1997, those who have been convicted of three crimes face permanent mandatory exclusion. Those who have been convicted of two health care offenses face a mandatory ten-year exclusion. *See* 42 USC § 1320a-7(b)–15(b).

There are two basic categories of permissive exclusions, derivative and nonderivative. Derivative grounds for permissive exclusion are those based on an action by a court, licensing board, or other official government agency. Because permissive exclusion in derivative cases is based on convictions or formal findings, no further findings by the secretary are necessary.[15]

In contrast, permissive exclusion based on nonderivative grounds requires the secretary to make a prima facie showing of improper behavior. Nonderivative grounds would include, for example, "submission of claims for excessive charges or unnecessary services, failure to furnish medically necessary services, engaging in fraud or kickbacks, and failure to disclose or supply information."[16]

On December 24, 1997, the inspector general published guidelines to be used in determining whether to impose permissive exclusion.[17] Although the guidelines are not binding, these guidelines bear close scrutiny by anyone facing even the possibility of permissive exclusion.

Finally, as of this writing there are fifteen grounds for permissive exclusion. In brief, they are:

1. certain prior convictions;

2. license revocation or suspension;

3. exclusion or suspension from a covered federal or state health care program;

4. filing excessive charges or supplying unnecessary or substandard services;

5. failure to provide medically necessary items and services;

6. false or improper claims;

7. fraud and kickbacks;

8. being an entity owned or controlled by a sanctioned individual;

9. failure to disclose or provide ownership information;

10. failure to grant immediate access to records;

11. failure to comply with a prescribed corrective action plan;

12. default on a health education loan or scholarship obligation;

13. violation of limitations on physician charges;

14. billing for services of assistant during cataract surgery; and

15. retaining ownership or leadership interest in a sanctioned entity.[18]

Developing an Effective Compliance Plan

Developing a comprehensive compliance plan is essential in today's regulatory environment for two basic reasons. First, a properly designed and implemented compliance plan will substantially reduce the risk of becoming a government target. Second, as pithily put by Gordon Apple, an attorney who specializes in health law, if a provider is investigated, a compliance plan "can make the difference between being seen as making an honest mistake and being labeled a crook."[19]

With these two goals in mind—avoiding investigation and liability altogether but, if investigated, minimizing penalties and other negative results—an effective compliance plan must include the following.

1. Experienced Professionals

Attorneys who understand health care law, including both civil and criminal specialists, should be involved at both the drafting and implementing phases. An accountant or financial officer who understands the financial documents, billing forms and records, and accounting procedures is also an essential participant. At least one physician or corporate compliance officer who has the ear of top management and understands the practical effects of any decisions on the day-to-day medical practice should also be on the professional compliance team.

2. A Comprehensive Compliance Manual

The first task of the professional compliance team is to prepare or assemble a comprehensive compliance manual—or to review and revise any existing compliance manual, policies, or procedures. Checklists, forms, and clear written procedures should be drafted (or reviewed), initially by the attorneys and subsequently by others on the compliance team, to implement the complex network of regulatory requirements. The good news here is that law firms specializing in health law have already done much of this work so that this part of the process is more fine-tuning than it is creation of policies and procedures from scratch.

3. A Compliance Officer with Real Authority

Providers who have tried to outsmart government regulators by putting in a compliance plan or chief compliance officer without real authority have learned the hard way that this can be seen as worse than no plan at all. In fact, it is often seen—with disastrous, punitive consequences—as what it may actually be: an effort to cover up or deceive. Rather, a compliance officer must be given real authority to investigate and an open line of communication to top management to report problems and recommend corresponding action. This authority and open line of communication should be clearly stated in the compliance officer's written job description and be true in fact throughout the organization.

4. An Ongoing Education/Training Component

All the good policies and procedures in the world will not help much if those handling the organization's day-to-day business are not aware of them. Therefore, an essential part of any compliance plan is the education and training of all affected personnel. Of course, the kind of training will be different for top management and data entry personnel. What is important is that individually tailored training and ongoing education be provided across the employee spectrum. Records of all training and educational efforts, including classes or sessions attended and any written materials given out, should be carefully maintained by the compliance officer.

5. Ratification by the Board

It is crucial that the board of directors (or other governing body) of the provider ratify the compliance plan—and any subsequent amendments or changes to the plan. As stated previously, the compliance officer should have regular and open communication with top management, as should the provider's attorneys and others on what has been called the compliance team. This is particularly true when the compliance manual or any significant changes to the manual

are adopted and when any significant or potential problems are identified.

6. Overall Responsibility for Compliance Vested in High-Level Personnel

Although already touched upon (in the emphasis on a compliance officer with real authority and the central role of the board of directors or other governing body), it bears repeating that the overall responsibility for compliance must be vested in high-level personnel. Indeed, it would be deadly to the intended goals—avoidance or mitigation of liability—to treat this whole subject as a minor annoyance and relegate its containment to lower-level or even mid-level personnel. This, too, is a lesson that certain providers have had to learn the hard way.

7. Internal Monitoring and Outside Audits

In addition to establishing correct policies and procedures, the compliance plan should prescribe regular internal monitoring and periodic outside audits to ensure that policies and procedures are being followed. Records of all monitoring and auditing, and documentation of any corrective actions prescribed and taken, should also be carefully maintained.

8. Established Channels to Report Apparent Violations

As noted under the section on the False Claims Act, providers with a hotline for reporting apparent violations experience a much lower incidence of employee whistleblowing. However, whether through a hotline or other means, it is crucial that a compliance plan include clearly established and well-publicized channels for employees to report suspected violations. Once these channels are established, it is equally important that no reporting employee is punished or otherwise left with the impression that the communication is unwelcome, and that clear and visible action is taken to correct any actual violations that are reported. Finally, whatever means of reporting is established, records of all calls or written reports and the totality of the provider's response should be carefully maintained by the compliance officer.

9. Disciplinary Policies and Actions

The compliance plan should include a detailed discipline policy, including an appeals procedure, for employees subsequently found in violation. Where individual factors or circumstances lead to variance from the prescribed discipline, the reasons for any variance should be clearly stated. A record of every disciplinary matter, including a statement of the facts and the actual discipline imposed, should be carefully maintained by the compliance officer.

10. Continuous Review and Revision

It would be nice if once the compliance manual and officer were in place, this whole compliance business could be placed on the back burner. Although there is a good deal more effort and expense in implementing new policies and procedures than in maintaining existing ones, effective compliance nevertheless requires continuous review and revision. New laws, cases, and regulations continue to come at a fever pace. Personnel turn over and new personnel (or existing employees taking on new assignments) must be trained. Top management must be regularly informed and consulted. Just as eternal vigilance is the price of liberty, continuous review and revision of the compliance plan are an unavoidable price of the right to provide health care with minimal government interference in today's regulatory climate.

Conclusion

The purpose of this chapter has been to inform physicians and other health care providers, and the professionals who represent them, of the genuine risks of civil or even criminal liability. We have sought to alert the indifferent and reassure the terrified, balancing tales of woe with practical steps to avoid or limit liability. Good and honest providers who take this practical counsel to heart will significantly reduce their chance of becoming government targets. Those who fail to take these practical steps will almost certainly encounter regulatory troubles—or worse—in the years to come.

1   Robert J. Milligan, "Risk Management for Physician Fraud and Abuse Liability: Internal Investigation and Voluntary Disclosure," 24-26 (for seminar sponsored by American Health Lawyers Association, April 24, 1998).

2   *Id.*

3   Bucy, Diesenhaus, & Imperato, *Health Care Fraud: Criminal, Civil and Administrative Law* 1-3 and 1-4 (Law Journals Seminars-Press, 1998).

4   *Id* at 1-2 and 1-3.

5   *Id* at 3.01.

6   Health Insurance Portability and Accountability Act, Pub L 104-91, § 241, *codified* in 18 USC § 24.

7   *Id.*

8   Mark Pastin, "New Study Sheds Light on Why Employees Become Whistleblowers, How Firms Can Reduce That Risk" (Bureau of National Affairs, 1996).

9   *Id.*

10 *Id.*

11 On this point, *see, eg,* 19 USC § 1615; *United States v Wollman,* 945 F2d 79 (4th Cir 1991); *United States v Thomas,* 913 F2d 1111 (4th Cir 1990); *United States v $95,945.18, 913* F2d 1106 (4th Cir 1990); and *United States v One Parcel at 7715 Betsy Bruce Lane,* 906 F2d 110 (4th Cir 1990).

12 *See, eg, United States v Rylander,* 460 US 752, 758-759 (1983); *United States v A Single Family Residence,* 803 F2d 625, 629, n4 (11th Cir 1986); and *United States v Little Al,* 712 F2d 133 (5th Cir 1983). *Accord Baxter v Palmigiano,* 425 US 308, 318 (1976)(adverse inference may be taken against party to civil case who remains silent in the face of adverse evidence); *United States v Thomas,* 913 F2d 1111, 1115 (4th Cir 1990)(same); and *In re Edmond,* 934 F2d 1304, 1308 (4th Cir 1991)(affidavit submitted in summary judgment disregarded since affiant had refused to be deposed).

13 Bucy, Diesenhaus, & Imperato, *supra* note 3, at 5.02.

14 *Id.*

15 *Id.*

16 *Id.*

17 62 Fed Reg 67392 (1997).

18 Bucy, Diesenhaus, & Imperato, supra note 3, at 5.02 (citing statutes, *Code of Federal Regulations* sections, and other authority).

19 Gordon J. Apple, "Tips for Developing an Effective Corporate Compliance Plan," *1998 Physicians & Surgeons Mid-Year Update* (St. Paul Medical Services, 1998). All references taken from St. Paul Medical Services' publications are reprinted with permission. ©1988 St. Paul Fire and Marine Insurance Co. All rights reserved.

Chapter 2

Income and estate taxes:

Tax-wise planning can substantially reduce tax liability

Taxation is another broad area in which law and regulation regularly touch the life of a physician. There are the better known taxes—state and federal income tax, capital gains tax, property tax, gift tax, and estate tax—and a host of lesser-known, specialized taxes. As one frustrated taxpayer quipped, "Death and taxes may be all that is certain—but at least you only have to die once!"

Calculating the various taxes, which used to be the simpler part, has grown steadily more complicated. The Internal Revenue Code has grown from around 400,000 words in 1954 to over 1.3 million words today. Regulations interpreting the code run about 6 million words—and compliance costs American citizens an estimated 3 billion hours and tens of billions of dollars—each year. The IRS now has more than 100,000 employees to check returns, impose penalties and interest, and otherwise ensure compliance.

Even in this era of growing government, however, tax-wise planning can sub-

stantially reduce the amount of taxes one is legally required to pay. This chapter will identify and briefly discuss a number of tax-saving steps and strategies, all perfectly legal and many often overlooked.

Of course, this brief overview is not intended as legal advice. Nor are the general suggestions in this chapter a substitute for the counsel of qualified experts (attorneys, accountants, or financial advisers), who are best equipped to decide whether a specific step or strategy is advisable in a particular case.

Federal Income Tax

The tax that comes up most notably each year, and the tax that regularly takes the biggest bite out of an individual's net available assets, is the federal income tax. While the amount of the tax is clearly excessive for higher-income taxpayers, and while the rules and regulations implementing the tax are indefensibly complicated, many taxpayers fail to take certain basic steps to reduce their federal income tax liability.

Put most simply, there are two fundamental ways to reduce federal income tax liability: (1) decreasing taxable income or (2) increasing allowable deductions. Either way, by decreasing what is considered taxable income or by increasing allowable deductions, taxpayers may reduce the federal income tax (and probably the state income tax) they are legally obligated to pay each year.

Decreasing Taxable Income

If a financial planner is asked for key tips on how to reduce income taxes, one suggestion is bound to be to maximize the annual contribution to your tax-deferred retirement plan. Higher-income taxpayers will usually have a 401(k) or Keogh plan, but whatever tax-deferred retirement plan (or plans) a physician may have, the contribution should be maximized each year.

Another basic way to decrease taxable income is to invest in appreciating—rather than income-producing—assets. For example, by purchasing real estate or stock that is appreciating in value but produces little or no annual income, the asset side of the balance sheet will grow with little or no income-tax consequences. In addition, when the appreciated property is sold, assuming it was owned for at least twelve months, the sale will be taxed at the much lower capital gains rate.

A look at the difference in tax rates is instructive. Since passage of the 1997 tax act, the top tax rate on capital gains has been 20 percent—compared to a top tax rate on ordinary income of 39.6 percent. In other words, those in the top marginal tax bracket cut their tax in half for every dollar shifted from ordinary income to capital

gains income. For tax years beginning after December 31, 2000, the picture is even brighter for assets owned over five years, with a top capital gains rate of 18 percent.

Before selling appreciated property and realizing a capital gain, however, consider whether a nontaxable like-kind exchange of property is possible. Most sophisticated real estate brokers can provide information regarding the necessary requirements for a tax-free exchange, which often involves three (or more) parties. Although the taxpayer will have to pay a capital-gains tax on cash or other "boot" received in the transaction, and there may be some tax under the complex depreciation recapture rules, like-kind exchanges of property remain an attractive and tax-wise alternative to consider.

If a man's home is his castle, as the saying goes, it is also often his most significant asset—and biggest tax shelter. This is particularly true following the 1997 tax act, which allows exclusion of up to $250,000 in capital gain on the sale of a principal residence ($500,000 for married persons filing a joint return). All one must show to exclude this significant gain from any tax at all is that the property was occupied as a principal residence for two of the preceding five years. Furthermore, unlike the former one-time exclusion for taxpayers at least fifty-five years old, there is no age limit under the new law, and the exclusion is available once every two years.

Physicians may want to consider reducing taxable income by giving income-producing assets to their children, depending on the children's ages and the physicians' personal philosophies. Each year an individual may give $10,000 ($20,000 per couple) to each child, tax-free, amounts to be indexed for inflation (in $1,000 increments) beginning in 1999. Obviously, it would not take too many years of maximum gifts to become a substantial sum with significant income-reducing potential for the giver.

If this strategy for reducing taxable income sounds appealing, be aware that there are limits on how much income a child under age fourteen can receive and still be taxed at the lower rates. For children under the age of fourteen, the first $700 in income is basically tax-free. The next $700 is taxed at 15 percent. But under what has been dubbed the "kiddie tax," annual income over $1,400 is taxed at the parents' tax rate. When a child reaches age fourteen, however, this limitation no longer applies.

Note that the issue here is not the amount of gifts to children (or grandchildren) but limits on the tax advantages on the income that these gifts produce. As previously stated, the estate tax is often a primary motive for lifetime giving, and whatever the income tax savings or consequences, gifts at or under the annual limits will escape estate taxes altogether.

A final strategy to reduce taxable income is an "old faithful" alternative: the purchase of tax-exempt bonds. The interest paid on most state and local bonds will be exempt from federal income tax. If the bonds are issued by the physician's state of residence or a municipality within that state, they may also be exempt from state income tax. Of course, considering the real value of a tax-exempt investment, a physician should compare the tax-exempt return to the taxable return less any taxes that she would have to pay on the latter amount.

Increasing Deductions

The other half of the tax-reducing equation involves increasing deductions. This section will identify and briefly discuss some of the more basic tax-saving ideas that fall into this broad category. Again, however, these general concepts are no substitute for the advice of one's personal legal and financial advisers, who should be consulted regularly.

Another highly effective—and often overlooked—way to increase income tax deductions is to convert nondeductible consumer interest into deductible mortgage or home equity interest. Of course, this is not to advocate unnecessary debt just to deduct the interest payments; indeed, excessive debt should be avoided as much as excessive taxes.

However, by paying off nondeductible consumer debt (such as a car loan, for example) with money borrowed from a deductible source (such as a mortgage or home equity loan), one can almost always improve the bottom line. The same is true when a physician uses money secured by a mortgage or from a home equity line of credit to make a purchase in the first place.

Under current tax law, an individual may claim two "qualified residences," a principal residence and a secondary residence. Surprisingly, this is one area in which the tax code remains fairly friendly—for example, including in the definition of qualified residences not only single family homes but also condominiums, cooperatives, timeshare arrangements, and even certain recreational vehicles and boats.

Assuming a property is a qualified residence, interest on mortgages up to $1 million for couples filing jointly ($500,000 if filing singly) and on home-equity loans up to $100,000 ($50,000 if filing singly) is fully deductible. One caveat: For the interest on a home-equity loan to be deductible, the combined balances of the mortgage(s) and home-equity loan must not exceed the current market value of the property.

Those who own more than two homes are limited to deducting interest on their principal residence and one secondary residence, although different secondary residences can be used in different years. Take care, however, not to run afoul of the personal or family occupancy rules for any vacation or secondary home that is rented. This rule requires that, for a house to qualify as a secondary residence for tax purposes, the owner or a member of his family must occupy the property for fourteen days or 10 percent of the total number of days it is rented (whichever is greater).

The income-reducing benefits of appreciating property, including real estate, have been noted. In addition, if the appreciating property produces rental income, sizable deductions may also be allowed.

Generally speaking, any expense incurred to rent, maintain, or repair rental property is deductible. These expenses would include noncapitalized acquisition costs, advertising, maintenance and repairs, utilities, supplies, insurance, commissions, professional fees, transportation and travel expenses, taxes, and interest, among others. Perhaps most significantly, a deduction is also allowed for depreciation based on the initial cost of the property (less the value of land) plus any capital improvements—even though the property is actually increasing in value.

This combination of income-reducing and deduction-increasing benefits has led some to describe rental property as the last remaining tax shelter. There is a lot of truth in this observation. Consider, for example, related rules allowing tax-free receipt of up to fourteen days rental income and rules allowing partial deductions where rental property is used by the owner (or immediate family) more than a prescribed maximum amount. In each instance, taxing authorities appear to have carved out rental property as a taxpayer-friendly exception to their general passion for tax increases and "loophole" closing.

Another strategy to increase deductions requires a more creative than usual look at the subject of charitable giving. Many are surprised to learn that, in addition to the personal benefits inherent in being a charitable person, the tax benefits are not half bad either. Indeed, in many instances, the deductions legally available for donated property are considerably more beneficial to the taxpayer than the property itself.

Those donating personal property should have a copy of IRS Publication 561, *Determining the Value of Donated Property,* which includes value ranges for many commonly donated clothing, household, and furniture items. Since most affluent Americans (especially families with growing children) have far more "things" than they really need or even want, regular donations of personal items to Salvation Army, Goodwill, and other charitable organizations can produce sizable deductions each year.

The law also allows a deduction for any out-of-pocket expenses incurred on behalf of a tax-exempt organization. For car expenses, an alternative deduction of fourteen cents a mile is allowed. How many taxpayers (or their spouses) routinely take this deduction when they help with a school function, transport an athletic team, or otherwise incur expense on behalf of a charitable organization? Again, with regular and careful record-keeping, the numbers add up and the tax bill goes down.

Anyone contemplating a larger gift to a charitable organization should consider giving appreciated stock (or other appreciated property). This is what one expert calls tax-wise giving because it avoids all capital gains tax and lowers the real out-of-pocket cost of the gift.

For example, consider a gift of $10,000 in appreciated stock that was purchased some years ago for $4,000. If the owner sold the stock, he would pay a 20 percent capital gains tax on the $6,000 gain ($1,200) and would therefore have $8,800 left after-tax. Assuming the taxpayer is in the top marginal tax bracket (and a state tax bracket of 7 percent), a $10,000 tax deduction will save about $4,660 in taxes. Therefore, by giving the appreciated stock, one is able to give the designated charitable organization $10,000 for a real out-of-pocket cost of only $4,140 ($8,800 that could have been kept after taxes less the $4,660 in tax savings). Put most simply, the more the property has increased in value, the less it will really cost to give it away.

Those who have a close relationship with a school or other nonprofit organization may want to consider a charitable remainder trust. A charitable remainder trust is an irrevocable gift to a tax-exempt organization of the right to receive an individual's cash or other property in the future, reserving the right to receive income for a period of years or even for life. The annual income that the donor is to receive can be stated either as a percentage of the value of the property (called a "unitrust") or as a specific amount (called an "annuity trust"). Once a charitable remainder trust is signed and funded, the donor receives a current income-tax deduction based on the present value of the charitable organization's right to receive the future gift.

A final deduction-increasing—and therefore tax-decreasing—strategy involves prepayment, toward the end of each year, of as many of next year's deductible expenses as possible. Assuming the financial ability, each taxpayer should consult an accountant (or whoever prepares the tax returns) around September or October of each year to be on the lookout for deductible expenses likely to be incurred next year that can be legitimately paid this year. These expenses might include, for example, professional fees, investment expenses, expenses related to rental property, or charitable pledges, just to name a few. When implementing this simple strategy, prepayment of any deductible expense will have the same beneficial effect on the bottom line.

Establishing Domicile

Although the average physician cannot pick up and move to another state just to reduce taxes, there are those who can—especially when approaching or past retirement. For those in a position to consider it, a change in domicile from a high-income-tax state (such as New York or Massachusetts) to a low- or no-income-tax state (such as Texas or Florida) is another way to yield substantial tax savings.

If a physician decides to establish domicile in a lower-tax state, certain steps must be taken to withstand any future challenge. For example, in the new state, the physician should register and license cars; register to vote and actually vote; obtain a driver's license; file any required state or local tax returns; open bank accounts; change addresses with insurance companies and brokerage firms and, where practical, establish relationships with companies or firms located in the new state; execute a new will; and, if the new state has a form for doing so (as Florida does, for example), file a declaration of domicile.

Conversely, the physician should cancel any previous car registrations and license tags, voter registration, and driver's license; inform any banks, insurance companies, brokerage firms, or other companies with which there is a continuing business relationship of the new, permanent address in the new domicile; and, if possible, spend a majority of time in the new state.

Finally, although one's change in domicile may never be challenged, a separate file should be maintained indefinitely with copies of all relevant documents. This file should include personal records of what dates the physician was living in each location, together with any other information helpful to prove relocation of the primary residence, or domicile, to the new state as of a particular date.

Estate Planning

In 1789, one year before his death, Benjamin Franklin penned his often-quoted aphorism about the certainty of death and taxes. In a generally optimistic letter to Jean-Baptiste Leroy, Franklin wrote, "Our new Constitution is now established, and has an appearance that promises permanency; but in this world nothing can be said to be certain, except death and taxes."

In the federal estate tax—the government's last chance to take a share of a person's assets before they pass to his or her heirs—there is the convergence of these two certainties. Yet another certainty is that even the most basic estate planning can save one's heirs a tremendous amount of money. Indeed, if income-tax planning can save thousands, estate planning can save a substantial estate hundreds of thousands of dollars in entirely unnecessary death taxes.

In contrast to the many angles and nuances involved in income-tax planning—and this chapter has explored only some of the most basic ones—estate planning is relatively simple. An effective estate plan makes maximum use of two major exemptions, (1) an exemption from federal estate tax of the first $650,000 in assets, an amount that increases incrementally until it reaches $1 million in 2006; and (2) an exemption of any property passing to a surviving spouse (called the "marital deduction").

Because the estate tax is very high—beginning at 37 percent of the first taxable dollar and rising to a confiscatory 60 percent—it is important to make full use of these two exemptions. In the case of a traditional family (husband, wife, and children), this is usually accomplished by a combination of lifetime gifts and qualified trusts established no later than the death of the first parent.

The basic concept can perhaps be best illustrated by a hypothetical example, a physician with several children and an estate valued at $2 million. Although $2 million may sound like a higher-than-average estate, with the escalating value of real estate, the inclusion of life insurance proceeds, retirement savings, and other investments, it is probably pretty close to an average physician's estate. In fact, it may well be lower than the average physician's estate in 2006, when the exemption will reach $1 million.

For purposes of the illustration, we will be traditional and assume the physician is the husband, that he will live until at least 2006, and that he will die before his wife. Assume further that the couple has three children, none of whom has been sufficiently disappointing to be disinherited, and all of whom have children of their own.

Left to their uncounseled preferences, our hypothetical couple might reasonably arrange for the survivor to inherit and own all their assets outright until his or her death, then pass what is left along to the children and grandchildren. They would probably jointly own their home and perhaps other real estate, bank accounts, or securities. In any event, their intention would be for most of their assets to pass first to their survivor and then, upon the survivor's death, to their children and grandchildren.

Although there is nothing inherently unreasonable or wrong with this uncounseled estate "plan," wouldn't the couple be surprised to learn that it will cost their heirs more than $400,000 in entirely unnecessary death taxes?

By leaving everything outright to his wife, the hypothetical physician failed to make use of any of the $1 million exemption at his death. Instead, he overloaded his wife's estate (beyond her $1 million exemption), thus creating a huge, entirely avoidable, tax liability.

The most basic estate planning tool—a "family trust," providing for the surviving wife during her life, with any assets remaining going to the children and/or grandchildren upon her death—would have avoided this huge tax liability altogether. Although there are certain limitations on the use by the surviving spouse of the assets in a family trust, these limitations are generally not burdensome. In fact, if the assets are really needed, they remain almost as available to the surviving spouse as if they had been left to her outright.

If a physician does create a trust, he must be certain to title any property that he intends to place in the trust in the trustee's name. In the case of an account or insurance policy, this can usually be accom-plished by signing a simple form. To transfer real property, one must execute and record a deed. In any event, a physician should make a list of any assets he wishes to place in the trust and use it as a checklist to ensure each item has been properly titled in the trustee's name.

Finally, as noted in the discussion of income-tax planning, one can give as many individuals as one chooses $10,000 per year ($20,000 if married and one's spouse agrees) with no tax consequences at all. Therefore, if lifetime gifts to family members (or others) are consistent with one's personal philosophy and goals, this is another strategic way to reduce or even eliminate estate taxes.

Conclusion

Taxes in this country may be too high, and they are definitely too complicated. However, even in this era of growing government and excessive complexity, there remain some basic steps and strategies that can substantially reduce the tax man's claim on our income and assets. There is no time better than the present to begin a lifetime of tax-wise planning. After all, every tax dollar saved is another dollar that can be saved or spent, given to charity, or one day passed along undiminished to loved ones.

Section 2

Medical malpractice

Claim prevention, protection, and litigation

Chapter 3

Claim prevention:

Heading off malpractice claims before they happen

A simple way to open a discussion of what physicians can do to avoid medical malpractice claims would be to say, "Practice good medicine." Unfortunately, such a statement is woefully incomplete advice. Practicing good medicine—a goal to which all reasonable physicians aspire—is simply insufficient to avoid being hit with a medical malpractice claim. First, everyone makes mistakes. None of us is on top of the game 100 percent of the time. Further, since medicine has become more multidisciplinary, and the types and number of levels of care (primary care physician, specialist, physician's assistant, respiratory therapist, and so forth) have multiplied, a wise physician has to be concerned not only with his own mistakes but also about the potential errors of many others ostensibly under his supervision.

Second, even when no mistakes are made, medicine is a discipline often fraught with tough choices—judgment calls that must be made within seconds. Since physicians must often make quick calls choosing from among imperfect options, patients must make emotional decisions while con-

fronted with confusing medical terminology and the stress of illness or infirmity; research is continually producing challenges to previously accepted ways of treatment; and the susceptibility to "Monday morning quarter-backing" is unusually high in the medical profession. When the results are bad and emotions are running high, second guessing of medical judgments is, unfortunately, not always an exercise in pure rational thought.

Third, even when there are no physician or staff errors and the calls are fairly routine, the practice of even the best medicine sometimes yields bad results. Physicians performing medical or surgical procedures may run into unforeseen complications, or they may simply be brought into the picture too late to help a dying patient. Since the stakes are often so high—physical injury, pain, emotional suffering, and even death—bad results are difficult to ignore or to soothe with kind words, more so than in other disciplines such as law or business. Combine a bad result with an angry and distrustful patient or family, a clever and persuasive plaintiff's attorney, or even a rival physician with a grudge, and you have a recipe for a malpractice claim—without having done anything wrong.

Fourth, and perhaps most important, there are obviously some intangible factors—aside from the pure quality of the medical care rendered—that determine whether and against whom claims are filed. Research has shown that although "one percent of hospital discharges are associated with evidence of medical malfeasance . . . less than two percent of patients who are injured through negligence ever file suit."[1] Meanwhile, "four to five times as many patients with injuries but without valid claims file suit as well."[2]

Thus, to meaningfully confront the specter of malpractice litigation—which will by most estimates engulf every physician at least once in his or her career—a physician must be prepared to deal with the inevitable mistakes that will be made or bad results that may occur, be adequately insured to protect against frivolous claims and to compensate legitimate ones, and be informed about how a claim will be litigated in the unfortunate circumstance that a suit is filed. Although not intended to be an exhaustive treatise on medical malpractice law, this chapter is structured to provide enough information to enable the prudent physician to know what he or she is up against, to ask the right questions when discussing insurance coverage or impending litigation, and, above all, to help physicians enter into practice with their eyes wide open—to both the pitfalls of malpractice liability and the potential for heading off claims through wise practice management.

To help prevent patient frustration from turning into burdensome litigation, it is crucial for all physicians—whether in solo practice or employed by a large hospital—to

have a meaningful, coherent plan for minimizing the risk of malpractice, dealing with dissatisfied patients, and navigating the emotionally turbulent river of the pre-claim process. The following suggestions, culled from medical malpractice cases and the professionals—attorneys and malpractice insurers—who handle them most frequently, are designed to help the busy practitioner ward off potential claims before they ripen into lawsuits. Although some of the advice contained herein may seem obvious or sound like yesterday's news, many are the physicians who would like to go back in time and apply these basic but important principles.

Developing a Good Bedside Manner

The importance of a genuinely caring, warm relationship with one's patient and the patient's family cannot be overstated. Although cultivating such a relationship is often hard work, and the desire to do it comes more naturally to some physicians than others, it is a vital skill for all physicians involved in patient care to develop. Genuine care and, dare it be said, healthy affection for one's patients will only increase the quality of the medical care offered. The more a physician emotionally cares for her patients, the more likely she is to gain their trust and obtain from them all of the information she needs to provide the best diagnosis and treatment. When a patient is seen as a whole person with real physical, emotional, and psychological or spiritual needs, as opposed to "the appendectomy in Room 221," the physician is more likely to pay adequate attention to those needs and can better provide the needed treatment.

Patients pick up on whether the physician is paying attention to them. "There is a growing body of empirical evidence that a patient's perception of the adequacy of the communication process is a major determinant of his/her satisfaction with the physician-patient relationship."[3] In 1977, a pair of researchers "found that patients' perceptions of their physicians' interpersonal conduct accounted for 41 percent of the variance in patient satisfaction with care and was far more important than availability of services or continuity of care."[4] Another study revealed a strong correlation between a new mother's satisfaction with her obstetrician and her perception that the physician had provided enough information about what she could expect during the pregnancy.[5] The development of a caring, healthy patient-physician relationship unquestionably facilitates the transmission of needed information between the two parties, which inevitably leads to better care and a better experience for both.

Increasing the emotional connection with patients not only enables the physician to practice better, more responsive, and ultimately more helpful medicine, it also erects an additional barrier to suit in questionable cases. If a physician has shown the patient and the patient's family genuine compassion, from the initial consult, through pre-op counseling, and in the midst of the surgical or medical procedure, it is going to be easier for the physician to communicate with that family when and if the physician is forced to deliver bad news. If family members perceive that the physician has been caring for their loved one—genuinely—from the outset, they will have a hard time later accusing the physician of being careless, blaming him for their loss, or filing suit over the bad result. Moreover, if they trust the physician and are confident that she has their loved one's best interest at

heart, they are more likely to hear, understand, and credit her explanation of what went wrong.

Conversely, if the physician has been gruff, uninterested, impatient, or blunt with his patient and family contact, it becomes much easier for the family to picture him callously or carelessly making a crucial mistake. When he comes to give the bad news, the family might question whether he cares more about their loss or the damage to his reputation. Any last-minute efforts to turn on the charm will fall on deaf ears and angry countenances. Any offers of condolences or remedial efforts will have no impact on the family's decision regarding what happens next.

Not surprisingly, a number of research studies on the incidence of malpractice claims bear out this commonsense principle. One study asked patients who had previously filed and resolved perinatal injury claims, "What exactly prompted you to initiate a claim?"[6] Only 25 percent of the respondents cited a need for money as their reason, while 20 percent indicated that "they needed information and decided that the courtroom was the only place where they could really find out what happened," and an equal number "believed that their physicians had hidden things from them."[7]

Similarly, a study conducted by a number of leading legal and medical scholars examined behaviors in patient claims and concluded that "problems with communication between physicians and patients were often crucial factors in precipitating individuals to file suit. Families perceived that physicians did not want to talk, would not listen, and in some cases attempted to mislead."[8] Many of the miscommunications reported to these researchers were a result of patients' "failure to understand medical terminology, . . . reluctance to raise their most deep-seated concerns or to seek clarification of points about which they were confused" or "difficulties they experienced in obtaining information about circumstances surrounding the adverse outcome before they filed their suits."[9] It is clear, therefore, that the physician's role in establishing good rapport and trust with the patient is absolutely crucial in providing quality care—and avoiding malpractice claims.

Practically speaking, how can a physician cultivate a more caring relationship with a patient? Much of the answer lies in the content and manner of communication. In one study published in the *Journal of the American Medical Association* in 1997, several researchers compared the communications skills of 124 physicians across a wide range of experience levels and specialties. By taping ten routine office visits of each of these physicians, the researchers were able to detect "significant differences in communication behaviors" between primary care physicians who had engendered two or more malpractice claims and those who had no claims experience. Specifically, the physicians with no previous claims were noted to have:

used more statements of orientation (educating patients about what to expect and the flow of a visit), laughed and used humor more, . . . tended to use more facilitation (soliciting patients' opinions, checking understanding, and encouraging patients to talk) [, and . . .] spent longer in routine visits.

The researchers identified a number of helpful orienting statements and facilitative comments, such as: "First I will examine you and then we will talk the problem over." "Go on, tell me more about that." "What do you think about taking these pills?" Although this study noted greater correlation between claims and the communication behaviors of primary care physicians as opposed to surgeons, the lesson for all health care providers should nevertheless be eminently clear. As the study concluded, physicians who use these behaviors in their office practice can very well "improve their communications skills and decrease their malpractice risk."[10]

A physician therefore must not risk engendering a claim—even for a bad result that was out of his control—by remaining distant, detached, and disconnected from the emotional reality of the patient's situation. A caring bedside manner will not prevent all claims, of course, but in dealing with unfortunate occurrences, honey works better than vinegar every time.

Obtaining Informed Consent

As all physicians know, it is extremely important to document one's explanation of the risks and benefits of any potential medical or surgical procedure or treatment and to obtain the patient's written authorization to proceed, with a full understanding of those risks. This concept—which is discussed in greater detail in chapter 6—is probably beaten into the heads of most medical students and is standard operating practice in most medical facilities, but it is also important enough to bear repetition. Obviously, in discussing any procedure or treatment with a patient (or his or her guardian), the physician's goal should be to explain all the risks in sufficient detail to permit the patient to make a well-educated decision. Again, this is a basic tenet of good medicine. Going through the various risks with a patient serves to refresh the physician's own recollection of what to watch for as the treatment unfolds, and it also shows to the patient that the physician knows what he is doing.

It is axiomatic that written informed consent should be obtained. Simply getting the patient to sign a standard form, however, is not the end of the matter. First, a practitioner should review all informed consent forms used in her practice and by any other co-treating physicians, as well as by the pertinent hospital or other medical facility. All such forms should be easily understood and written in clear, basic terms (and, conversely, not crowded with complex medical terminology or legalese). It is unwise for a physician simply to adopt or use whatever forms are provided by the hospital without giving them careful scrutiny for comprehensiveness and ease of understanding.

Second, the physician must make sure that the consent form is properly filled out (where there are blanks for explanations of the particular risks associated with a particular procedure) and, even more important, carefully and thoughtfully explained to the patient or guardian. If the physician cannot oversee this procedure directly, he or she should ensure that it is done only by high-level nursing staff with adequate medical knowledge and a proper bedside manner for explaining difficult concepts. The practitioner walking through the form must be patient and knowledgeable enough to answer any and all of the patient's questions or diligent and caring enough to find out the answers to the questions she cannot field. Every effort should be made to obtain not only the patient's signature also but his demonstration of a mental and emotional understanding of what he is signing. Besides the consent form, it is helpful to have any

notes reflecting the physician's or nurse's informed consent discussion and the patient's expression of understanding and willingness to proceed. Again, this decreases the chance of either an actual misunderstanding or a patient's later claiming not to have understood what he or she signed.

Few practitioners forget altogether to have some kind of documentation of informed consent in the patient's chart. Liability for failure to obtain informed consent may, however, arise when complications develop or new problems are discovered that call for a revision or cessation of the original plan to which the patient or guardian consented. For example, the Supreme Court of Wisconsin recently considered the claim of a woman who originally consented to a vaginal delivery of her third child, having had two previous deliveries by cesarean section. Partway into labor, the patient changed her mind and told her physician twice that she wanted to have a cesarean. The physician on each occasion continued to urge her to proceed with the vaginal delivery, in spite of the severe abdominal pain that she had begun to experience. Ultimately, the baby's heart rate dropped significantly, and the baby was delivered by an emergency cesarean section. It was determined that the patient's uterus had ruptured and deprived the baby of oxygen, leaving the baby a quadriplegic for life. The court ruled that under Wisconsin's informed consent statute, "a substantial change in circumstances, be it medical or legal, requires a new informed consent discussion." The court concluded that the physician's failure to have a new informed consent discussion after the patient withdrew her legal consent to a vaginal birth was a violation of his duty and was the proximate cause of the child's injuries.[11]

It is therefore crucial not only to obtain the patient's informed consent initially but also to give the patient or her family immediate updates about changing conditions. If possible, the physician should relay the information, explain its significance, and outline the options available from that point forward. Documentation of the patient's or family's consent to any new procedures is always helpful, where possible.

Finally, a physician might also want to consider preparing an informed consent statement to accompany a patient's refusal of recommended treatment. Such a document should include a thorough explanation of the physician's diagnosis, the patient's prognosis, and the treatment options (and their attendant risks and side effects) discussed and ultimately rejected. It will take some sensitive and skillful writing to word this document to make it effective yet not come across as if the physician is more concerned with getting sued than with the patient's welfare. The need for such a document should seldom arise, but in those rare cases, having a signed statement in the file may make the difference between an early dismissal and protracted litigation in a case of missed diagnosis.

In obtaining informed consent, the prudent physician will maintain a proper balance, providing full disclosure of risks and options without overwhelming the patient or talking over his or her head. The patient should come away from any discussion of informed consent with a genuine, but realistic, hope for the success of the procedure, an honest appraisal of the nature and extent of any anticipated side effects, and a continued sense of respect and trust for the physician. When the patient and the patient's family feel that the physician adequately informed them of the risks and cared about

their understanding of the explanations of them, they are both better able to handle the materialization of any of those factors and less likely to claim malfeasance on the physician's part. Should a claim nevertheless materialize, the more documentation of genuine understanding and assent the physician can show, the less likely that an unmeritorious claim will be filed or be successful.

Documentation

Of course, the need for good documentation extends beyond the mere documentation of informed consent. Obvious though it may seem, many a malpractice case is made or strengthened by poor documentation. For example, in one recent case of missed cancer diagnosis, a physician contended that he had recommended that the patient have a mammogram after detecting a "slight fibrous area" in her right breast. At trial, however, the physician was forced to concede that he had no documentation of his recommendation and the patient's refusal. A medical expert testified that "the standard of care requires that a general practitioner recommend a mammogram, and if the patient refuses, that he document the refusal and instruct the patient to return for a follow-up exam in one month." Although the jury initially found in favor of the physician, its verdict was overturned and a new trial was ordered, in part based on the factual issue of his failure to warn the patient that the fibrous area could be cancerous and to recommend follow-up testing or treatment.[12]

Although often tedious and time-consuming, proper documentation is important for several reasons. First, it is good medicine, and it serves the patient's best interests. Even the best memories fade, and patients' cases often run together, so it is always helpful for physicians to be able to look back at their notes when writing a prescription, developing a treatment plan, or preparing for a surgical procedure. Second, documentation enables a physician to run a more efficient practice. With proper documentation of a particular patient's history and chief complaints, one need not reinvent the wheel on each successive visit. That leaves more time to get to the heart of the matter during the limited time one may have with a patient on a given visit, and it also shows the patient that the physician cares enough to remember who she is and when and why he has seen her before. Anything that improves the quality of care and deepens the patient-physician relationship is good for the patient, good for the practice, and good protection against future claims.

But documentation becomes absolutely crucial when and if claims do materialize. Liability may often hinge on who said what to whom, and at what point in the treatment process. Did the patient forget to tell the physician that she was nine weeks pregnant—or did she tell the physician, who simply forgot to note that fact and take it into consideration when prescribing Haldol for her newly diagnosed schizophrenic disorder? Was the physician made aware of the patient's family history of diabetes? Did the paramedics inform the physician that they had detected an odor of alcohol on the ER patient's breath? Issues like these frequently turn on the credibility of the parties, and if either party can produce contemporaneously recorded notes of the conversations that took place and the information that was exchanged, she will have a distinct advantage in defending—or heading off—a claim.

Keep in mind, also, that a liability case may not just be the physician's word against the patient's. Malpractice cases typically involve multiple physicians and hospitals, as well as medical equipment and supply companies and other third parties. For example, in a case where it is established that the patient died following the rupture of his coronary bypass, the physician, the hospital, and the suture manufacturer will likely be named in the suit, and each may have a vested interest in showing that one of the others is at fault. Key issues may be whether the surgeon properly tied off the suture, whether hospital staff verified that the suture package was intact and undamaged when removed from its carton and prepared for use, or whether the suture was properly designed and manufactured. The evidence on these factual issues is likely to conflict in key respects, and the credibility of the evidence may rest in turn on the accuracy and trustworthiness of the records kept by each party.

To the extent possible, all medical personnel should therefore keep detailed notes and records, including (but not limited to) a patient's history, a chronology of his current problem, a record of his present symptoms, the physician's or nurse's findings upon examination, the alternatives considered in developing a differential diagnosis, the treatment options discussed with the patient, and a detailed description of the treatment recommended or provided. It is also extremely important to document all contact with patient and family, whether in person or by telephone, on matters of any significance to the diagnosis and treatment process. Care should be taken to avoid keeping notes that look too much as if the physician is more concerned with saving his own skin than the patient's but still reflect an accurate record of the information exchanged between the parties. It goes without saying, too, that one should take extra care in documentation when dealing with difficult patients or hard cases. If a physician finds herself negotiating consent with an unusually difficult individual, she may wish to have a witness present when describing the proposed treatment or procedure.

Bear in mind when keeping records and dictating or transcribing treatment notes that if they are one day read in the context of a court proceeding, someone—usually a skillful attorney—is going to be looking for holes, inconsistencies, and other inadequacies to exploit. As much will be made of what is *not* in the records as of their actual contents. Although a physician does not have to write beautiful prose, the more comprehensible—and comprehensive—her notes, the less explaining she will have to do years down the road when her actions are being reviewed under a microscope.

A good system for storage and retrieval of medical records is also essential. Attorneys will have a field day with lost or missing documents. They will portray the physician to a judge or jury as incompetent in record-keeping (and thus in overall practice) or, worse yet, having something to hide. Although the task of record storage and retrieval is frequently delegated to nursing staff or office managers, the physician needs to have a good understanding of—as well as confidence in—the manner in which records are kept. A malpractice attorney will be looking for any opportunity to portray the physician as out of touch with or out of control of the office.

When the records become too voluminous, many physicians often may have to resort to off-site storage facilities, conversion to microfiche, or computer imaging of records. Thankfully, the technology for scanning, imaging, storing, and retrieving of documents is becoming more widespread and cheaper every day. Oversight of computerized storing or imaging of documents must be entrusted only to technically competent and trustworthy personnel.

There is no hard and fast rule regarding how long records should be maintained. As discussed more fully below, each state has different time periods, known as statutes of limitations, for filing suit in medical malpractice claims. States also have different rules for determining the event that starts that time period running and what events may suspend it. Some states, for example, have laws providing that the time period for filing suit does not even begin to run until the alleged results of the physician's alleged negligence manifest themselves (if the alleged error was not reasonably discoverable before manifestation), which in some cases can take several years. It is therefore a good idea to consult with a malpractice attorney when setting up a system and a policy for storage of old medical and personnel records. An attorney should be able to provide advice about the statute of limitations on claims, any other special applicable rules in the physician's state, and what types of records physicians should be concerned about retaining in their areas of specialty.

Specific office procedures also must be established for the circumstances under which medical records will be provided to outside sources. Each state recognizes the patient-physician privilege, and several states have gone even further and codified rules governing the confidentiality of medical records.[13] In some situations, even if no medical malpractice is involved, a patient may have a cause of action against the medical care provider for improper disclosure of confidential records. Even if no statutory penalty or cause of action applies, a physician may be sued for improper disclosure of confidential records based on grounds of defamation, breach of fiduciary duty, or invasion of privacy. These cases frequently involve the disclosure of a person's HIV-positive status.

Again, an attorney can be especially helpful in reviewing or helping establish office procedures for disclosure of confidential records to appropriate persons by appropriate means.

Staff Selection and Training

As noted previously, physicians may generally bear responsibility for their own mistakes, as well as those of the assistants, nurses, and even fellow physicians allegedly under their supervision or control. Indeed, many cases are filed against a physician solely under the legal doctrine of *respondeat superior,* liability for the actions of agents or employees. As the number of nurses, specialists, and tertiary-care providers involved in a case increases, so does the exposure of the physician in charge.

Therefore, a physician can never take too much care in staff selection, training, and supervision. The nurses, physician's assistants, and even receptionists will not only help set the tone for each patient's visit but at various points in time will have a crucial aspect of the patient's care in their hands—whether taking a history or filing lab test results. The person or persons on whom responsibility for all these crucial personnel falls—the physician—cannot afford to be too disconnected from the process of choosing, equipping, and disciplining them.

While staff recruitment and hiring are tasks frequently delegated to office man-

agers, the physician should maintain an active role in the process, making all of the close calls and ascertaining that—however the process unfolds—she can fully trust the persons selected to assist her in all aspects of patient care. Although an office manager or nurse manager may do most of the initial screening or interviewing of candidates, the physician should always set the hiring standards—in terms of education, skills, professionalism, and personalities desired, among other factors—and oversee the hiring process.

Protecting against allegations of sexual misconduct or abuses, founded or unfounded, should also be a high priority in the recruiting and hiring process. Especially where care will be rendered to small children and others in vulnerable positions, it would be wise to have some sort of screening mechanism to determine whether an applicant has a criminal record and, if necessary, run a criminal records check. At a minimum, all applicants should have to fill out a written employment application, on which there should be a question about prior or pending criminal charges and convictions in any jurisdictions. The costs of this intrusion into an applicant's privacy pale in comparison to the emotional and physical consequences—to say nothing of the financial impact—of an incident of sexual assault or abuse involving a patient, especially one that could have been prevented. No doubt, opposing counsel will have this information before he files suit, so the physician should have it before there arise any incidents that may lead to a lawsuit.

A medical practice should seek out potential employees who are technically proficient and who will also maintain the indispensable caring, supportive office environment discussed above. Both of these types of skills are necessary in order to provide a better patient-care experience and to minimize the risk of claims developing out of personality conflicts or misunderstandings. The physicians in a practice also set the tone for hiring by their allocations of funding for particular positions, and they should take care to allocate sufficient resources to attract and retain competent, teachable caregivers. Again, spending a little bit more money on the front end is a small price to pay for trustworthy and competent employees and can save a lot of money in malpractice premiums, legal fees, and monetary damages in the long run.

As the ultimate source of liability for the care given to a particular patient, physicians should also take an active role in the training and professional development of nurses and other staff in their employ. Physicians should make time and, if necessary, financial resources available for staff to attend outside continuing education classes, and they should also provide well-planned, regular in-service training and practice updates for all staff. The best way to make sure that one's employees know how to do their tasks right—from record-keeping to administration of medication—is to have a hand in designing or providing the training they receive. The physician simply has to know what her employees and assistants are capable of in order to delegate tasks most efficiently, safely, and wisely.

The physicians in charge must also manage the practice's overall use of staff time and resources. If staff members are routinely forced to work overtime or frequently feel so overburdened that they cannot give each patient their full attention and best effort, there is a staffing problem. If two staff members have a personality conflict so ingrown that they cannot work peaceably in one another's presence, patient care is bound to suffer. Fatigued and distracted employees cannot provide the most competent and sensitive patient care, and they may unwittingly damage the patient-physician relationship. The physician can ill afford to find out about such problems after the fact, once a costly mistake has been made. Again, one does not want to be portrayed as out of touch or uncaring in front of a judge or jury down the road.

Finally, when accidents or allegations of misconduct do occur among staff, the physician or group must have a thorough, efficient, and adequate means for disciplining the persons involved. If a physician is sued for supervisory liability because of a mistake one of his nurses made (while under the physician's ultimate, if not immediate, supervision), one of the first things the opposing attorney will want to see is that nurse's personnel file and any write-ups or other disciplinary records. This kind of evidence can be a catch-22. If a file contains no disciplinary records whatsoever, the opposing attorney will try to create the inference that the physicians covered up past incidents or are not supervising their employees at all. If an employee's file contains a number of incidents of unacceptable or negligent conduct, the attorney will contend that the physicians were negligent in retaining this careless employee.

On balance, it is much better practice to maintain employee disciplinary records and to be able to demonstrate that efforts were made to address any problems with a particular employee. For this reason, each practice should have a comprehensive employee review and disciplinary policy, about which all employees are informed before there are any incidents. The policy, which an attorney can assist a physician to develop in detail, should include:

- a standardized, documented, periodic review of all employees for any issues in technical skill, personality conflicts, or compliance with office practices and procedures;

- a procedure by which errors or incidents are recorded, addressed with the employee in a meaningful way, and remedied as appropriate;

- a tough, yet fair, range of remedial measures from verbal reprimand through termination for any acts of incompetence or insubordination; and

- full documentation of all disciplinary actions.

With such a procedure in place, a practice can not only cut down on the number of errors made but also demonstrate to a court of law, when necessary, that its physicians were making every effort to maintain a competent and careful staff and should not be held responsible for a particular employee's actions.

Of course, not all the persons with whom a physician works in each particular case will have been under her control day to day. A physician may sometimes be held responsible for the actions of nurses or therapists whom she did not hire or train. Therefore, physicians must be extremely careful in evaluating which hospitals and fellow physicians to work with, choosing—where possible—only those with a demonstrated commitment to hiring and maintaining highly qualified, easily adaptable staff. A physician can also take the time and effort necessary to inform employees with whom he must work on a limited, temporary basis of the standards and con-

duct expected while they are under his authority. When a problem arises with a particular colleague or his employees, every effort must be made to document the incident and make sure that the person's supervisors are adequately informed. The more a physician can do to minimize the risk of working with other people—as is inevitable in the medical profession—the less the chances of being hit with a supervisory liability claim from out of nowhere years down the road.

The Physician's Own Training

A physician may not be able to exercise full control over the persons working with or for him, but there is one person whose training, competency, and abilities he can control—himself. It is time-consuming, but crucial, for a physician to stay on top of new developments in her given practice area. Today's accepted standard of care can become tomorrow's archaic quackery a lot faster than used to be the case. Indeed, in the recent wave of litigation over the prescription of the off-label combination of fenfluramine and phentermine (fen-phen), one of the key issues has been whether and when physicians who prescribed the drugs became aware of research indicating that the drugs could cause heart valve defects and primary pulmonary hypertension.

A physician should therefore allot sufficient time for his own continuing education and actually thumb through a few of the more worthwhile practice journals that pile up on his desk. Most physicians make a habit of discussing hard cases and tough calls with their colleagues to share ideas and insights. This is a wonderful practice when treating a difficult case, but it can reap even more rewards if done before the fact, using hypothetical situations and case histories presented in journals. In these days of ever-tightening schedules and significant competition for patients and insurance pools, constructive dialogue has become harder to find, but perhaps it is even more necessary than ever before.

Knowing One's Limits

On a related, more practical note, in certain situations a physician must be willing to admit that she is in over her head and call for assistance. As Solomon wisely observed in the Book of Proverbs, "Pride goes before destruction, a haughty spirit before a fall."[14] All too often, many of us are inclined to think we are superhuman, and we take on greater tasks than our training or energy level would suggest are prudent. But an awareness of one's limits—physical and intellectual—can help reduce the risk of error and/or claims.

For example, suppose an otolaryngologist has biopsied a lump on a patient's jaw and diagnosed a unilateral recurrence of a benign pleomorphic adenoma of the parotid gland. He schedules the patient for outpatient surgery, a deep lobe resection with attempted preservation of the facial nerve. On beginning the procedure, he observes multiple nodules of mixed-cell growths, in many places in the parotid bed and almost inextricably intertwined with portions of the facial nerve. What began at 10:00am and was anticipated to be a three- to four-hour outpatient procedure now looks as though it may take more than twelve hours, lasting until well past midnight. What should the otolaryngologist do?

The smart course of action is to call for backup. A surgical procedure of this intricacy—much of which must be performed with the aid of a microscope—is tedious and exhausting. It is crucial that the physician enlist another competent physician to relieve him for considerable periods of time. Obviously, the patient's family should be immediately told of the unforeseen complications, offered any other alternatives to completing the entire procedure, adequately informed of the increased risk of facial paralysis, and, most important, informed of the need for the additional surgeon's assistance.

Once again, the family (and the patient, when he comes to) will feel that they have been given competent, compassionate medical care. Rather than doubting their physician's ability to handle the procedure himself—as some physicians might fear—they will admire his placement of the patient's needs above his desire to look all-powerful. If extensive permanent facial paralysis does result from the procedure, the patient will be much less likely to press a claim if his family can tell him that the physician was unequivocally looking out for his best interests during the entire ordeal. Alternatively, the physician who tries to be the hero and carry the full load himself may not make a mistake. Because of the perception that he may have been too fatigued to carry out the procedure, however, he may be forced to answer a lot of pointed questions about how much sleep he had the night before, how many patients he had already seen and procedures he had already performed that day, and whether he was able to give this patient his full concentration. Once again the patient's and his family's perception—how they feel about the care that they have been given—can be almost as important as the reality.

Likewise, knowing one's intellectual and professional limits is also important, especially given the ubiquity of managed care, wherein general practitioners are tacitly or explicitly encouraged to handle as much as they can themselves and are rewarded for minimizing the number of specialist referrals. Pride, expedience, and economic concerns may sometimes pressure a physician to attempt treating a particular condition where a specialty consult is warranted. One research study has indicated that "over the past 2 years 30 percent of primary care physicians report an increase in the severity and complexity of patient conditions that they care for without referring to a specialist. Fifty percent of specialists similarly report an increase in the complexity and severity of patient conditions at the time of referral to them by primary care physicians."[15] This is a recipe for an increase in claims. Again, perception matters in this realm as well, for most patients feel better, in the hard cases, when they have had an expert's input (just as a physician would probably prefer that her malpractice attorney not be the one to draw up her will). The wise physician, within the potential constraints of the HMO or insurance company in question, will err on the side of referring borderline cases to a specialist with the appropriate training.

On a related note, the wise physician who desires to minimize exposure to malpractice claims will also graciously accept his patient's desire to seek a second opinion. Typically, the worse the outlook or the more complex the case, the greater the patient's desire for a second opinion. Since hard cases and distraught patients provide some of the more fertile ground for malpractice claims, it is in precisely such cases that the physician's unreserved commitment to the patient's well-being ought to be most evident. If the initial physician selfishly discourages a second opinion, she again may unintention-

ally come across as territorial or prideful. If she lets her wounded pride fester, her anger at the patient may manifest itself in small ways that damage the vital patient-physician relationship. When something goes wrong, even through no fault of the physician, the patient has an easy scapegoat: "I knew she should have let me get a second opinion!"

On the other hand, the patient who is encouraged to get a second opinion knows that her physician is confident enough in his diagnosis or recommendations to have them tested by a peer, cares less about losing a patient than doing right by her, and can be trusted if eventually allowed to provide the recommended treatment, if chosen. If the patient goes elsewhere for treatment and is satisfied, the physician has done his duty to care for the patient, is maybe only a few dollars poorer, and need not worry about a malpractice claim. If the patient goes with a second opinion that she likes better and has a bad result, the malpractice claim at that point is the second physician's concern. The confident, competent physician has nothing to lose—and everything to gain—by placing the patient's needs above his own, even if pride is one of the bitterest pills to swallow.

Controlling the Standard of Care

As mentioned in the previous section, physicians are facing increased pressure from HMOs and insurance companies to conform their care to a predetermined regimen. Specialty referrals are to be doled out like Nobel prizes, courses of treatment for "routine" conditions are considered to be uniform, and office staff must frequently navigate a labyrinthine voice-response telephone system in the hopes of getting a live person to approve of expensive yet necessary laboratory testing. Even worse, the standards are not uniform from insurer to insurer or from one HMO to another. Thus, it is often a Sisyphean effort to determine whether a particular test or procedure is authorized by a particular company. As a result, patients are frequently denied the most accurate and least intrusive lab tests because they cannot afford them.

Despite legislative initiatives to hold managed care organizations accountable, for the most part, the physician carries a significant portion of the risk of liability in such cases. It is therefore important for a physician to establish his own standard of care, notwithstanding the pressures applied by HMOs and insurance companies (or any other financial considerations, for that matter). A physician will always have a stronger defense against a claim if he can demonstrate that he acted in the sole interest of the patient, regardless of any financial constraints imposed by the patient's HMO.

As a practical matter, such conflicts between the physician's preferred course of treatment and the level of care authorized by the HMO can be expected to arise more frequently as HMOs proliferate and health care costs continue to rise. When such conflicts do arise, the physician should resolve to give the best care, that is, to do what is best for the patient, even if it means that the physician may not ultimately be compensated. Of course, few physicians can disregard cost altogether, but a physician's choices in the end cannot be dictated by the bottom line. Most physicians already put this idea into practice. The pressure to cut costs is going to increase, however, and the importance of making independent medical judgments may, too, as the landscape of HMO and insurance company liability changes.

A wise physician should have her practice standards in mind when determining the HMOs and preferred-provider networks with which she will contract. If the HMO's restrictions on the physician's treatment autonomy are too great, or if the scope of care provided to patients is too narrow or shortsighted, the physician ought to take a pass on that company's business, no matter how lucrative it may look from the outside.

A related issue concerns the provision of counsel to physicians accused of medical malpractice arising out of an HMO's or a managed care provider's denial of allegedly necessary testing or treatment. As discussed below, almost all malpractice insurance carriers contract to provide a legal defense of any claim filed against the insured physician, no matter how frivolous. It is not clear that a malpractice carrier would be obligated to provide a legal defense—or coverage, for that matter—for a physician whose challenged treatment decisions were made pursuant to an HMO's guidelines, however, especially if the physician "expected" that harm would result from the prescribed course of treatment. Thus, following an HMO's standard of care when it conflicts with the physician's own may not only expose a physician to liability but may also require him to pay for his own legal defense in certain circumstances.

This possibility is an additional reason to provide the best reasonable care in the physician's own judgment (regardless of financial impact). It also counsels in favor of thorough selectivity when signing up as a preferred provider or contract physician with an HMO. A physician should carefully review an HMO's or managed care plan's guidelines before agreeing to be bound by them and should also try to negotiate a provision in the contract whereby the HMO or plan agrees to provide a legal defense and indemnity for all claims arising out of the HMO's or the physician's adherence to plan or policy guidelines. In particular, the defense counsel provided should be separate and independent from that provided to the HMO or insurance company, as a conflict of interest may arise between it and the physician.

Physicians should keep a close eye on the overall legal landscape of these issues and, where possible, get involved in the legislative process. Congress has proposed numerous initiatives to reform regulation of managed care, but it is uncertain when and in what form legislation will ultimately be passed. Remedial legislation may shift liability from physicians to HMOs, or vice versa. In any event, whatever legislation results will undoubtedly be hard to wade through and comprehend. A good relationship with an attorney knowledgeable in this field can help a physician to navigate the rough waters and changing seas of individual and institutional liability for medical judgments. Also, a physician's malpractice insurer may be a good resource for learning about legislative charges, confronting particular situations in this context, or locating experienced counsel for assistance in dealing with these issues.

Early Warning Signs of Substance Abuse

Unfortunately, there is little research about the instance of substance abuse among health care providers as a group. The main study of this issue did determine, however, that while physicians were less likely than the general population to be current users of illicit drugs, their alcohol consumption was higher than that of the general population (although similar to that of similar socioeco-

nomic groups).[16] It is generally known that physicians and health care providers are no less susceptible than other people to alcohol or drug abuse and addiction and that such problems can have an impact on physicians' professional lives as much as their personal lives.

Alcohol and substance abuse by a physician or his staff can therefore be a factor in exposing a practice to malpractice claims. Although there have certainly been medical malpractice claims where the sobriety of the treating physician or staff has been an issue, such cases are not usually heard of as, needless to say, there is usually no point in even litigating them. They usually settle early on in the discovery process; if the substance abuse element is exposed, the stakes are raised significantly.

If a physician is concerned that a colleague or staff member has been consuming alcohol or drugs before coming to work—regardless of the quantity or the person's own assessment of her abilities—he must relieve that employee or physician from her duties (at least temporarily) post haste. Further, if the physician suspects a recurrent alcohol or substance-abuse problem, the issue must be confronted head on. Doing so is much easier if the practice or hospital has a clear policy on alcohol and substance abuse in place and, more important, a disciplinary mechanism for addressing such problems and making certain that they do not impair an individual's ability to function on the job. When the suspected addict is a fellow physician, the issue is likely to be more difficult to raise without some formal guidelines or opportunities for review and evaluation.

If a physician is concerned that his own drinking or substance abuse might be affecting his work, he should seek professional help immediately.[17] Most state medical societies have, or have an affiliation with, a physicians' health program (PHP), established specifically to help physicians identify substance abuse or other mental health or behavioral problems, obtain appropriate treatment or therapy, and maintain their state licensure. For example, North Carolina's Physician Health Program, one of the most advanced and well-funded such nonprofit organizations in the country, receives referrals from physicians with such problems, their colleagues or coworkers, and the state medical board. When a health care professional approaches (or is approached by) the NCPHP, he may sign a contract whereby he agrees to submit to an appropriate inpatient or outpatient treatment plan and five years of monitoring by the organization. In exchange, the NCPHP agrees to preserve the physician's anonymity (so long as he does not pose a physical danger to himself or others), to supervise him and assist him in getting counseling or plugging in to a recovery program, and to advocate for him in licensure and certification proceedings where necessary.

PHPs often work closely with existing recovery groups in the general population to connect physicians with similar problems and needs. Nearly every local chapter of Alcoholics Anonymous® has special, closed, extremely confidential meetings (referred to in many states as "caduceus groups") for physicians and health care professionals battling addiction. Participants in such groups are typically assigned not only an AA mentor, called a sponsor, but also a fellow physician monitor to keep them on track both professionally and personally during the recovery process. Such groups may be contacted and utilized outside of the auspices of the state medical society or PHP, as well.

Physicians concerned that they or a colleague might have a problem should not hesitate to contact their state medical society, PHP, AA, or a chemical dependency center before it is too late. A directory of state PHPs is available, for a nominal fee, from the Federation of State Physicians' Health Programs (312 464-5073). Once again, this is an area where an ounce of prevention is far less costly than a pound of litigation.

Crisis-Management Skills

When and if things are starting to go wrong in the OR or the treatment room, it is important that the physician be prepared and equipped to manage the crisis to avoid making any further mistakes and to minimize the potential for harm to the patient. Two experts affiliated with the National Patient Safety Foundation, an outgrowth of the American Medical Association (AMA), suggest the following behavior in a time of crisis (particularly in an operating room):

- *Show leadership:* The lead physician (or anesthesiologist) must take charge, assign priorities, and delegate tasks.

- *Ensure communication:* Speak directly to specific people within the operating room, making certain the message is received and understood.

- *Distribute the workload:* Ensure that no one is overloaded and that every team member is doing something useful.

- *Call for help early enough:* Safety is optimized by getting help before it is crystal clear that the situation is really serious.

- *Use all available information:* Cross-check important data. Don't become fixated on any one item.

- *Use cognitive skills:* Memory is not always reliable. Use checklists, manuals, calculators and other aids.[18]

With the goal of developing good crisis-management skills, a physician may choose to have in-service training and perhaps even crisis simulation drills to prepare staff for what may happen in the operating room. Again, the time spent in this kind of exercise pays off in both improved quality of care to patients and minimization of risk exposure.

Discussing the Bad Result

Everything looked great as Mr Bowen was sewn up following the replacement of his mitral valve and the repair of a previously implanted aortic prosthesis. A tiny fungal infection had formed on his heart valves during the procedure, but a dose of penicillin was supposed to clear that right up. Unfortunately, a few weeks after the surgery, a clot of the fungus broke loose and caused a fatal cerebral infarction. Mrs Bowen, the patient's wife of only one month—most of it spent at her husband's bedside helping him recuperate—has not even begun to understand what happened, let alone to deal emotionally with the loss of her husband. Sitting in front of the physician, all alone, emotionally distraught, she peppers her with questions: "Why did the fungus grow in the first place? Why didn't the penicillin kill it? Why did it have to go to a blood vessel in his brain? Isn't there anything you could have done to prevent this?"

The physician is emotionally drained, sleep deprived, and genuinely surprised by this unfortunate turn of events. What will she say? What should she say? What can she say to care for this suffering woman—as much the patient now as her husband was

previously—yet protect herself from the misunderstandings or miscommunications that might send Mrs Bowen, angry and upset, to an attorney's office?

Many competing considerations must be balanced in this delicate situation. First, this is not the time to stop caring for the patient. In fact, the physician must redouble her efforts to communicate compassionately with the patient's family. (As noted previously, this will be easier if the physician has done so from the outset.) The words chosen will vary depending on each situation, but the tone and manner of communication should, ideally, flow smoothly from the patient or family connection that the physician and her staff have previously cultivated. How one acts at this crucial stage of events may well determine whether a lawsuit is ultimately filed. The medical staff should also be advised of this sensitive matter and be cautioned to be careful in communicating with the patient.

Nonetheless, a physician in this circumstance has to be somewhat guarded. Any statements she makes may be used against her down the road. One must be especially careful not to make any admissions of legal liability or fault unless one is absolutely certain of the error and willing to accept whatever consequences may flow from it. Sometimes, all a patient is looking for in filing a claim is for someone to take responsibility. Early acceptance of responsibility (where warranted) may help a patient decide not to file a claim at all or at least increase the chance that, if he does so, it will be resolved quickly, fairly, and amicably. In cases of high risk or unclear liability, however, legal counsel should be involved at an early stage and should assist in determining what steps need to be taken.

Involving the Malpractice Insurer

Doni Haas, RN, a risk management specialist who has worked extensively as a board member of the National Patient Safety Foundation, offers the following specific suggestions to physicians facing the arduous task of discussing a bad result in this kind of situation:

1. *Let the family member know you care.* Sit down with her; make eye contact; and take her hand. Speak slowly, using simple terms.

2. *Don't speculate.* You may not know all the facts; do not guess. Do not blame others or yourself. Simply state the clinical facts of what happened, and specifically what efforts were taken to save the patient's life (or to prevent further damage).

3. *Assist the family through their grieving process.* Be sure to consider the family's need to know if the patient was afraid or in pain, or if he said or did anything in the course of the procedure to indicate suffering. Slowly sharing this difficult message in a compassionate manner is vital to the family members' grieving process. Sit in silence for a few moments, giving them time to react, to question, or simply to cry. Often in grieving, the family may feel guilty for what happened for a variety of reasons. Strangely enough, the disclosure of error, if there was any, can help diminish their guilt and allow closure.

4. *Leave the lines of communication open.* Before you leave her side, tell the family member that you know this is a lot of information and that she will probably have more questions later on. Give her a number where she can reach you and license to call you any time of day.

5. *Keep the family updated.* Let the family know immediately of any new information you receive. As new facts are discovered or clarified over time, work with your insurance carrier and their legal counsel to guide further disclosure. If you find there was a problem or an error, work with them to see if there is a way to disclose it, apologize for it, and compensate the patient or his family. Most people respond favorably to a sympathetically presented, honest admission of fault.

6. *Get some support or assistance for yourself.* These incidents are stressful for physicians as well as the patients and their families. It is difficult to know what to do, what to say, and how much blame to take. Also, a physician may need assistance in communicating effectively with the family. A fellow physician or a supportive risk manager can both help the treating physician to deal with the situation and assist a family with their immediate needs. She can help them cope with their loss or injury and encourage them to move forward with their lives as best possible under the circumstances.

As Haas's suggestions and the foregoing discussion indicate, communication following a bad result involves a mixture of clinical, emotional, psychological, and even legal elements. Attaining the right balance of these elements is a difficult but crucial skill for a physician to develop. If he is too defensive, indifferent, or cold and clinical in talking with the family, the family will not feel cared for, and they may file an unwarranted lawsuit either to "get some answers" or to make the physician feel sorry for what he did. Conversely, a physician who fails to somewhat restrain his empathy may admit fault or error where there was none and incur unnecessary liability. This balance will play out differently in different situations, but at all times the physician's central focus should be on maintaining the dignity, mutual respect, and compassion necessary to the patient-physician and family-physician relationships.

When the patient-physician or family-physician relationship appears to have broken down, considerations of liability begin to become paramount. Most insurance policies require notification as soon as practical whenever the insured is on notice of a potential claim. Notice of a potential claim is not limited to receipt of a lawsuit. Any time a patient indicates that a claim may be filed against the medical care provider, immediate notification should be made, regardless of whether the claim has merit. Failure to provide timely notice of even a potential claim may be grounds for denial of coverage. Thus, it is extremely important to set up a record-keeping system that documents whenever a potential notice of a claim is received and forwarded to the insurance carrier.

Since a physician may change insurers frequently, a determination of which liability insurance policy applies must often be made in order to know which malpractice carrier to notify. Thus, the physician must know what type of policies he has ("claims-made" or "occurrence," as discussed below) and when each potentially applicable policy period begins and ends. (Policy years do not typically coincide with the calendar year.) Under an occurrence policy, it will be the policy in effect on the date of the alleged act of malpractice that applies. Under a claims-made policy, the date on which the claim is made to the physician triggers policy coverage. This determination will also be significant because an insurance policy—even one written by the same insurer—may contain different policy limits and coverage terms from year to year.

Even if the patient has not provided notice of a potential claim, the physician should still give notice to the insurance company any time there has been a misdiagnosis, an error in treatment, or some other action from which a claim could potentially result. When an event occurs that indicates a claim is possible, the insurance carrier should be notified and the matter should also be reviewed carefully internally by the insurance claims representative and by counsel. It may be important at this stage to get the physician's personal attorney directly involved. The importance of doing so is that information communicated to an attorney at this stage may be privileged, meaning that it must be held in confidence. An attorney can advise what further course of communications, charting, involvement of other specialists, or other future handling of the matter may be required. It should be assumed by the medical care provider that any information communicated about this incident to anyone other than the attorney (and in rare cases even information communicated to the attorney) will be subject to legal discovery and could be shown to a jury.

In very sensitive cases, it may be wise to meet personally with counsel and let the attorney make all of the notes and records of the conference. This arrangement will most likely protect these disclosures from discovery, at least to the extent they do not appear elsewhere in records. In many cases, information prepared "in anticipation of litigation" is also protected.

Remedial Efforts

Whenever it becomes apparent that a claim is likely, the physician should be extremely cautious about attempting to settle the matter informally. Sometimes there is a temptation to avoid notice to the insurance carrier, and an effort is made to offer some compensation or services to the patient in an effort to resolve the claim. While some claims may be resolved in this fashion, the procedure is extremely risky. Not only may the actions of the physician be later claimed an admission of fault, but the absence of prompt notice of the claim to the insurance carrier may result in a denial of coverage due to late reporting.

Thus, best practice is for a physician to report a potential liability incident to his or her insurance carrier immediately once it becomes apparent that a patient may file a claim. Most insurance carriers have a "claims repair" procedure by which they can assist the insured in trying to resolve potential claims at an early stage. Bringing the insurer into the process early enables both physician and insurer to address the situation in a manner that not only meets the immediate medical needs of the patient but also protects the legal position of the insured if the matter is not resolved. The physician may also wish to consult his or her personal attorney to obtain advice on the appropriate means to deal with the situation.

If a patient's condition can clearly be improved with little risk or further harm or allegations of negligence, the physician may be counseled to attempt to provide further necessary treatment. Indeed, whenever a good patient-physician relationship can be revived or maintained, there is less likelihood that a lawsuit will materialize. In most instances, therefore, a physician should consider offering the patient the option of continuing under his care. If the patient does not feel comfortable doing so, the physician should offer to assist the patient in finding a new physiscian with whom she does feel comfortable.

In a few rare cases, the physician should proceed with caution in offering to render remedial care. First, when the patient suggesting the possibility of a claim has been a "problem patient"—difficult to deal with over a long period of time, quick to threaten legal action, uncooperative with the treatment plan, and/or malingering—it may be wise to discontinue treatment. Sometimes a patient's actions, threats, and contentious nature may render a healthy patient-physician relationship all but impossible. Second, in cases where the original treatment or alleged error took place a long time ago (eg, several years), a physician has to be concerned about reviving a potential claim that has grown "stale" (meaning that it is no longer legally viable due to the passage of time). Courts in some states may extend the statute of limitations—the time limit within which an action must be filed, as discussed in further detail later—where subsequent medical treatment creates a "continuing course of treatment." While the physician's focus in a given situation cannot be on liability alone, wise risk management demands that he not proceed in such cases without first attaining some level of certainty that the actions undertaken will not revive a possible claim that is time barred.

Conclusion

Some of the foregoing suggestions may be obvious, and some of them may be burdensome. But the law reporters are filled with the real-life stories of physicians who failed to heed them. If a physician has any question as to whether current practices and procedures provide sufficient protection against future negligence claims, he or she should contact a malpractice defense attorney or insurance company for a checkup immediately.

1. Gerald B. Hickson, "Physician Behaviors That Lead to Malpractice Claiming," The Digest (spring 1997):2 (St. Paul Medical Services); California Medical Association and California Hospital Association, *Report of the Medical Insurance Feasibility Study* (San Francisco: Sutter Publications, 1977); T.A. Brennan, L.L. Leape, N. Laird et al, "Incidence of Adverse Events and Negligence in Hospitalized Patients: Results from Harvard Study," 324 New England Journal of Medicine 370–76(1991). All references taken from St. Paul Medical Services' publications are reprinted with permission. ©1988 St. Paul Fire and Marine Insurance Co. All rights reserved.

2. Hickson, "Physician Behaviors . . . ," *supra* note 1.

3. Frank A. Sloan et al, *Suing for Malpractice* 55 (Chicago: Univ of Chicago Press, 1993).

4. *Id, citing* Barbara J. Doyle and John E. Ware, Jr, "Physician Conduct and Other Factors That Affect Consumer Satisfaction with Medical Care," 52 Journal of Medical Education 10:793–801 (1977).

5. *Id, citing* Myron Glassman & Nanci Glassman, "A Marketing Analysis of Physician Selection and Patient Satisfaction," 1 Journal of Health Care Marketing 4:25–31(1991).

6. G.B. Hickson, E.W. Clayton, P.B. Githens, & F.A. Sloan. "Factors That Prompted Families to File Medical Malpractice Claims Following Perinatal Injuries," 267 Journal of the American Medical Association 1359–63 (1992).

7. Hickson, "Physician Behaviors . . . ,"*supra* note 1.

8. Sloan, *supra* note 3, at 69.

9. *Id.*

10. Wendy Levinson et al, "Physician-Patient Communication: The Relationship with Malpractice Claims among Primary Care Physicians and Surgeons," 277 Journal of the American Medical Association 553-59 (1997).

11. *Schreiber v Physicians Insurance Company of Wisconsin,* 223 Wis 2d 417, 588 NW2d 26, 33 (1999). *See also Gorab v Zook,* 943 P2d 423, 430–31 (Colo 1997) (holding that, under Colorado law, a physician has no general duty to continue to explain the treatment options and their corresponding risks once the physician obtains consent and begins the procedure, but "where a new, previously undisclosed, and substantial risk arises, there may be an additional and independent duty to warn" the patient of that risk).

12. *May v Jones,* 675 So 2d 275, 279 (La App 2 Cir 1996).

13. Christopher Kerns, C.J. Gerner & C.R. Ryan, Health Care Liability Deskbook § 7:20 (West Group 1998).

14. Proverbs 16:18 (New International Version).

15. President's Advisory Committee on Consumer Protection and Quality in the Health Care Industry, March 1998, p 47, *citing* Robert St. Peter, Marie C. Reed, David Blumenthal & Peter Kemper, "The Scope of Care Provided by Primary Care Physicians: Physician Assessments of Change and Appropriateness," paper presented at the Association for Health Services Research Annual Meeting, Chicago, June 1997.

16. P.H. Hughes, N. Brandenburg, D.C. Baldwin, et al, "Prevalence of Substance Abuse among U.S. Physicians," 267 Journal of the American Medical Association 2333–39 (1992).

17. The World Wide Web site for Alcoholics Anonymous® (www.aa.org) has a checklist to help a person objectively assess whether he or she might have a drinking problem.

18. Jeffrey Cooper & David Gaba, "Medical Crisis Management Skills," *1998 Physicians and Surgeons Mid-Year Update.* St. Paul Medical Services.

Chapter 4

Claim protection:

Selecting the right malpractice liability insurance

Even the best bedside manner, the most careful selection and training of staff, and the most attentive and technically precise application of one's craft cannot prevent a bad situation from ripening into a medical malpractice claim. As noted in the last chapter, there are too many bad results, unpredictable emotional factors, and external pressures swirling about within the day-to-day practice of medicine. For this reason, it is paramount that a physician be well protected in the event of a malpractice or other kind of liability claim.[1]

The following is an overview of the major concerns involved in securing adequate insurance protection against medical malpractice claims. A more thorough consideration of these issues may be found in the AMA's award-winning publication *Medical Professional Liability Insurance: The Informed Physician's Guide to Coverage Decisions,* also available from the AMA.

Professional Liability Insurance

Professional liability insurance typically is obtained by contacting an insurance agent (who sells policies for a particular company) or an insurance broker (who sells policies on behalf of several different companies). Although it is often wiser to use a broker to get the best selection of rates and coverage terms, one should note that some insurance companies will sell their policies only through their own approved agents, so getting the most coverage for the money may require some independent shopping around.

As a general rule, whenever new coverage is requested or any changes are made to an insurance policy, these communications should always be made in writing or confirmed in writing to the insurance agent or broker. Agents have their own malpractice coverage, called errors-and-omissions coverage, and they may be liable to their customers for failure to purchase the requested insurance. However, failure to have such a request in writing may seriously hamper a physician's ability to prove that specific coverage was requested. Written confirmation of the insurance coverage sought and actually obtained can also serve to reduce the likelihood of a miscommunication, misunderstanding, or failure to act on the part of the insurance broker or agent.

A broker or agent is also useful in helping to select the coverage one needs, explaining the terms of the policy, and answering any questions that come up during the life of the policy. While a broker's or agent's consultation is extremely helpful, however, it is also wise for a physician herself to read the insurance policy before purchasing it. No one—not even attorneys, and probably not even insurance brokers or underwriters—enjoys reading insurance policies. Nevertheless, professional liability insurance policies must be given equal, if not even greater, scrutiny than any other contracts entered into by a physician or practice group. Given the ever-increasing complexity of insurance documents, and the multitude of instances in which one will make reference to them, it is vital to have an understanding of what a contract for medical malpractice liability insurance actually provides.

The following are a few of the essentials of any professional liability policy that must be considered and understood before purchasing an insurance policy. Familiarity with these terms and how policies work in general will assist a physician in comparing policies, selecting the proper amendments or endorsements, and understanding how the chosen policy will work when needed.

Type of Policy

First, a physician must determine which general type of malpractice liability policy is right for his or her practice. There are two major types of professional malpractice policies, referred to as "occurrence" policies and "claims-made" policies. Under the terms of an occurrence policy, coverage is provided only to the extent that it was in effect on the date of the occurrence that gives rise to the claim. This fact is significant because most professional liability insurance policies are renewed yearly, and they may as a result have some different material terms and even coverage limits from year to year. Thus, it is imperative to keep copies of all occurrence policies for a number of years after expiration since those old policies may still be applicable to lawsuits filed many years later.

Occurrence-based medical liability policies have become less common since the advent of claims-made coverage in the mid-1970s. In a claims-made policy, the applicable coverage is the coverage that is in force at the time the claim is first made or reported—either to the physician or to the insurance company, whichever happens first and regardless of when it actually occurred. Thus, claims-made coverage applies only to claims that are actually presented during the policy period. Even though a claim may have arisen from events that took place during a different policy period, if no claim is made until after the expiration of the policy, that particular policy will not apply. It is important to be familiar with the language used in a claims-made policy, as different policies may identify different triggering events (such as ambiguous requests for a patient's medical records by an attorney) that are required to be reported to the insurer.

A notable feature of this type of policy is that in a given year, all claims actually presented are governed by the same policy, both in terms of coverage provisions and applicable limits. This fact can be good for uniformity, but not so good if, in a given year, multiple claims are presented which threaten to exhaust the policy limits. Claims-made policies tend to be cheaper, given the fact that it is easier for the insurance company to determine its exposure on such policies.

A claims-made policy will also typically have a retroactive date, meaning that there will be no coverage for negligent acts or occurrences that happen before that date, even if the claim is made during the policy period. Therefore, before selecting a claims-made policy, a physician must make sure that the retroactive date goes back far enough to leave no gaps in coverage for any past years. The insurance company in many cases will be willing to provide an earlier retroactive date in exchange for a somewhat higher premium.

Likewise, a physician in some instances needs to be concerned about future coverage. Once the particular policy term has expired, there is no coverage whatsoever for any future claims. This means that any time a person switches from a claims-made policy to an occurrence policy, switches to a different carrier or a different practice, or retires, the old policy will provide no coverage, even for claims that arose during the policy period, unless the claim was made during that period. To avoid such a gap in coverage, it is often necessary to purchase what is referred to as "tail coverage" or an "extended reporting endorsement" to extend a claims-made policy to provide coverage for future claims arising out of past activities. Otherwise, a physician who retires after having had only claims-made coverage may find that there is no coverage when a lawsuit is filed after the expiration of the policy.

Which type of policy to choose will depend on different considerations at different stages of one's practice. Likewise, certain

portions of state law governing malpractice claims may figure into the calculus as well. It is important for the medical professional to receive full information from legal counsel about the statute of limitations for all states in which he or she practices, since this statute must be taken into account in determining what insurance coverages are required and how long such coverages must be maintained.

Coverage Terms, Exclusions, and Endorsements

Perhaps the most important feature of a policy is the scope of its coverage. Simply knowing that the policy provides medical malpractice or professional liability coverage is not enough. While there is some standardization of policies, each policy contains its own combination of industry-approved provisions and grants or excludes coverage through somewhat different means.

The declarations portion of the policy sets forth a general statement of the areas covered by the policy. It usually states the policy limits, any applicable deductible, and other basic information, such as what individuals are specifically covered under the policy. Following that section will typically be a section describing the particular coverage provided, often referred to as the policy terms and conditions. These portions of the policy must be reviewed to make certain that the coverages provided relate to every area of one's practice or every area in which one might possibly practice during the policy period. They also will generally indicate whether the policy is a claims-made or an occurrence-based policy.

The terms and conditions and declarations must be read in conjunction with three other portions of the policy that play a role in extending or restricting coverage. The definitions section, as one might expect, defines critical terms in the policy. In some circumstances, it may take away coverage that the terms and conditions appear to provide on their face. In this section will be found further information about the policy, what persons are considered to be insured, what constitutes a claim or occurrence, and information about what office personnel are covered under the policy.

The exclusions contained in the policy expressly withdraw coverage that might otherwise be included under some tenable reading of the policy language. For example, many policies exclude coverage for any personal injuries "expected or intended from the standpoint of the insured." In lay terms, that phrase means that the policy simply will not pay for injuries intentionally caused by an insured. How this exclusion applies to a particular set of facts will depend on its exact wording and any constructions given that wording in the courts of a particular jurisdiction. In medicine, as in other disciplines, intentional acts undoubtedly may have entirely unintended consequences; thus, this definition can often be tricky to apply.

Finally, so-called endorsements to the policy are attached to add a particular form or type of coverage that the policy does not expressly provide—or even one that it excludes—in its remaining sections. Such endorsements may often be purchased at additional cost to expand coverage—or provide more favorable terms thereof—to suit the needs of a particular physician or practice.

It is important for a physician to read the policy thoroughly, paying particular attention to all of the exclusions and definitions, to make certain that the policy as a whole does not exclude some particular aspect of his practice from which claims might arise. If there is anything in the policy that he does not understand completely, he should ask an insurance agent or lawyer for an explanation of the provisions and, if possible, written confirmation of that explanation. Different policies may contain different exclusionary language, and even the same language may have been interpreted differently by courts in different states. The advice of counsel located in the state in which the physician is practicing is therefore absolutely crucial in making sure that adequate coverage is obtained.

The following is a brief consideration of several critical policy features and options to keep in mind when reviewing the terms, conditions, definitions, exclusions, and endorsements of a particular policy.

Policy Limits

The first basic feature of the standard malpractice insurance policy that must be understood is the policy limits. Most policies permit the physician to choose and pay a corresponding premium for the policy's limits of liability, that is, the maximum amount that the company will pay, per occurrence, per claim, or per policy year, or some combination of the three. For example, a majority of policies provide liability limits of at least $1 million per claim and $3 million in the aggregate per policy period. Unless he has purchased what is called excess insurance, a physician will be personally liable for all amounts paid in settlement or following an adverse verdict in excess of the stated policy limits.

The typical size of potential jury verdicts varies dramatically from one jurisdiction to another, and perhaps even more dramatically with the type of practice.

Surgeons and obstetricians/gynecologists, for example, tend to select higher limits of coverage (and also to pay higher malpractice premiums) because of the relative frequency with which they experience claims and the costliness of adverse verdicts and settlements in their fields of expertise. A knowledgeable insurance agent or a personal attorney should always assist the physician in determination of the appropriate level of coverage protection for a particular field of practice and a particular state.

Almost all liability insurance policies include a provision whereby the insurer agrees to pay for the cost of defending a lawsuit against the insured, including attorney's fees and other incidental costs associated with the defense. While many policies impose no specific limit on defense costs, some policies count all sums paid in defense of the claim against the overall policy limits, meaning that defense costs can erode a substantial portion of the amount available to settle the claim or pay an adverse judgment. This kind of provision can place a physician's personal assets at greater risk in the event of a significant liability claim. A physician should therefore determine how defense costs are treated by a given policy and be prepared to purchase higher policy limits in order to ensure adequate coverage

If a physician is concerned that the policy limits available from a given insurer are not high enough for her particular needs, or higher limits on the primary policy do not appear to be cost efficient, she should look into obtaining an excess insurance policy. Such a policy, which may be written by a different carrier altogether, promises to kick in additional money to pay any portion of a judgment or settlement in excess of the primary policy limits. Excess coverage should be carefully selected, however, because it brings

with it a new policy of insurance that includes its own set of limitations, exclusions, and endorsements, some of which may impact the handling of a particular claim that threatens to tap in to the excess coverage. For example, excess insurers, as one might imagine, typically like to see claims settled within the limits of the underlying primary liability policy, and the excess insurance policy may contain provisions to encourage or facilitate such settlement. Likewise, in some high-risk cases, the primary policy may advance its entire policy limit toward a settlement, leaving the excess carrier to defend the remainder of the claim and litigate over how much, if at all, the plaintiff should recover in excess of the amounts already paid. Therefore, the excess policy's provisions regarding selection of defense counsel and consent to settlement (as discussed below) will become extremely significant.

Provision and Selection of Defense Counsel

All policies provide that the insurance carrier has a duty to defend the insured (or other person covered under the policy) in the event that a lawsuit is filed. In practice, this usually means that the insurance company selects and compensates the defense attorneys retained to defend the lawsuit. Ordinarily, this presents no problem since most insurance companies have established relationships with well-qualified medical malpractice defense counsel. The insurance carrier obviously also has an interest in a successful outcome of the case. However, in some instances the medical professional may desire to have input on the selection of defense counsel, especially if he has an established relationship of trust or confidence in a particular attorney's ability and reputation within the community. Some policies (or endorsements) give the medical professional a measure of input with respect to the selection of defense counsel. If this feature is important to a physician, he or she should investigate what each potential policy says about this issue and what, if any, other options are available.

Likewise, in the event that a claim is filed and counsel is appointed, a physician should ask to be fully informed as to the retention arrangement between the insurance company and the counsel selected to represent the physician. Defense counsel who work exclusively for the insurance company—whether as members of the company's legal department or of a captive law firm actually owned or controlled by the company—may not be able to render impartial and independent service to the policyholder in the litigation of a claim. In particular, such an attorney may have a conflict of interest if in her representation of the physician she learns confidential information that is then used by the insurance carrier to deny coverage to the physician. This is precisely what happened in a recent case in Maryland. A physician's malpractice carrier decided to deny coverage for a liability claim against the physician after learning confidential information from its general counsel in the course of counsel's representation of the insured.[2] The physician ultimately prevailed in obtaining coverage based on the insurance company's and its attorney's conflict of interest, but not until after the physician had filed a separate lawsuit of his own, incurred substantial legal fees, and endured several additional months of stress and time away from work.

Control of Settlement

A related issue is which party wields the ultimate authority to settle a claim or lawsuit.

Many insurance policies vest the insurance company alone with that authority, leaving the decision of whether and for how much to settle in the hands of the entity that will actually be writing the check and its legal counsel. It is not unusual for cases to be settled for various practical considerations even though legal liability may be questionable. In such cases, the decision to settle may be made notwithstanding the objection of the medical professional unless the policy specifically provides otherwise. This provision has often proved unpalatable to physicians, who have a vested interest in their reputation and standing within the medical community and the community at large. Therefore, they may not want to capitulate on a questionable claim for economic reasons alone.

Even more unsettling to many physicians is language contained in many policies stating "The [insurance] company may make such investigation and settlement of any claim or suit as it deems expedient." As one commentator has noted, "Physicians who have 'deems expedient' provisions in their malpractice policies may find themselves vulnerable to quick settlement offers by their insurance companies even if the insurer's claims-handling department conducted little or no investigation on which to base a settlement decision." As a result, "When an insurer opts to settle claims quickly and cheaply, meritless malpractice claims may nevertheless be rewarded, to the detriment of the policyholder."[3]

Some policies, however, do allow the insured to have some input—or even the ultimate authority—on the decision of whether and for how much to settle a claim. Frequently, such a consent-to-settle provision comes in the form of an endorsement purchased at a somewhat higher premium.

However, a few states—notably, Florida, Kansas, and Wisconsin—prohibit consent-to-settle endorsements or provisions on public policy grounds, fearing that they serve as a disincentive to the swift and equitable settlement of claims.[4] Physicians concerned about this issue should find out through their attorney or broker/agent whether such an endorsement is available in their states and from each particular carrier with whom they are considering doing business.

Endorsements and policy provisions giving the physician the authority to grant or withhold her consent to settle must be scrutinized carefully, however. Some policy language may contain restrictions and qualifiers on the physician's ability to weigh in on the decision. Watch out, in particular, for what is known as a "hammer clause," that is, language that permits the physician to withhold consent to settle but leaves him or her on the hook for any portion of a damages award in excess of the value at which the insurance company desired to settle the case. Some policies also provide that if the insurance company and the insured disagree over the maximum amount for which the claim should be settled, they will be required to submit their dispute to an arbitration panel, which will hear each party's position and set the final amount of the settlement offer to be made.[5]

It is important that a physician understand how these provisions are going to work ahead of time in order to obtain the coverage and authority desired in the event of a claim. For example, suppose the insurance company is willing to pay (and the claimant is willing to accept) $50,000 to settle a case. The physician does not wish to consent to any offer over $25,000, feeling that the case is frivolous. Without a consent-to-settle provision or endorsement,

the physician is powerless to stop the settlement. If the policy in question contains a consent-to-settle provision with a hammer clause, the physician can prevent the settlement but will risk having to pay out of pocket any portion of a judgment ultimately obtained that exceeds $50,000. If the consent-to-settle provision requires arbitration of the parties' dispute over the value of the case, the arbitration panel may choose an amount that is too low to get the case resolved or much higher than what the physician is comfortable with. These risks will weigh heavier on some physicians than others. Thus, selection of this kind of provision is a matter of the preference of the individual physician and should be made with the considered input of personal counsel.

Coverage for Punitive Damages

Medical malpractice claimants are allowed to seek recovery for economic damages (medical expenses associated with remedial, rehabilitative, or palliative treatment necessitated by the alleged negligence), noneconomic damages (pain and suffering or mental anguish), and, in most states, punitive damages (additional amounts awarded to deter intentional or reckless behavior or actions motivated by malice). An award of punitive damages usually requires a showing of conduct far more egregious than mere negligence. Often, a claimant is required to show clear and convincing evidence of malice, gross negligence, willful and wanton conduct, reckless indifference to the patient's safety, or some other higher level of culpability. The laws with respect to punitive damages vary from state to state. Some states cap the maximum amount of punitive damages that may be awarded, and some prohibit them altogether.[6]

Similarly, the laws regarding insurance coverage for punitive damages also vary, as do the standard coverages provided by different insurance carriers. It is extremely important to know whether and under what circumstances a policy excludes or includes coverage for punitive damages, as such claims are frequently asserted in malpractice actions. In fact, when punitive damages are not covered, such a claim may be included by a claimant's attorney for tactical reasons to place additional pressure on the physician or hospital to settle and avoid any potential personal liability for punitive damages. The availability and desirability of coverage for punitive damages will be a function of the laws of a particular state with respect to punitive damages and their coverage, the options provided by each potential carrier, and the personal preferences and fears of the physician.

Staff Coverage

A physician may in some circumstances be held liable for the negligence of his or her nurses, physician's assistants, or other staff. Such liability frequently will turn on the degree of control that the physician is authorized to exercise over the persons in question. Liability for employees under one's direct daily supervision is highly likely, as is liability for hospital staff under one's supervision on a given surgical procedure.

For this reason, all portions of a malpractice insurance policy must also be reviewed to determine whether coverage is provided to all persons working for the insured entity. One must determine whether all subordinate staff on the office payroll are either listed as covered persons on the declarations page or otherwise covered under the definitions and terms and conditions of the policy. Consideration also must be given to coverage for temporary, part-time, or borrowed employees who may be operating from a physician's office for a short term. Such employees may not be properly listed in the declarations portion of the policy or included within the definition of covered persons, resulting in no coverage, even though there may be legal liability for the physician or practice as a result of their actions. All temporary or borrowed employees either should be immediately and fully covered under the subject policy or should, upon employment, present the practice with a certificate of insurance showing adequate coverage limits through some other source. On that policy, the physician and her office should be listed as additional insureds. One can never assume protection under another person's policy without a certificate of insurance from his or her insurance carrier specifically indicating that such an endorsement has been provided.

When a physician works for a group or other organization, it is wise to request an opportunity to inspect the insurance coverage for the group and to have this policy reviewed by an insurance agent and/or attorney to make certain that it includes all necessary coverages. If there are any gaps in this coverage, supplemental policies or endorsements may be required.

Picking a Reliable Company, Not Just a Cheap Policy

In selecting malpractice insurance, a physician should also bear in mind that he is essentially picking a business partner, not just entering a written contract. Therefore, it is important that he evaluate and feel comfortable with a prospective insurer's administrative competency, accessibility, efficiency, and financial strength. The value of an insurance policy diminishes considerably if the physician cannot get through to a knowledgeable person to obtain or report vital information or if patient claims get lost in a maze of bureaucracy, automated recordings, and hostility. Often, the manner in which the malpractice carrier handles a particular claim can be just as critical as the physician's conduct in giving rise to—or heading off—a potential claim. Thus, it is always prudent to check an insurance company's references (typically policyholders for whom it has previously handled claims), just as one would do when hiring a child-care provider or home-renovation contractor.

Of course, all the courtesy and coverage in the world will be meaningless if the insurer is not financially solvent and able to pay claims. It may sound unthinkable, but several insurance carriers in this field have recently gone bankrupt, leaving their policyholders in fear of personal liability for years' worth of potential and existing claims. Physicians in Ohio recently received such a shock with the liquidation and dissolution of twenty-three-year-old Physicians Insurance Exchange Mutual Insurance Company of Cleveland (known in the industry as PIE) in March 1998. Once the largest malpractice insurer in Ohio and a significant provider of coverage in several other midwestern states, PIE was endorsed by the Ohio State Medical Association because of its low premiums, captive legal defense counsel, and ownership by physicians. An investigation by the Ohio Department of Insurance begun in 1997, however, turned up evidence that PIE had been grossly and even corruptly mismanaged. Specifically, investigators determined that PIE had filed fraudulent financial reports, made illegal payments and loans to its officers and direc-

tors, bribed insurance regulators, and was substantially undercapitalized. Criminal indictments of a number of PIE's officers and the imposition of civil penalties soon followed, resulting in a judicial order in March 1998 requiring that PIE be dissolved and liquidated altogether.[7]

Once PIE was ordered out of business by the courts, thousands of physicians were forced to find alternative coverage on short notice, to worry about whether they might get any premium refunds from PIE, and, most important, to agonize over whether there would be any PIE funds left to cover nearly five thousand then-pending claims that arose during periods of coverage under PIE and an untold number of future claims. Moreover, the company's collapse has spawned a host of lawsuits against its officers and directors, lawyers, accountants, and other related entities that are certain to consume significant judicial resources sorting out the blame and fighting over the company's few remaining assets.

Similar collapses in 1998 by PIC Insurance Group—which once insured 7,000 physicians in Pennsylvania—and by Insurance Corporation of America—a PIE subsidiary in Texas with 2,350 physician-insureds—have placed a tremendous amount of pressure on other insurance carriers, state insurance guaranty funds, and physicians.[8] As a result, "Physicians are taking stock of the merits of discount insurance pricing, [and] many are looking beyond the rates to determine the real cost of protecting themselves."[9]

Based on her familiarity with the PIE liquidation and several similar company failures, Carol Brierly Golin, publisher of the *Medical Liability Monitor,* warns physicians against selecting the cheapest insurance available. Rather, Golin says, physicians should "[l]ook for stability and solvency, and thoroughly investigate every company [they're] considering doing business with."[10] A physician should consider several factors in evaluating the financial strength and viability of a particular insurer, including the following:

• Make sure the carrier is licensed to do business in your state and is in good standing.

• Verify the carrier's financial condition and/or rating (Standard & Poor's, Duffy's, A.M. Best, and Moody's provide annual letter-grade ratings based on a comprehensive review of numerous financial indicators).

• Make sure the carrier is backed by an adequate state guaranty fund. Such funds, which provide a backup source of coverage in the event of bankruptcy or insolvency of insurance companies, exist in most states. Where a fund is already significantly strained by a major carrier collapse such as that of PIE, one does not want to be on board the next ship that goes down.

• Find out how long the company has been in business, keeping in mind that longevity is a good, though not perfect, indicator of reliability and stability.

• Make certain that all hospitals and other facilities with whom the physician will be working will accept that carrier. A number of large hospitals have begun restricting hospital privileges to physicians covered by a well-known, trustworthy carrier.[11]

The failure of an insurance company affects not only its own insureds but other health care providers as well. Shrewd plaintiff's attorneys, when faced with an insolvent carrier for their target defendant, will attempt to refocus the case on other potential parties, such as hospitals or co-treating physicians, in hopes of finding additional funding for a settlement or verdict. In the wake of major collapses of established carriers like those in Ohio, Pennsylvania, and Texas, a physician cannot be too careful in choosing a malpractice carrier.

Business Premises or Office Property Insurance

Not all types of claims that might occur at a physician's office may be covered under a professional liability policy. Fortunately, business property insurance policies frequently afford some level of protection against liability for injuries that occur on office property, allegedly as a result of dangerous or hazardous conditions on the property (ie, "slip and fall" or inadequate security claims). An insurance agent and/or attorney should conduct a comprehensive review of all business insurance policies. Care should be taken to select appropriate types and coverage amounts for office and clinic property, as well as to provide workers' compensation benefits for employees injured on the job.

Many of the same principles discussed in the previous subsection on professional liability insurance also apply to the selection of business and property insurance policies. It is important that at least one person within each practice or hospital be knowledgeable about the definitions, coverages, and exclusions contained in these types of policies to make certain that all business activities and types of potential liability claims are covered. Such policies are likely to have different types of limits, deductibles, or claims-reporting procedures that may apply in a given situation. Care must be taken to know when and how to submit each different type of claim to the correct carrier.

One particular exclusion contained in a standard property or commercial general liability (CGL) policy is some form of pollution exclusion. In such a provision, the insurer typically restricts its coverage obligation for pollution cleanup to sudden and accidental discharges of pollution. There have been innumerable cases over the meaning of this wording (and other similarly worded provisions) in the context of a company's liability for environmental pollution and waste disposal. Such liability may arise in the form of a claim for bodily injury, property damage to adjoining land or appurtenances, civil penalties, or reimbursement of the costs of cleaning up a waste disposal site incurred by the Environmental Protection Agency. Health care providers—particularly hospitals—need to pay attention to what their pertinent policies say about coverage for this type of liability, especially depending on the extent to which their disposal practices for infectious medical waste might engender one of the types of claims listed.

One may be tempted to think that liability for disposal of medical waste is unlikely. In one noteworthy case in New Jersey, however, a number of medical care facilities incurred hefty civil fines and penalties for their medical waste disposal practices. The case is significant because the medical facilities were subjected to these penalties simply for contracting with a waste-removal company that turned out—despite its representations to the contrary—to be unlicensed and to be dumping infectious waste through unauthorized means, without a permit, and on property unauthorized for such disposal on Staten Island.[12] In light of the very real threat of this kind of liability, the wise physician should do some investigation of his or her practice's medical and infectious waste dis-

posal practices and at least ask its business or professional liability insurer whether an endorsement is available to provide coverage for any waste disposal or pollution-related liability.

An insurance professional or attorney should be able to help each physician's office tailor a package of business and professional coverages to fit the practice's particular needs. Many insurance companies may be able to provide a package of all necessary policies at a significant discount, but one must pay attention to the details of each policy as well as the company's experience in handling each separate type of claim.

Personal Insurance

In addition to examining the particulars of one's medical malpractice insurance and premises liability insurance coverage, a physician should also make certain that she has adequate personal liability coverage. Physicians are frequently considered "deep pocket" or "target" defendants. Because of their presumed wealth, physicians are more likely to be sued personally for garden variety automobile, premises liability, or other accidents. Cases involving claims of serious personal injury—even marginal ones—can expose a physician to liability for a sizable verdict or settlement. An individual may also be held personally liable for the value of any judgment in excess of any applicable automobile or homeowners' insurance policy limits.

Therefore, a physician must have a clear understanding of his personal liability insurance coverage. The most common forms of personal liability insurance are homeowners' insurance and automobile insurance. Each of these kinds of policies should be reviewed periodically to make certain that all of a physician's nonprofessional activities are adequately covered and that policy limits are high enough to protect his or her assets. Further, a physician should consider an excess or a personal "umbrella" insurance policy to provide additional protection over and above the coverages in the standard homeowners' and automobile policies. Umbrella policies are typically inexpensive, providing comprehensive coverage for numerous types of claims, and are thus a wise investment in a physician's personal assets.

Given the frequency of automobile accidents and the high potential for severe damages associated with them, careful scrutiny should be given to both one's auto insurance policy and the ownership of all family vehicles. All vehicles, whether recreational or used in business, should be properly insured with adequate limits of coverage. Individual exposure to liability for injuries to others resulting from automobile accidents can be reduced by having family automobiles owned individually by the family members who normally drive those vehicles. In most states, if a vehicle is owned jointly or by a different family member from the one who is driving at the time of an accident, the owner, as well as the driver, may face personal liability under the family purpose doctrine. If the owner of each vehicle is the primary driver, however, other family members may generally not be held liable for the driver's actions.

Also in the realm of automobile insurance, a physician should periodically evaluate the terms and limits of any underinsured and uninsured motorists coverage, which provides extra protection for injuries resulting from automobile accidents caused by other drivers. Such coverage is important to protect against one's own loss of income that could result from an accident. A dis-

abling injury could result in very substantial damages, including loss of present and future income, which may be a considerable sum for a physician. A claim for such damages may be virtually uncollectible against a motorist who is uninsured or who has very low liability limits.

For example, if a thirty-five-year-old surgeon is involved in a wreck and sustains a permanent injury to his dominant hand, resulting in a loss of his ability to work as a surgeon, the negligent motorist could be liable for millions of dollars in lost future income (not to mention medical bills and damages for pain and suffering). However, if the negligent driver is uninsured or has only $25,000 in liability insurance (the legal minimum in most states), the physician will have no way of being compensated for his lost income and other damages unless the driver has personal assets that may be seized (which is usually not the case) or the physician has purchased sufficient underinsured or uninsured motorists coverage on his own automobile insurance policy. UM/UIM coverage (as it is known) pays whatever damages the negligent motorist cannot, but only up to the policy limits selected. Thus, the wise course is to select a sufficiently high limit for this coverage—in the range of a million dollars or more—which should be available at a reasonable cost.

Conclusion

Reviewing insurance policies is time-consuming, arduous, and even frustrating. But the costs of the investment of a little time and energy on the front end—without an actual claim hanging overhead—are minuscule compared to the exasperation of realizing that an imminent claim is not covered, or that a policy is lacking some crucial feature, to say nothing of the potential economic impact of a misguided selection. Although hindsight is twenty-twenty, most physicians can improve their foresight with a little effort; and a little foresight in selecting a policy can go a long way toward ensuring peace of mind and preparing wisely for the ugly reality of a malpractice claim.

1. The authors are indebted to Rodney A. Dean, Esq, an insurance defense and medical malpractice defense attorney in Charlotte, North Carolina, for his substantial contribution to this chapter.

2. *Medical Mut Liab Ins Soc of Maryland v Miller,* 451 A2d 930 (1982).

3. Eugene R. Anderson & Joshua Gold, "Malpractice Insurance: Careful Choice Can Prevent Later Problems," 13 Medical Malpractice Law & Strategy no 7, 3–4 (May 1996), *citing Gardner v Aetna Cas & Sur Co,* 841 F2d 82, 85 (4th Cir 1988) (plaintiff physician claimed that his malpractice insurance company inadequately investigated the underlying malpractice suit before offering a settlement).

4. "Consent to Settle 101," *1997 Physicians and Surgeons Update,* St. Paul Medical Services. All references taken from St. Paul Medical Services' publications are reprinted with permission. ©1988 St. Paul Fire and Marine Insurance Co. All rights reserved

5. *Id.*

6. Michael Rustad & Thomas Koenig, "Reconceptualizing Punitive Damages in Medical Malpractice: Targeting Amoral Corporations, Not 'Moral Monsters,'" 47 Rutgers Law Review 975, 1001–1002 nn 80–89 (spring 1995).

7. *See* "PIE's Lessons—'Don't Buy on the Cheap,'" *1998 Physicians and Surgeons Mid-Year Update,* St. Paul Medical Services, 1998; Debra Baker, "One Big Headache," 84 ABA Journal 40(December 1998).

8. *Id.*

9. Baker, *supra* note 7.

10. "PIE's Lessons," *supra* note 7.

11. American Medical Association, *Medical Professional Liability Insurance: The Informed Physician's Guide to Coverage Decisions* (Chicago: AMA Press, 1998), *cited in 1998 Physicians and Surgeons Mid-Year Update,* St. Paul Medical Services (1998).

12. *See US v Paccione,* 751 F Supp 368 (SDNY 1990), *aff'd,* 949 F2d 1183 (2d Cir 1991).

Chapter 5

Litigating claims:

What happens after the suit has been filed?

Perhaps the only topic more unpleasant than the finer points of insurance coverage and exclusions is that of actual malpractice claim litigation. Those who have chosen to practice law may feel at home in a heated deposition or drafting answers to multipart interrogatories, but for nonlawyers, the litigation process can be a strange and confusing world. Medical professionals in particular see the burdens imposed on them by lawsuits as especially onerous. As one medical malpractice defense attorney recently wrote:

Litigation is disruptive to the practice of medicine. Even when physicians prevail at trial, they often feel it's a Pyrrhic victory. They are emotionally spent. Their lives have been disrupted. They feel personally and professionally attacked. They have lost time away from their office, but still have overhead to pay. If they are uninsured, attorney fees and litigation costs are astronomical. Insurance for medical negligence remains very expensive and tort reform will not come to the rescue. Before the dust settles on a ver-

dict in their favor, they get angry at the system, at plaintiffs and at lawyers in general, even their own. There is no satisfaction in a victory like this.[1]

The aim of this section of chapter 5 is to relieve some of the pain and stress that litigation can cause a physician—whether as the named defendant in a lawsuit, a material fact witness, or an expert consultant hired by one side or the other of a dispute involving colleagues. Of course, no amount of foreknowledge or preparation can remove all the anxiety or difficulty from the process, but it is hoped that a physician's navigation of these turbulent waters will go more smoothly with a better understanding in advance of what the legal issues will be, what the process will require, and what the possibilities are for the end game and resolution of a lawsuit. Physicians who have not yet encountered actual claims may benefit from familiarity with this information. Knowing the ins and outs of the litigation process will not only make a physician better prepared when and if it has to be endured but will also perhaps help him practice better medicine and motivate him to make whatever changes are necessary to avoid being sued.

The Beginning of a Lawsuit

A significant percentage of claims—especially the most egregious ones—are resolved by the insurance carrier without a lawsuit ever being filed. Some claims cannot be resolved without litigation, however, because either it is unclear whether there was a violation of the standard of care, it cannot be determined which of several persons or entities should bear responsibility for such a breach, or the claimant and the insurance company (or companies) and/or the physician cannot agree on the valuation of the claim.

Therefore, once a patient—or the family of a patient who has since died—has determined that a claim for medical malpractice will not be informally resolved by the physician's malpractice carrier, she must initiate formal legal action by the filing of a complaint. The patient (or the administrator/executor of her estate, if deceased), now known as the plaintiff, will have her attorney (who will frequently, but not always, have already been involved in presenting the claim to the insurer and attempting to negotiate a settlement) file in a state court a complaint describing the factual and legal bases for the lawsuit. There may be considerable delay between an insurer's final denial of a claim and the actual filing of suit, however. Although there are specific time limitations by which a lawsuit must be filed, a plaintiff's attorney will frequently delay filing a complaint until near the expiration of that period, either because of a busy schedule, to conduct more extensive presuit investigation, or to try to gain some strategic advantage. A physician should never con-

sider a potential claim to have been abandoned until after being advised by the insurer or an attorney that the applicable time for filing suit has expired.

An action is not fully commenced against a defendant until the complaint is officially served on that defendant. The proper means of service of a complaint is governed by each state's law, but service is generally accomplished by registered or certified mail or personal delivery by a sheriff's deputy or other registered process server. The timing and manner of service of the complaint is extremely important. Errors in the process may even in some circumstances result in the lawsuit's being dismissed. Whenever suit papers are received, both the insurance carrier and the medical care provider's personal attorney should be notified immediately, and copies of the suit papers should be forwarded to each. It is important for the defense attorney to know the exact circumstances under which the suit papers were received, to whom they were delivered, who signed for them, and the date and time of such receipt. Under no circumstances should the physician attempt to contact the plaintiff's attorney to discuss the case, even if it is obvious that the suit papers are in error.

A medical malpractice complaint often proves to be difficult reading, if not in its complexity, then certainly in its tone, especially to a named defendant. The physician should review the allegations of the complaint carefully and prepare himself to discuss them with counsel, point by point. But it is helpful to remember that the complaint purposefully—and to the full knowledge of all court personnel and attorneys involved—presents only one side of the story in a decidedly slanted fashion. Words such as *willfully, wantonly, carelessly, recklessly,* and *heedlessly* are typically sprinkled freely throughout the complaint. The physician's conduct will be described in the worst terms possible. The newly sued defendant should bear in mind that such hyperbole is boilerplate and that he will have an opportunity to respond to the allegations through his counsel at the appropriate time and manner.

Once suit is filed, the physician needs to make prompt arrangements to transfer the patient to the care of some other physician. Ideally, counsel should be contacted to review any such arrangement. At that point the physician should have no communication with any legal representative for the plaintiff except to provide copies of medical records to the patient or the patient's designated representative as formally requested, most likely through the attorneys for each side. The physician should also take measures to safeguard the pertinent medical records—and specifically to prevent loss or tampering—until their ultimate production in the course of litigation.

Liability Coverage Issues

At this point, control of the case will shift somewhat from the insurance company to the attorney whom it has retained to serve as independent counsel for the physician. Defense counsel will be the physician's primary source of information about the pertinent law and the progress of the case. All questions regarding the claim should be directed to defense counsel first. Although the insurance company pays the attorney's bills, the physician is the client, and the attorney has a duty to keep both informed of the progress of a case.

A physician should make certain that the attorney retained on his behalf owes professional duties to the physician alone. If

there has been any question of coverage or intimation by the insurance company that a coverage issue might have to be litigated, it should be clearly delineated which party each attorney is representing so as to avoid potential conflicts of interest.

A professional liability policy requires the company to provide a defense for the insured on all claims in a complaint for which there may potentially be coverage. Typically, if there is a potential coverage issue, the carrier will issue a "reservation-of-rights" letter informing the physician that the company is providing defense counsel to the insured but is reserving its rights to deny coverage for any adverse verdict or settlement should the facts learned in litigation support such a denial. A reservation-of-rights letter will set forth the facts of the claim as understood by the insurance company and recite any potential portions of the policy in question that the company contends would support a denial of coverage. For example, the company may deny coverage because the physician was treating outside his or her specialty, did not give proper notice of the claim when it first arose, or has defaulted on payment of premiums.

A physician should retain separate counsel (different from the firm retained to defend the actual claim) to review any reservation of rights by the insurer, to provide advice about rights and obligations under the policy, and, if necessary, to litigate against the insurance company in the event of a wrongful denial of coverage. If it becomes necessary for the physician to sue for coverage of the claim—or if the insurer brings an action asking the court to declare that there is no coverage under the subject policy—the coverage lawsuit will proceed independently of the underlying claim or lawsuit by the patient. However, a coverage lawsuit may be stayed (temporarily halted) during the pendency of the liability suit since, if the physician wins the liability case, the coverage issue becomes moot. Also, the specific findings by the jury in the liability case may ultimately determine the coverage issue as well. The physician's coverage counsel and liability defense counsel will most likely work together to avoid duplication of efforts and to make sure that the two suits are efficiently managed.

The Initial Meeting with Defense Counsel

Physician's Overview of the Case

One of the first things defense counsel will want to do will be to meet with the physician face to face to find out about the particular facts underlying the claim, provide an overview of the legal standards and issues that will control, and give a preview of the upcoming events. The attorney will want the physician to bring copies of all pertinent medical records, bills, and charts for the patient (especially if the insurance company has not already given them to the attorney), any devices or instruments used that may be pertinent to the claim, and a list of all medical personnel involved in the evaluation and treatment of the plaintiff. The physician should be prepared to describe in detail the diagnosis and treatment of the plaintiff, identify what persons handled which aspects of the course of treatment, and explain all notes and abbreviations in the medical charts. Since in most cases the attorney will not have practiced medicine, he or she will also need to be familiarized with the normal etiology, symptoms, and progression of the condition at issue; how the procedure, treatment, or diagnosis in question is typically performed; and any background informa-

tion regarding any controversies or seminal articles on the treatment in question found in the medical literature. In some cases, the physician's knowledge of a new research study or newly approved technique may be a key facet of the plaintiff's case, but in every case the physician must help the attorney to become well educated about the conditions and treatments in question.

The physician must be entirely candid with his attorney at this and every stage of the proceedings. Presenting the attorney with a false view of the facts does much more harm than good in the long run. The other side will be looking to exploit any weaknesses in the defense. If the defense attorney is working with false information, he or she is primed for a fall that will possibly cost credibility with the judge or jury and will certainly decrease the chances of winning the case or settling it favorably. The attorney simply needs to know what, if any, mistakes were made to properly account for them in evaluating the case and constructing the defense. As one medical liability defense attorney sums it up, "The only fact that your attorney cannot deal with effectively is the one that you fail to convey, one that pops out for the first time in your deposition or at trial."[2]

The attorney-client privilege—whereby the attorney and the attorney's staff are ethically bound not to reveal any confidential communications made by the client—exists specifically to promote such full disclosure. A similar privilege protects patient-physician confidential communications, also in order to encourage candor; but the patient has waived that privilege, at least to some extent, by filing suit against the physician. The attorney-client privilege is considered sacrosanct, and it will only be violated in limited situations, such as to prevent the commission of fraud or a future crime.

Identification of Other Parties

The physician's initial overview of the case will also help the attorney to identify all of the persons or entities also named in the lawsuit and to sort out their respective roles in the treatment or diagnostic process. It is not unusual for a lawsuit to name several physicians, the hospital or clinic at which the treatment was rendered, and other health care providers involved in treating the patient. Plaintiff's attorneys typically look for as many potential sources of recovery as possible, knowing that the case against some defendants may be stronger than it is against others. Understandably, no plaintiff wants to end up at trial with all of the defendants casting the blame on another person not even present in the courtroom, so plaintiffs usually err on the side of inclusion, rather than exclusion.

Nevertheless, it may be in the physician's best interest to have additional parties added to the case. Once the attorney has a good feel for how the events in question happened, she can determine whether any other persons ought to be brought into the case as defendants. Some health care personnel or hospitals involved in the patient's treatment may have already settled claims against them. Thus, they may not have initially been sued but may need to be nominally in the lawsuit for the purposes of allocation of fault. Other defendants may have been overlooked or considered not worth pursuing by plaintiff's counsel.

The physician may want to file what is known as a cross claim against these or other defendants or a third-party complaint against new, as yet unnamed parties. In it,

the physician would allege either that the other defendant(s) are solely responsible for the plaintiff's illness or injury, or that if the physician is found liable to the plaintiff, they are, too, and should be obligated to reimburse him for the damages he has to pay. Some employment contracts and other practice arrangements may require one party to indemnify or hold harmless another, that is, to bear ultimate responsibility for the other's actions. The ultimate determination of who else, if anyone, is brought into the lawsuit will be made by the attorney once he has all the relevant facts and has researched the pertinent law.

Evaluation and Litigation of Procedural Pretrial Defenses

At that initial meeting with counsel, the physician can expect to receive a general overview of the procedural and substantive legal issues presented by the case. The meeting will focus in part on procedural issues (if not conclusively addressed in prior correspondence). As mentioned above, one of the procedural defenses that must be considered is invalid or improper service of process, which involves the factual circumstances of the timing and method of delivery of the suit papers. If service was not properly effectuated, the attorney may consider filing a motion to dismiss the complaint. This is a tactical decision, and it may turn on the seriousness of the defect, counsel's prior experience with and opinions of the attorneys representing other involved parties, the identity of the judge who would decide such a motion, and the measure of final resolution such a motion would achieve. In many instances, the remedy for an improperly served complaint—whether by an unauthorized means or on the wrong party—is the granting of additional time to effect proper service. Some defense attorneys therefore may in certain circumstances cooperate with opposing counsel to clear up any such defects and proceed efficiently to the merits of the case.

A motion to dismiss may also be filed if the claim was arguably filed outside the applicable statute of limitations or if the plaintiff has failed to comply with some other statute or procedural requirement. A statute of limitations, which sets the time limit for filing suit, does not begin to run until a cause of action has accrued, meaning that the alleged harm or injury has manifested itself (or at least been detected). The statute of limitations on medical malpractice actions varies from state to state, but it ordinarily ranges from two years to four years. However, every statute has its exceptions. For example, the statute of limitations may be considerably longer for claims involving treatment of minors, those involving foreign objects left in a patient's body, or claims where the injury or cause thereof was not reasonably discoverable for some period of time.

In some states, malpractice actions are also governed by a statute of repose. While the statute of limitations measures the time within which a lawsuit must be filed after a cause of action has accrued (as evidenced by the manifestation of injury), the statute of repose sets out the maximum amount of time within which a lawsuit can be filed after the medical treatment at issue was rendered, regardless of when the injury appeared. To evaluate a possible statute of limitations or statute of repose defense, the attorney will want to know the beginning and ending dates of all treatment, the date of the alleged act of negligence, and the dates of all contact between the physician and the plaintiff, her family, or her attorney.

Some states have enacted statutes that require a plaintiff to certify that before a suit was filed, a competent medical professional in the same area of expertise has reviewed the claim and would be willing to testify as to the breach of the standard of care.[3] The particular requirements of these statutes vary from state to state, but many of them provide for summary dismissal in the event of noncompliance.[4] Thus, a plaintiff's failure to comply with any such procedures may be another ground on which the attorney may file a motion to dismiss early in the proceedings.

The defense attorney will discuss these issues with the physician and will determine early on which, if any, of these procedural defenses are worth pursuing. They may be litigated in the form of a pretrial motion to dismiss if the facts surrounding them are not in dispute, or they may have to be resolved after the factual record has been developed through discovery.

A motion to dismiss asks the court to find that even if everything happened as the plaintiff contends, the defendant is not liable and should not even be required to defend the lawsuit, as a matter of law. Such a motion can usually be presented to and argued before the court without much more effort on the part of the defendant physician, although he may have to sign an affidavit or sworn declaration describing the particular circumstances of service of process, for example. Each side will have an opportunity to present its legal argument on such a motion, either in the form of legal briefs, oral argument at a hearing, or both, after which the judge will issue an order ruling one way or the other. The judge may take some time while considering the motion, and the case will essentially be on hold until a decision is rendered.

Evaluation of the Merits of the Case and Substantive Legal Defenses

The substantive legal issues must also be discussed at length by the physician and attorney at the initial meeting. Most cases in the malpractice arena will allege simple negligence, although a physician who does not secure proper informed consent to do surgery or who operates on the wrong organ or appendage may be sued for battery (unconsented touching that causes harm), which is considered an intentional tort, as well as negligence. Since informed consent issues are discussed in greater detail in chapter 6 of this book, the present discussion will focus on a medical negligence action.

The elements of a medical negligence action are fairly simple conceptually: The plaintiff must establish that the physician breached the standard of care in his evaluation and/or treatment and that such breach was the proximate cause of the patient's alleged injury. The plaintiff will try to establish that the physician did not act as a reasonable physician with similar training would have under the circumstances, and that the physician's error or omission made the plaintiff sicker, caused her to get well slower, or caused her injury or death.

Of course, the plaintiff will have to present factual testimony—from the patient or her family, nurses, or other medical staff—to establish her version of what happened and when. More important, however, to establish both the standard of care and whether that standard was breached in this particular case, the plaintiff will have to present the testimony of one, or several, expert witnesses. These experts should be

other physicians in the relevant field of expertise—frequently, but not always, medical school professors or well-respected practitioners—who will testify about the correct procedure for evaluation and/or treatment of a particular condition and identify any deviation by the defendant physician. Expert testimony must also be used to establish that the physician's alleged negligence proximately caused the further injuries or illness, pain, and suffering allegedly endured by the plaintiff.

Assuming that the case does not settle early in the process, the defendant physician will ultimately have the opportunity to present both factual and expert testimony as well, including that of other physicians or medical personnel assisting in the procedure and experts retained to testify that the physician followed the pertinent standard of care under the circumstances. The issues of breach of the standard of care and proximate cause will often boil down to a "battle of the experts," and the outcome will depend largely on which side's experts come across as the most knowledgeable, objective, and credible. As discussed below, the physician will have an important role to play in the identification and selection of expert witnesses to testify on his behalf.

In many medical negligence cases, the substantive issues are conceptually straightforward. Did the physician breach the standard of care in providing a particular drug to a patient with this patient's particular history, or by performing an operation in a particular manner? Was the patient's postoperative infection caused by the carelessness of the nursing staff or by factors out of their control? Did the cardiologist fail to tie the suture properly, or was the suture damaged or mishandled before application?

The two most straightforward and commonly asserted defenses are, of course, to argue that the physician did not breach the standard of care and/or that any error that the physician may have made was not the proximate cause of the plaintiff's condition getting worse or failing to improve. The burden at all times is on the plaintiff to establish these elements of her case (that is, a "tie" goes to the defendant). The defense, however, must present evidence tending to disprove either or both of these elements. Frequently, denying the existence of a breach and of proximate cause will go hand in hand, but the attorney may occasionally have to choose one path or the other to present a consistent defense.

Regardless, both of these issues require the physician to present expert testimony—her own and almost always that of other knowledgeable physicians. Therefore, at some point fairly early on in the case, the physician will need to help the attorney find reputable experts in the pertinent field(s) of medicine to testify on behalf of the defense. The attorney may have a list of medical experts with whom he has worked previously, but the physician's additional input will be crucial for a number of reasons. First, the attorney may not have needed an expert in a particular field before and may not be familiar with its preeminent practitioners or scholars. Second, some of the experts on the list may have provided prior or subsequent care to this particular patient, in which case they may be needed—and may ultimately be more helpful—as fact witnesses, and in some circumstances cannot be contacted without consent of the plaintiff's counsel. Third, some of the "usual suspects" among the experts may already have reviewed the file consultatively and/or signed on to testify on behalf of the plaintiff. Finally, for strategic reasons the attorney may want to avoid experts who spend a great deal more time testifying as experts than practicing medicine. Such experts often, over time, become susceptible to being portrayed by the opposition as "hired guns" rather than scientific, objective arbiters of the standard of care.

Thus, it might be a wise idea for a physician to bring to the initial meeting with counsel a list of practitioners (local or national) and noted experts in the pertinent specialty who might be willing to testify on his behalf. Since the plaintiff will be out looking for experts in support of her side as well, time will frequently be of the essence. If the insurance company has not already lined up supporting experts before the suit was filed, then the attorney will want to do so speedily. If there are several defendants, this effort will often be coordinated among defense counsel, both to present a consistent defense and to economize on litigation expenses.

Other defenses exist that shield a physician from liability even if the plaintiff proves all the elements of her case against the physician. These affirmative defenses (called so because the defendant bears the burden of proving the facts to support them) include the statutes of limitations and repose discussed earlier, independent intervening negligence of some other person, and contributory or comparative negligence by the plaintiff.

The independent intervening negligence defense is, practically speaking, another way of attacking proximate cause. It requires the attorney to show that despite the physician's negligent conduct (as proved by the plaintiff), a subsequent negligent act or omission by another party was the real cause of plaintiff's death, continued illness, or other injury. For example, suppose that the plaintiff can prove that her surgeon negligently failed to prevent, detect, or treat a postoperative bacterial infection later detected by plaintiff's primary care physician as it began to ripen into pneumonia. The primary care physician prescribes a course of penicillin, neglecting to ascertain that the patient is allergic to the drug. The patient develops a severe reaction to the drug and has to be rehospitalized for several more agonizing days. The surgeon will probably try to argue that the primary care physician's intervening negligent act—the erroneous prescription—was the reason that the patient sustained additional damages and thus in effect cuts off her liability for allowing the patient to develop pneumonia in the first place.

Of course, the plaintiff will contend that she never would have needed the prescription but for the surgeon's mistake, and the second physician, for tactical reasons, might not vigorously oppose her arguments in this regard. The case may then boil down to a determination of what the defendant's prognosis would have been but for the misprescription. Suffice it to say that for an intervening act of negligence to insulate the first negligent actor from all liability, it must be sufficiently separated from the first negligent action or omission. If, for example, instead of developing an allergic drug reaction, the patient was injured in a car accident while returning to the hospital for treatment of the pneumonia, the physician will have a better chance of avoiding liability for the plaintiff's subsequent hospitalization for injuries sustained in the accident.

Contributory or comparative negligence is a complete or partial defense to liability when it can be shown that the plaintiff failed to act with the care of a reasonable person, regardless of the physician's negli-

gence, and in so doing caused or contributed to her death or injury. For example, change the previous hypothetical case so that the patient is prescribed a proper antibiotic but neglects to take it and is subsequently hospitalized when her condition worsens. The physician is still responsible for plaintiff's illness, but the plaintiff's failure to follow the prescribed treatment helped worsen her condition and cause her damages. The patient's negligence may be a partial or complete defense to liability, depending on the applicable law.

All but four states have abandoned the common law concept of pure contributory negligence, whereby a plaintiff is completely barred from all recovery if found to be even 1 percent at fault for causing her injuries.[5] Most states instead allow some form of comparative negligence defense. In pure comparative negligence states, the jury must determine the plaintiff's total damages and percentage of liability for which each party is responsible. The plaintiff's recovery is then reduced by her proportionate share. For example, if the physician is found 60 percent responsible and the plaintiff is found 40 percent responsible, plaintiff's award is reduced by 40 percent. If her total damages are $50,000, she recovers only $30,000. In modified comparative negligence states, parties are similarly assigned a percentage of the total liability, and plaintiff's reward is reduced by her share, unless it is greater than 50 percent, in which case she recovers nothing.

There may be other affirmative defenses that apply according to the particular facts of the case and the statutes and case law of a particular state. Every state has, for example, enacted some form of Good Samaritan law, which shields a medical professional from liability for negligence—but not for criminal misconduct or gross negligence—if she was rendering services in response to a medical emergency, unless doing so in the ordinary course of business, that is, in an emergency room. Similarly, in Florida, a statute codifies a form of "charitable immunity," whereby health care providers who offer free medical services to indigents are completely immune from suit for negligence.[6]

Once provided with all the relevant facts, the defense attorney will advise the physician as to the availability of these or any other affirmative defenses and the advisability of asserting them in light of other tactical considerations. Sometime after the initial conference with the physician and the resolution of any motions to dismiss on procedural grounds, the attorney will prepare an answer to the complaint, in which she will admit or deny each of the plaintiff's factual allegations or conclusions of law, assert any cross-claims or third-party claims, and set forth any applicable affirmative defenses. In most cases, the physician will have an opportunity to review the answer before it is filed in order to make certain that it recites the facts correctly and uses proper medical terminology where appropriate. The filing of the answer will trigger the beginning of the discovery period in the case, whereby the parties begin providing to and obtaining from each other the evidence needed to support their positions.

Valuation of Plaintiff's Claim and of Defendant's Exposure

One of the more significant subjects on the physician's mind is likely to be that of damages: How much is the plaintiff suing for, and how much is he likely to get? Although the physician will have some idea of how the plaintiff and the insurance company value the case, the attorney will bring a fresh, experienced perspective to the issue. More important, the attorney will be looking to combine her practical litigation experience with the physician's medical knowledge of expected outcomes and prognoses to come up with a realistic assessment of the likelihood and potential size of an adverse verdict. To help the attorney to value the case, the physician ought to know a little bit about the law of damages recovery going in.

Medical malpractice plaintiffs are permitted to seek reimbursement of economic damages (for example, lost earnings and expenses for medical treatment incident to and necessitated by the alleged act of negligence), noneconomic damages (typically referred to as "pain and suffering"), and punitive damages (additional sums awarded to deter intentional, malicious, or reckless behavior).

Past economic damages are typically fairly easy to quantify—the plaintiff will simply present evidence of how much he spent for the negligent care and any past remedial care, as well as the value of plaintiff's lost salary or wages from work. However, in cases where the degree and cost of necessary future medical care or lost future earning capacity are involved, each side will likely rely on expert testimony to establish what type and level of care the plaintiff will need, as well as his opportunities for future gainful employment. In particular, each side may present expert testimony from an economist or life-care plan specialist to assist the jury in determining its award.

In many states, a rule known as the collateral-source rule has caused no end of consternation among physicians and defense attorneys. According to this rule, in considering the amount of plaintiff's economic damages, the jury is not allowed to hear evidence that the plaintiff was compensated for medical bills or lost time from work from any other third-party payers, such as private health insurance or workers' compensation insurance. Nor is the defendant allowed any type of credit against or reduction in the verdict against him for these amounts already paid from other sources. Thus, where the collateral-source rule is in effect, there is a general perception that plaintiffs frequently "double recover," that is, they get compensated for medical bills that they have already paid from these other sources and pocket the extra money.

In truth, however, workers' compensation insurers, Medicare/Medicaid, and other sources of first-party insurance benefits will often (although not always) be entitled by statute or contract to a lien on any recovery the plaintiff obtains from a negligent third party. Nevertheless, over half of the states have abolished the collateral-source rule in an effort to prevent real or perceived double recovery in medical negligence and other tort actions.[7] Therefore, the attorney will need to know whether the plaintiff's medical bills have been paid, and by whom, to be able to apply the law of the pertinent state and calculate the value of plaintiff's economic damages claim.

Noneconomic and punitive damages are perceived to be more of a wild card than economic damages. The good news is that punitive damages awards in professional liability cases are rare, given the high threshold a plaintiff must meet (that is, gross negligence, recklessness, or willful misconduct) to recover them. Damages for pain and suffering, however, may still be quite substantial and can often form the greatest portion of a liability judgment. Many state legislatures have placed limits on recovery of

noneconomic damages, partly in response to the perception that juries award them in excessive amounts. As a presidential advisory commission on the quality of health care found in 1998, "approximately two-thirds of the States have imposed some limits on the size of malpractice awards made by the courts."[8] According to the commission, these caps on noneconomic damages may range from $250,000 to $750,000. In some states, total awards are capped at as much as $1 million.

In light of the complexity of computing potential damages, another way in which a physician can be of great assistance to the attorney in the early stages of the case is in helping to evaluate the risk exposure. Up to this point, all the evaluation of plaintiff's damages and likelihood of prevailing has been conducted by the insurance company. Now, it is in the hands of the warrior who must actually ride the horse into battle, so to speak. The attorney is likely to have some familiarity with the range of potential jury verdicts in the jurisdiction and the degree to which any applicable defenses are likely to succeed, given the judges who will be handling the case. The physician can bring to the table information regarding odds of survival or recovery associated with given conditions, as well as the costs of remedial, rehabilitative, or palliative care for the injuries in question.

How these two learned professionals value a particular case—as a function of maximum potential liability and likelihood of winning or losing—will help decide the approach they must take in defending it. Some cases may be frivolous and easily disposed of. Some may be questionable and high risk, calling for all-out litigation war. Still others may require a quick and easy settlement once the litigation battle lines have been drawn. Even the insurance company's evaluation will evolve over time, especially as defense costs and expert witness fees become a reality.

However, some cases are tougher to value because they do not fit the traditional mold of a standard negligence case. In particular, missed-diagnosis cases—where it is not alleged that the physician caused injury or illness but rather failed to detect or properly treat an illness in time to save the patient's life or obviate the need for more invasive or expensive treatment—can present particular problems of proof of causation and measurement of damages.

Consider the claim of a forty-five-year-old woman who is being treated for a fractured left femur when a preoperative chest x-ray reveals an abnormality in one of her lungs and recommends further x-rays or a CT scan. The woman alleges that her orthopedist did not make any mention of this finding by the radiologist. One year later, following another chest x-ray, the radiologist notes "probable scarring" in the left upper lobe of her lung and again recommends a CT. Once again the orthopedist does not follow up on this finding. One year later, the woman is diagnosed with lung cancer, and she dies shortly thereafter. According to expert testimony, the patient's odds of survival were about 50 percent had she begun receiving treatment shortly after the first x-ray. By the time of the second, those odds had decreased to 20 percent or 25 percent. By the time the cancer was diagnosed, they had dropped to 15 percent to 20 percent.[9]

What showing should be sufficient for a malpractice claim by this woman's husband to succeed? What, if anything, should he be allowed to recover from the physician who missed this diagnosis? Change some of the variables a bit, and the analysis grows even more complicated: Suppose that she has not yet died at the time of suit and is now given a 10 percent chance of survival for the next five years. On the other hand, suppose that with chemotherapy and radiation, her cancer has gone into remission by the time of the trial. Or suppose that she is eighty instead of forty-five years old and had already outlived her life expectancy. What are her damages worth in each of these cases?

Put simply, what is the value of a decrease in a plaintiff's chance of survival if proved to have been caused to some degree by a physician's negligence? Does it matter whether the decrease was from 85 percent to 66 percent, from 50 percent to 20 percent, or from 10 percent to 5 percent? How does the analysis change if the risk does not materialize in death? State courts and legislatures have adopted several different approaches to these kinds of dilemmas, known as "lost-chance" cases. Under the traditional approach to these kinds of cases, followed in eighteen states, a plaintiff is not compensated for a lost chance of survival unless that chance was greater than 50 percent to start with.[10] If it was, the plaintiff can recover all of the damages suffered. The net effect of this approach is that "a patient who probably would have suffered the same harm had he or she received the proper treatment is entitled to no compensation."[11]

Eleven states have tried to take a more proportional approach to these kinds of cases, allowing recovery "even if with proper care the plaintiff's chance of recovery would not have exceeded 50 percent" but restricting plaintiff's recovery to "the proportion of the total amount of serious injury or death-related damages reflecting the reduced chance."[12] As one commentator has described this approach in action:

For example, if a patient had a forty percent chance of recovering from breast cancer and a negligent physician's misdiagnosis results in her chances dropping to ten percent, then the plaintiff can recover thirty percent of her total death-related injuries. Thus, if her damages totaled $100,000, the plaintiff could recover $30,000.[13]

The plaintiff still must prove by a preponderance of the evidence that the defendant's negligence caused the reduction in the patient's chance of recovery.

Finally, in five states, courts have adopted what may loosely be termed a relaxed-causation approach, which "allows a plaintiff's case to reach the jury by relaxing the burden of proof" so that a "plaintiff need only show that the physician's negligence led to a percentage increase, no matter how small, in the patient's risk of harm" to obtain full recovery of her damages.[14]

Many other kinds of cases present similar difficulties in valuation. For example, in a prescription case, both the prescribing physician and the pharmaceutical manufacturer may be found partially responsible for a patient's death from a particular drug. Other types of cases may involve manufacturers of medical devices, such as pedicle screws or breast implants. How liability will be allocated by a jury in such cases depends greatly on a particular state's law. Some states maintain the concept of joint and several liability for such injuries, which means that every party proved to be partially at fault for the injury in question is considered individually liable for the full amount of the damages award. The assumption underlying this approach is that the liable parties can best negotiate among themselves the allocation of liability for the full amount. To facilitate that process and to make sure that the plaintiff is fully compensated, courts enable the plaintiff to enforce the entire judgment against any responsible party. Joint and several liability can prove especially troubling for a defendant found to be only partially at fault but who happens to be the only defendant remaining solvent or adequately insured.

Other states have adopted some sort of comparative allocation of liability, whereby a liable defendant is responsible only for a proportionate share of the jury verdict. This approach, too, has its problems. It is frequently difficult to predict how a jury will allocate responsibility—especially in a case, for example, involving many physicians, a hospital, and a multimillion-dollar medical device manufacturer.

One final type of case presenting difficult issues of valuation is worth mentioning. What is the value of a claim for increased exposure to a particular risk that has not yet materialized? For example, although many of the pending fen-phen claims have been filed by patients who actually developed primary pulmonary hypertension or heart-valve defects allegedly as a result of the off-label combination of these two weight-loss drugs, many other claims have been filed by patients who have not yet developed cardiac or pulmonary problems but fear that they might in the future. Courts and state legislatures are now having to decide the extent to which a physician (or, for that matter, a pharmaceutical company) should have to pay for the future costs of testing and monitoring a patient for the onset of these conditions, as well as for any future costs of treatment in the event the conditions materialize. Understandably, plaintiffs have a real fear that these conditions may develop (even if they have discontinued usage of the drugs) farther down the road. The manufacturer may by that time, however, have exhausted all available insurance coverage, be bankrupt, or be out of business—and therefore judgment-proof. On the other hand, the feared conditions may never materialize, resulting in no real compensable injury other than anxiety and fear of future illness perhaps. (Similar issues are presented in cases for fear of HIV infection from contact with a contaminated needle.) Somehow, courts considering these claims must foretell the likelihood of injury, place a present dollar value on that injury, and determine how much, if anything, a patient should recover to be compensated for a future injury or fear of one.

Needless to say, such calculations can make one's head spin. They are important for the physician to understand, though, because the valuation of a medical malpractice claim is dependent on a number of legal, medical, and interpersonal variables. Therefore, it must be a joint function of physician and attorney. The physician may be one of the attorney's main sources of scientific knowledge. His contribution to the damages calculation may be crucial and may have a significant impact on case management and strategy. Likewise, the more the physician knows about the risk of the case, the better equipped he is to make a practical, economical decision about settlement options.

Pretrial Discovery Procedures

The physician's role in the case by no means ends just because the answer has been filed and her attorney has a general overview of the case. Once the complaint has been filed and answered, any procedural pretrial motions have been resolved, and a general litigation strategy has been mapped out, the process of pretrial discovery will begin.

By some estimates, it takes an average of four to five years to resolve a malpractice claim from incident to disposition.[15] Discovery will usually consume the greatest portion of that time once suit has been filed. While relatively few malpractice actions actually go to trial (most are settled, abandoned, or dismissed somewhere along the way), almost all nonfrivolous ones go through some portion of the discovery process. It is in discovery that the battle is frequently won or lost. In discovery, the parties' attorneys will begin truly digging into the case. It is important for the physician to understand what is going on behind the scenes all this time in order to be better prepared when the time comes to return to active participation—as it most certainly will.

It should be noted that the attorneys typically control the discovery process. The presiding court will only be involved to the extent necessary to set deadlines for the completion of discovery or to resolve any disputes among the parties about the propriety of requests or the timeliness and sufficiency of responses. The trial judge will have the ultimate say as to what information and evidence may be considered by the jury at trial but will typically not be a noticeable player during discovery.

The rules of civil procedure that govern the discovery process provide two primary means by which an attorney may learn what evidence or expert opinions the opposition is planning to offer at trial, written requests for information and live testimony of witnesses at depositions. The typical case will involve some of both kinds of discovery. Although there is some tactical variation among attorneys, written discovery is usually exchanged before taking depositions. Each of these elements can make or break a case if not handled properly by the attorney—or by his client.

Written Discovery

The plaintiff's written discovery requests must, like the initial complaint, be served on the defendant in some form prescribed by law. Although written discovery may sometimes be served directly on the physician along with the complaint (a tactic some plaintiff's attorneys use in an attempt to overwhelm the defendant or set him up for a procedural default), more often such discovery requests are served on the parties' attorneys. Regardless of the manner of service, the defense attorney bears primary responsibility for making sure that the required responses get filed in the right form and within the mandatory time period—typically thirty days, with extensions of time frequently obtained as needed.

Written discovery requests may take one of three forms, requests for admissions, interrogatories, and requests for production of documents. Requests for admissions are statements of fact that the recipient is asked to admit or deny under oath, such as, "Admit that Mrs Jones told you about her family history of breast cancer at her initial office visit on July 1, 1999." If the recipient of the request fails to respond to any request for admission, the statement is automatically deemed to be admitted as true. The recipient is also typically instructed to provide a full explanation of the factual basis for his denial of any particular request. Therefore, these types of discovery requests are considered useful for three purposes. First, they may serve to narrow the issues in the case by determining the basic facts upon which the parties will be able to agree. Second, they help the propounding attorney gain in-

sight into the opposition's legal strategy and view of the evidence. Third, they are often sent in hopes that the other side will fail to respond and thereby judicially admit facts which help the party that propounded the request. Thus, it is extremely important that if requests for admissions are served along with the complaint, they are passed on to the defense attorney immediately to make sure a response is timely filed or an extension of time is obtained.

Requests for production of documents typically ask for the party on whom they are served to provide all documents described by the requests. This is how the plaintiff will typically obtain a copy of all of the physician's medical charts, notes, records, bills, test results, x-rays, and so forth—sometimes even if he has already obtained some of these records before filing suit. Conversely, the defense attorney may serve similar requests on the plaintiff, asking him to provide, for example, all of the records of his treatment by any other physicians (before, after, or during the physician's own treatment), opinion letters or reports prepared by plaintiff's expert witnesses, and evidence of any payment of plaintiff's damages from other sources.

Finally, interrogatories are written questions submitted to the parties alone asking for general information regarding the case, including explanations of the recipient's view of the facts, lists of all persons believed to have knowledge of the facts of the case, and information regarding previous claims filed against the defendant (or filed by the plaintiff). Interrogatories must be answered under oath by the responding party, and they may be used in a trial as if they were live testimony. Therefore, the accuracy and consistency of interrogatory responses are especially crucial.

The defense attorney will review all incoming written discovery requests and keep track of the response deadlines. She will necessarily enlist the physician's aid (and perhaps that of other members of the treatment team) in preparing the responses, either by sending the questions to the physician for a first draft of the answers or by going through them one by one in person or over the phone. It is important for the physician to provide responses speedily, as the defense attorney will need some time to review the responses and put them into the proper form on time.

The attorney will also identify any requests that are legally irrelevant, unduly burdensome, or, in the words of the governing rule of civil procedure, not "reasonably calculated to lead to the production of admissible evidence," and will object in writing to each such interrogatory or request. If the opposing counsel does not believe the objections are warranted, he may try to negotiate to obtain the information requested voluntarily. If the parties cannot agree on the objections or sufficiency of the responses, the dissatisfied party may file a motion to compel the other side's responses, asking the presiding judge to rule on whether the information sought is discoverable.

The physician will not only assist the attorney in responding to discovery but may also have a role to play in the preparation of discovery requests to propound on the plaintiff as well. (Thankfully, discovery is a two-way street.) The physician may, for example, identify certain facts in favor of the defense and help the attorney draft questions about them. Moreover, as always, the physician will probably assist the attorney with proper use and understanding of medical terminology in the preparation of discovery requests. Like much of litigation, this process is tedious and time-consuming, but being meticulous on the front end may save time and money spent on the claim in the long run.

Finally, the physician will participate in the written discovery process by reviewing the responses of the plaintiff to help the attorney evaluate their credibility, accuracy, or sufficiency; identifying any medical or factual mistakes and information omitted or unaccounted for in them; and reviewing the reports of plaintiff's expert witnesses to help the attorney understand them and prepare to take their depositions. This considerable involvement in written discovery helps give a physician a feel for how the case is going, helps give the attorney timely notice of any inaccuracies or inconsistencies to exploit, helps identify any further investigation needed, and most of all helps the physician to prepare for the day when he will give his own testimony for the first time at his deposition.

Depositions

There is perhaps no more important facet of the discovery process in any civil case—and especially in any malpractice case—than a deposition of a key witness. A deposition is a witness's recorded testimony, given under oath, upon being questioned by the attorneys for the parties in the case. A deposition is a chance for the attorneys to find out what facts and opinions the witness will testify to at trial. Therefore, one side's attorney will typically depose witnesses identified by the other side in support of its case.

In the typical medical liability case, the plaintiff's attorney will take the deposition of the physician, the physician's expert witnesses, and any fact witnesses the physician has identified as favorable. The defense attorney will also take the depositions of plaintiff and plaintiff's witnesses. If the witness is one of the parties, his or her attorney will of course be there to object to any allegedly improper questions, hear for himself how his own witness comes across, and ask any follow-up questions necessary to clarify the witness's answers or any misimpressions created on the record by the other attorney's questioning. Neutral witnesses may be subpoenaed for deposition by either party and usually will be questioned by each side in the course of a deposition.

Attorneys do not use depositions only to learn what a given witness will say. They will also be seeking to pin down the witness's testimony to keep it from changing, to ferret out and explore any weaknesses in a fact witness's recollection or an expert's opinion, and to assess the witness's overall credibility and jury appeal. The strength or weakness of a party's or a key expert's deposition testimony is often a crucial factor in a party's decision to settle the case or press on to trial. Deposition testimony may also be tendered to the presiding judge on a motion for summary judgment, whereby either party may argue that the facts as revealed in discovery are not in dispute and therefore it is entitled to judgment as a matter of law.

With so much riding on a deposition, a physician absolutely must be well prepared for his own testimony. Naturally, preparation involves a thorough and exacting review of the patient's medical records and the physician's treatment notes. Most, if not all, of these documents will already have been provided to opposing counsel, who will have examined every word looking for inconsistencies or omissions. A physician's failure to know the treatment history could well be used by the plaintiff's attorney to show carelessness, callousness, or ignorance. The physician should also, to the extent possible, review the more important contents of the attorney's litigation file, including all discovery responses (especially his or her own) and expert reports to make sure that his or her testimony is consistent with the known facts and sufficiently addresses the concerns of plaintiff's experts. In the course of this review, the attorney should assist the physician to "focus preparation and thinking on areas of care that create liability exposure, not every nuance of the care provided."[16]

Where possible, the physician should attend all of the other depositions in the case but especially those of the plaintiff and plaintiff's experts. Again, this will be time-consuming, but the physician is the person best able to help the defense attorney understand the other expert's testimony and look for holes or inconsistencies in it. Moreover, as an in-house staff attorney for one medical liability insurer puts it, the physician's presence "not only helps [him] become more familiar with the process, it also helps the deposed parties think more carefully about their responses."[17] At a minimum, the physician will need to spend a significant amount of time helping the attorney prepare to depose the plaintiff's experts.

Dispositive Motions—Round Two

At the completion of discovery, one or more of the parties may file a motion for summary judgment, asking the court to rule in its favor as a matter of law even if the opposition's version of the facts is considered to be true for the purposes of the motion. The moving party must show that there is "no genuine issue of material fact" and thus nothing for a jury to decide. Toward that end, the moving party will file portions of the discovery exchanged and deposition transcripts, as well as legal briefs setting forth its argument. Once the movant has met its burden, the nonmoving party must file its own brief and evidence of specific facts demonstrating a genuine issue for trial. When considering summary judgment motions, courts must view the undisputed facts and the inferences to be drawn from them in the light most favorable to the party opposing the motion.

Because of the many factual issues and conflicting expert opinions often involved, summary judgment is rarely granted in medical negligence actions. However, the defense attorney may want to file such a motion if plaintiff has failed to turn up any evidence of one of the elements of her case (such as any actual damages or breach of the standard of care) or if there is legal authority establishing as a matter of law that the plaintiff's version of the facts does not give rise to legal liability. Such a motion, if successful, may dispose of all or part of a plaintiff's case and may be worth pursuing depending on the circumstances.

Alternative Dispute Resolution

Once the parties have exchanged written information and documents, heard the fact and expert witnesses' anticipated testimony during their depositions, and learned whether the case may be resolved as a matter of law, they may be in better positions to sit down and talk about resolving the case before trial. Increasingly, courts like to encourage parties to resolve their disputes by agreement rather than trial; therefore, the judge may at some point either conduct a settlement conference or appoint a neutral third party to be a mediator or arbitrator of the dispute. Some courts interpose dispute resolution earlier in the process than others.

In the closer medical liability cases, meaningful mediation may not be possible until after the completion of discovery.

The most common form of dispute resolution in civil litigation cases—and the one most suitable for medical malpractice cases—is mediation. At a mediation, all parties, their attorneys, and, typically, representatives from any involved insurance carriers must attend a face-to-face meeting with a neutral third-party mediator appointed by the court and/or agreed to by the parties. Unlike an arbitrator or the medical review panels found in some states, a true mediator does not decide the case. Rather, the mediator's goal is to get the parties to agree to settle the claim on mutually agreeable terms. Actually, there is an old saying that a successful mediation is one in which the parties are equally unhappy with the result. Mediation is often useful because it

gives the power to the parties themselves, to resolve disputes at an earlier and less expensive point in the process, before the specter of trial forces a settlement. It is a generally recognized fact that most lawsuits settle before trial, but usually only "on the courthouse steps." By then, years have gone by, money has been spent, emotions have been exhausted and wounds are still open.[18]

At the beginning of a mediation session, the mediator will typically present an overview of the session, hear presentations or summaries of evidence from each party, and then lead the parties in a discussion of settlement possibilities. The parties may break out into separate rooms, and the mediator may go back and forth between the rooms relaying offers and counteroffers, as well as the parties' concerns and their opinions of the relative strengths and weaknesses of each other's case or defenses.

The defendants' insurance carriers will also be involved heavily at the mediation as well, and depending on the particular provision of the policy, they may have the authority to settle the case. With multiple defendants, some of the most serious negotiations may take place among defense counsel about how liability should be apportioned among their respective clients.

Mediators differ widely in style and approach: Some are hands-off, while others will twist the parties' arms to get a settlement. A good mediator is one who can apply gentle but firm pressure to each side to bring about an agreement or who can persuade a stubborn party that the facts and/or law are not in his favor. Both plaintiff's and defense attorneys are often thankful for mediation because it gives their clients a chance to hear what an unbiased third party thinks of the merits of the case. Often the mediator is able to convince a party that her case is weak when no one else can: She certainly will not believe it when the opposing attorney or party tells her, and she does not want to hear it from her own attorney either.

The physician's role in the mediation is especially crucial. This may be the first time, other than in the context of an adversarial deposition, that the plaintiff and the physician have come face to face, with an opportunity to address what has happened between them. The physician's demeanor will communicate to the client whether he or she is genuinely concerned for the plaintiff's well-being or is more influenced by anger and frustration at having been sued. What the physician says and how she says it may have a big impact on the parties' ability to reach an agreement on favorable terms.

Typically, a mediation session offers each party a chance to speak with impunity; that is, statements made in the course of a mediation are considered privileged and may not be used by either party against the other if the case proceeds to trial.[19] Therefore, if a physician-defendant is concerned that an error was made or is at least genuinely sorry for what happened to the plaintiff, whatever the cause, he or she should take the opportunity to say so. Since many malpractice suits are brought because of a plaintiff's desire to have someone take responsibility for an injury or loss,[20] such an admission, when warranted, may go a long way toward resolution of the case. Before the mediation session, however, the physician should consult with the defense attorney to make sure that any statements are indeed protected from disclosure.

The mediation will conclude when either an agreement is reached or the talks come to an impasse. The parties may agree on all the specific terms of a settlement agreement, or they may leave some of the details to be hammered out by the attorneys in the days and weeks to come. In a typical settlement agreement, the parties will agree that the physician's settlement of the claim does not constitute an admission of liability and to keep the terms of the settlement agreement confidential. The attorneys will help with the drafting of any other terms that may be necessary or desired by the parties under the particular circumstances.

Even if an impasse is declared at the mediation conference, the effort spent is not necessarily for naught. The parties' discussions may yet prove to be the catalyst later on for a settlement reached before trial. Frequently, one party or another will want to make the final concessions necessary to reach an agreement but will desire to do so a few days later to save face. A number of psychological and interpersonal factors are at work in any mediation. A physician should go into the process with a willingness to explore all avenues of peaceful resolution. Surrender, even partial surrender, is often painful, but then so is trial of a medical liability case.

Trial

A blow-by-blow explanation of a medical malpractice trial is beyond the scope of this chapter, but a physician ought to have at least a basic understanding of how a trial works in general. The key fact to remember is that a physician's demeanor at the trial at all times—not just while on the witness stand—is especially important. The judge and jury will be able to observe the physician's posture, body language, and casual interactions with witnesses and court personnel throughout the trial. What they see and hear will help form their impressions and may even shape their deliberations. Therefore, to the extent she can know a little bit about what to expect as the trial progresses, a physician can be prepared to project a quiet confidence without coming across as arrogant or uninterested.

Before the trial begins, the attorneys will confer with the presiding judge to discuss any last-minute settlement options and the evidence and testimony to be offered and to work out any procedural or technical issues. In particular, the attorneys may ask the judge, orally or in writing, to exclude any particular items of evidence that they know will be offered during the trial. Such motions, called motions *in limine,* are based on the rules of evidence and may be ruled on by the judge or may be held for consideration as the issues arise.

The trial will begin in earnest with the selection of the jury. The selection process varies from state to state and from court to court. In general, a large pool of potential jurors will be brought in and questioned—both all together and individually—by the lawyers for each side about their background, work experience, jury or litigation experience, and any personal biases and prejudices that may impair their ability to render a fair decision in the case. This is each side's first chance to give a preview of its case and to begin to build rapport with the jurors. Therefore, the physician's demeanor during this phase—whether while being introduced or reacting to the plaintiff's attorney's summary of the case—will no doubt be scrutinized.

Jurors with an obvious conflict of interest—such as relatives of one of the parties or persons with similar claims pending in the same court—may be removed from the jury "for cause." Each side will also be given a number of peremptory challenges or strikes, which enable them to remove potential jurors from the panel for virtually any other reason (save race or gender). Jury selection is not an exact science, and attorneys have many different styles and guidelines that they use. Generally speaking, however, a malpractice defense attorney is going to be looking for more educated jurors who can understand technical terms and appreciate the nuances of medical decisions, business owners who have a stake in the community and can relate to what it might feel like to be sued, and persons without a significant history of filing claims.

Once both sides have exercised their peremptory challenges and are satisfied with the final composition of the jury, the selected jurors and any alternate jurors will be sworn in and presentation of the case will begin. In a medical liability case, the plaintiff carries the burden of proof, which in a civil trial usually requires establishing the elements of the case "by a preponderance of the evidence" or "by the greater weight of the evidence." Thus, the burden is on the plaintiff to put forth evidence and persuade the jury. If the evidence balances, defendant wins. The defendant bears the burden of proof on any affirmative defenses, however, as discussed previously. As the party with the burden of proof, plaintiff is permitted to give the first opening statement and (after defendant's opening statement) to put on its case first. The opening statement will merely be a preview of the evidence. It is not supposed to be argumentative in tone.

Plaintiff's counsel will call each of plaintiff's witnesses, one at a time, and ask them questions to elicit their direct testimony. Defense counsel will then have an opportunity to cross-examine each witness in an attempt to undermine his or her credibility, demonstrate bias, or point out other facts of which the witness was not aware or did not acknowledge in testimony. Cross-examination is not usually as dramatic as it is portrayed on *Perry Mason, Matlock,* or *Law & Order.* Nevertheless, it is very important to the case. The physician should pay close attention to all of the testimony and evidence offered by the plaintiff to assist the attorney in watching out for inconsistencies or misstatements and also to prepare for testimony and cross-examination.

Once the plaintiff has finished presenting witnesses and evidence, the judge may entertain any motions by the defense for the entry of a directed verdict. Such a motion asks the judge to rule that the plaintiff has not provided sufficient evidence to let the case be considered by the jury. Such a motion is rarely granted at this stage of the proceedings. The attorneys may also use this break to deal with any procedural or technical aspects of defendant's presentation of evidence.

The defense attorney(s) will then begin to present their evidence, which in most cases will include the testimony of the physician and any supporting experts. Plaintiff's attorneys will have the opportunity for cross-examination as well. The tone and tactics of the cross-examination of the defendant will be somewhat different from those employed by the plaintiff's counsel at deposition. In the deposition, attorney was looking for holes or other problems with the defendant's or expert's testimony. During cross-examination, plaintiff's counsel will be trying to make use of what she has already learned to undercut the physician's testimony before the jury. Any inconsistencies with defendant's deposition testimony or discovery responses will be exploited. The attorney may attempt to get the physician to lose his cool or show arrogance or indifference on the stand. The defense attorney will have counseled the defendant on how to avoid the pitfalls of cross-examination and how to cultivate a juror-friendly attitude.

The attorneys will, of course, object to the admission of certain testimony or pieces of evidence throughout the trial as appropriate, and the judge will typically sustain (grant) or overrule (deny) these objections on the spot. Occasionally, however, there may be a need for the judge to hear further argument—or to hear the evidence itself—out of the presence of the jury.

Throughout pretrial preparation and the trial itself, the physician should help the attorney find ways to make the defense testimony easily accessible and engaging for the jury. More and more attorneys are using computer-assisted demonstrative evidence and presentations to keep the jurors' attention and give them a better feel for what the witnesses are talking about. Any models, demonstrative videotapes, or chalkboard-type illustrations that the physician can provide may help in these efforts. As stressful as it may be, a trial is a chance for a physician to play educator—to help twelve people learn all that they can about her field of practice in a limited time. Anything that aids that process will help the case.

At the conclusion of defendant's presentation of evidence, the plaintiff will have the opportunity to put on rebuttal evidence if needed to address matters raised during defendant's presentation. After any such evidence is offered, the attorneys will have another conference with the judge while the jury is excused. This time, the defendant may again request that the judge decide the case based on the law and not submit it to the jury for findings of fact. Such a motion at this stage may have more chance of success than the motion at the halfway point. Unless the argument for a judicial ruling tossing out the case is crystal clear, however, most judges will let the case go to the jury having come this far. The attorneys at this time will also conduct a charge conference, during which they discuss and argue the elements of the instructions to be presented to the jury.

When the jury returns, two tasks remain. Typically, each party's attorney will present a closing argument, with the plaintiff, who has the burden of proof, getting the last word. Then the judge will instruct the jury on the law applicable to the case and how they are to deliberate and arrive at a verdict.

The jury will retire to deliberate, and the waiting game begins. The jury is permitted to ask to see particular items of evidence or to ask the judge in writing to clarify the instructions or the applicable law. In most, if not all, cases, the jury must reach a unanimous verdict about both liability and, if necessary, the amount of damages to which plaintiff is entitled. Once the jury reaches such a verdict or determines that it is hopelessly deadlocked, it will return. The foreman will announce the verdict or impasse. A split or "hung" jury means that the case ends in a mistrial, and may, depending on the determination of the parties, have to be tried all over again (although the discovery process will not recommence, mercifully) or be settled.

A lawsuit may still be settled at any point before the jury's rendering of its verdict—even while the jury is out deliberating. Attorneys, parties, and insurers may change their views of the likelihood of an adverse outcome dramatically based on the effectiveness of a particular witness, the admission or exclusion of certain key items of evidence or testimony, or even the composition and demeanor of the jury. Therefore, a physician should not be surprised if settlement talks resume at any time during the proceedings, even this late in the game.

Posttrial Motions and Appeals

Following the jury verdict (either immediately or within a few days), the losing side may move that the judge enter judgment notwithstanding the verdict. The threshold for this motion to succeed is extremely high, as the party so moving must establish that no reasonable juror could have found in favor of the winning party based on the evidence of record. On the other hand, a losing defendant may ask the court to reduce the amount of damages as being excessive under the circumstances or for a new trial based on some mistaken procedural or evidentiary ruling by the court. A successful motion for judgment notwithstanding the verdict, new trial, or reduction of damages is somewhat rare and will almost always be appealed.

The losing side will have a statutorily prescribed time period in which to file notice of its intention to appeal the verdict. Surprisingly, depending on how the trial was conducted, a number of cases settle at this point—following a jury verdict but before the decision on appeal. The parties may be battle-weary by this time, and they may also have a more realistic appraisal of their hopes of prevailing. Appeals can be expensive and, of course, time-consuming. Moreover, the relief sometimes awarded to the winner on appeal—a new trial—is a frightening prospect at this point.

An appeal may not be made simply because of dissatisfaction with an adverse jury verdict. Rather, the losing side must base its case for reversal or a new trial on alleged errors committed by the judge in conducting the trial. Parties may challenge a judge's rulings regarding admissibility of evidence, the scope of the opinion an expert was allowed to give, an error in the instructions to the jury, or the denial of a motion for directed verdict or judgment notwithstanding the verdict. Even if one of these kinds of errors is established, it may not entitle the appealing party to any relief unless the error materially prejudiced the outcome of the trial. Either side may appeal, and in some cases both sides may appeal aspects of the outcome or rulings with which they are dissatisfied.

The attorneys will work together with court personnel to compile the record on appeal, consisting of all exhibits and transcripts of all of the testimony and proceedings on the record. The party appealing the decision (or the party appealing first) will file a brief in support of its assertions of error, after which the opposition will have the opportunity to respond in defense of the court's rulings and/or argue its points of error. The court—typically a panel of three or five judges—may or may not allow the attorneys to present oral argument before it renders a decision by majority verdict. Most states have two levels of appellate review. The first level is usually as of right, while the decision to hear an appeal by the highest court in a state typically lies within that court's discretion.

The physician can expect to be less involved at this stage of the proceedings and in all likelihood will not be called back into action unless the case is remanded for a new trial. The appeals process can be quite lengthy, sometimes taking over a year from the rendering of a verdict to a resolution on appeal. A successful appeal may mean outright reversal and entry of a judgment in favor of the defense, or it may only succeed in obtaining a new trial. Add this time (and the stress of waiting while one's fate hangs in the balance) to that already spent in negotiation before the suit was filed, pretrial discovery, and the trial of the case, and one can see how long and grueling a process litigation can be. Suddenly, modifying one's bedside manner and other aspects of one's practice to avoid engendering claims does not sound quite so burdensome.

1. Sheila M. Johnson, "A Medical Malpractice Litigator Proposes Mediation," Dispute—typically to a panel of three or five judges—Resolution Journal 42, 45 (spring 1997).

2. Robert C. Rouwenhorst, "In Your Defense: The Physician's Role in the Defense of Medical Liability Claims," The Digest (fall 1996), St. Paul Medical Services.

3. *See* Jefferey A. Parness & Amy Leonetti, "Expert Opinion Pleading: Any Merit to Special Certificates of Merit?" 1997 Brigham Young Law Review 537, 590 nn 3–4 (1997) (*citing* pre-suit certificate of merit requirements in Florida, Georgia, Illinois, Michigan, Minnesota, Missouri, New Jersey, New York, and Texas). *See also* NC Gen Stat § 1A-1, rule 9(j) (North Carolina rule requiring prefiling expert certification).

4. Parness & Leonetti, *supra* note 3, at 574.

5. *See Jones v Rochelle,* 125 NC App 82, 89, 479 SE2d 231, 235 (1997) (noting that "[a]lthough forty-six states have abandoned the doctrine of contributory negligence in favor of comparative negligence, contributory negligence continues to be the law of [North Carolina] until our Supreme Court overrules it or the General Assembly adopts comparative negligence"). The remaining states that retain contributory negligence as a complete bar are Alabama, Maryland, and Virginia. Steven Gardner, "Contributory Negligence, Comparative Negligence, and Stare Decisis in North Carolina," 18 Campbell Law Review 1, 37 (winter 1996).

6. *See* Fla Stat Ann § 766.1115 (West 1995).

7. *See* Michael Flynn, "Physician Business (Mal)practice," 20 Hamline Law Review 333, 347 (winter 1996); Calvin Wright, "Comment, The Collateral Source Rule in Georgia: A New Method of Equal Protection Analysis Brings a Return to the Old Common Law Rule," 8 Georgia State University Law Review 835 (1992); Michael F. Flynn, "Private Medical Insurance and the Collateral Source Rule: A Good Bet?" 22 University of Toledo Law Review 39 (1990).

8. "Final Report of President's Advisory Commission on Consumer Protection and Quality in the Health Care Industry," chap 10, p 157, *citing* Health Care Liability Alliance, *State Enactments of Selected Health Care Liability Reforms* (Washington, DC: 1995).

9. These facts are taken from a real case, *Jones v Owings,* 318 SC 72, 456 SE2d 371 (1995).

10. Bryson B. Moore, "South Carolina Rejects the Lost Chance Doctrine," 48 South Carolina Law Review 201 208 (1996)(citing the following as states that follow the traditional approach: Alabama, Alaska, Arkansas, California, Florida, Kentucky, Maryland, Massachusetts, Mississippi, Nebraska, New Hampshire, New Mexico, Ohio, South Carolina, Tennessee, Texas, Rhode Island, and Virginia). *See also Jones v Owings,* 318 SC 72, 456 SE2d 371 (1995) (reviewing approaches to lost-chance cases taken by courts in other jurisdictions).

11. Moore, *supra* note 10, at 208–209, *citing* Lisa Perrochet et al, "Lost Chance Recovery and the Folly of Expanding Medical Malpractice Liability," 27 Tort and Insurance Law Journal 615, 617 (1992).

12. *Id* at 202, n 9 (Indiana, Iowa, Kansas, Michigan, Missouri, Montana, Nevada, New Jersey, Oklahoma, Vermont, and Washington).

13. *Id* at 202.

14. *Id* at 207, nn 39–43 (Arizona, Louisiana, Pennsylvania, Utah, and West Virginia).

15. Daniel P. Kessler & Mark B. McClellan, "The Effects of Malpractice Pressure and Liability Reforms on Physicians' Perceptions of Medical Care," 60 Law and Contemporary Problems 81 (1997); Patricia M. Danzon, Medical Malpractice: Theory, Evidence and Public Policy 3 (1985). *See also* Frank A. Sloan, et al, Suing for Malpractice (Chicago: Univ of Chicago Press, 1993): 26, tbl 2.4.

16. Daniel Cotter, "Deposition Can Be Physician's Most Important Contribution to Defense" The Digest at 4–5 (fall 1996) St. Paul Medical Services.

17. *Id.*

18. Johnson, *supra* note 1, at 48.

19. *Id* at 52.

20. Sloan, *supra* note 15, at 68–69.

Chapter 6

Informed consent

Background

Informed consent is the cornerstone of the contemporary clinician's ability to treat and the linchpin of the patient's right to accept or reject clinical care. This has not always been the case. That patients have a right to full disclosure of a proposed treatment, including the assessment of risks and benefits, as well as a discussion of possible side effects and unintended but possible consequences, is a relatively modern notion.[1]

As early as 1914, Supreme Court Justice Benjamin Cardozo articulated this principle, writing, "Every human being of adult years and sound mind has a right to determine what shall be done with his own body; and a surgeon who performs an operation without his patient's consent commits an assault, for which he is liable in damages."[2] Most of the issues that have subsequently arisen to plague clinicians, patients, attorneys, and courts alike stem from this deceptively simple statement. The issues packed within it, awaiting the right condi-

tions to sprout, include questions such as these:

1. Who is an adult?

2. What does sound mind mean?

3. What constitutes an operation?

4. Are there exceptions to the rule or to parts of the rule?

5. How much information should be provided?

What Is Consent to Treatment?

Too often, physicians believe that consent to treatment is a form. Consent is equated in their minds with the release through which patients agree to procedures that their physician believes are advisable or necessary. This definition is incorrect and misleading and can produce dangerous results.

Consent requires dialogue between patient and physician in which both parties exchange information and questions culminating in the patient's agreement to a specific medical or surgical intervention. On the one hand, the patient needs certain basics to decide whether or not to accept the treatment. On the other, the physician also needs information from the patient to tailor the disclosure of risks and benefits to him. To be effective, both parties must participate.

A piece of paper called a consent form can never replace the exchange of information between a patient and a physician. In some instances, serious injury or death can result from a practitioner's failure to question a patient about drug sensitivities or health history.

The Traditional Approach: Liability for Assault and Battery

Under common law, touching another person without his or her express consent is a battery, while placing someone in the fear of being touched is an assault. To prove a claim of medical assault or battery, the plaintiff would have to show that she was examined or treated without having given expressed or implied consent. Unlike the more modern negligence view of consent, there is no need to prove actual harm to recover damages, although harm may certainly occur.

The Modern Standard: Negligence

Over the years, it became evident to the courts that the assault-and-battery concept was no longer adequate. The wrong done by a physician who carries out an unauthorized diagnostic test is quite different from that done by a surgeon who conducts a procedure to which the patient consented on the basis of inadequate information. The assault-and-battery concept of consent could not serve as a basis for suit in the latter instance since the procedure was author-

ized. Unless fraud, misrepresentation, or breach of contract could be demonstrated, the injured patient would have no recourse.

To remedy this situation, many states have recognized through court decisions and legislation a so-called negligence concept of consent.[3] Although the standards of required disclosure vary from state to state, the basic elements of the action remain the same. There must be a failure by the health care practitioner to meet the applicable standard of disclosure, and the patient must have consented to and undergone a procedure based on the physician's disclosure. It must be shown that as a reasonably foreseeable consequence of the inadequate information the patient was injured. Finally, the patient must be able to prove that had he been given all relevant and significant information, he would not have agreed to the procedure.

The negligence concept of consent has not yet received universal acceptance, but it is now the majority view among state courts. To prove a case of negligent consent may be more difficult than to establish a lack of consent under either of the principles of assault and battery. The negligence concept should not be perceived, however, as an easy way for plaintiffs' attorneys to obtain large judgments. Proving causation, or that a patient would have forgone surgery had he or she been properly informed, is hard to establish to the satisfaction of a judge or jury.

Criteria for Valid Consent

The basic criteria for valid consent are the same in both the assault-and-battery and the negligence causes of action. A patient must be capable of giving consent and must possess sufficient information with which to reach a decision about treatment. Failure to meet the requirements of consent due to a departure from recognized standards of care may result in a claim for negligent failure to obtain consent. Performing unauthorized treatment may result in a civil suit based on assault and battery. The circumstances of each case are important determining factors, as well as whether or not a state permits claims actions based on either cause of action.

For some patients, the atmosphere of a hospital, clinic, or physician's office creates psychological or sociological pressures that affect the voluntariness of their consent. The pressures applied may be overt or subtle. The validity of the consent obtained under such circumstances may be called into doubt if allegations of coercion, duress, or undue influence are proved.

If a physician tells a patient that she must have a particular procedure or else she must find another physician, her consent may or may not be valid, depending on the circumstances of the case. If the physician were one of several dozen equally qualified physicians in the community, the ultimatum would be but one factor to consider in a charge of undue influence or coercion. If the physician were the only one available for hundreds of miles and the patient lacked the resources to seek treatment elsewhere, this hard-line approach may constitute duress, undue influence, or coercion.

Short of giving ultimatums, physicians are entitled to gently urge patients to follow a particular recommendation. For physicians to tell patients that under similar circumstances they themselves would have a particular type of surgery should not be considered undue pressure. However, a recommendation for surgery couched in exaggerated "do or die" terms—when other

reasonable means of care exist—may be a basis for complaint.[4]

The law is now clear in almost every jurisdiction that a physician has the duty to disclose to the patient, before any treatment or procedure, sufficient information to enable the patient to make an informed decision. In the interpretation and application of this rule, however, courts have dealt with a series of questions about the scope of the physician's responsibility and have emerged with answers that have not always been consistent.

The major issue in informed consent is the question of what information the physician must provide to the patient. Courts have generally agreed that the patient must be advised of the nature and purpose of the treatment, the risks and consequences involved, and the alternative courses of treatment, including the consequences of no treatment. The physician must explain the steps that will be involved and the diagnostic or therapeutic results that are sought. For instance, if the patient is told that exploratory surgery or a biopsy is to be performed and instead an organ is removed, the physician may be held liable.[5]

Failure to explain to the patient the relevant risks of a treatment or procedure is by far the most common source of liability for lack of informed consent. Physicians have been held liable for failure to disclose such risks as paralysis following spinal surgery,[6] clotting following an angiogram,[7] cardiac and respiratory arrest resulting from anesthesia administered to an asthmatic,[8] nerve injury from surgery,[9] injury from birth control pills,[10] or paralysis from an arteriogram.[11]

To make an informed decision, patients must be fully advised of the choices of treatment available to them. For example, in a

Washington state case, the failure of a physician to advise a patient regarding alternatives to cesarean delivery and the relative risks associated with vaginal and cesarean births led an appellate court to overturn a verdict in favor of the physician.[12] In a Florida decision, a physician was held liable for failing to inform his patient of alternative treatments for a fracture.[13]

Patients must also be advised of the risks if they decide not to consent to the procedure or treatment in question. This requirement of informed refusal has developed only recently. Although some commentators have argued that the rule is novel and a departure from previous legal doctrine, a minority of the courts have viewed it as a logical extension of the informed consent process. In one highly controversial California Supreme Court decision, a patient was under the routine care of a general practitioner for several years. Although the doctor urged her to have a pap smear, she refused to consent, and he never advised her of the risks of her decision. When she eventually died of cervical cancer, the court found that the physician could be held liable if he had failed to disclose the risk of refusing the test.[14]

The Amount of Disclosure Required

A question that has troubled courts from the earliest decisions on informed consent is how detailed and inclusive the disclosure to the patient must be. To tell the physician to describe risks offers little guidance when risks can range from minor to life-threatening and from common to rare.

First, the nature of the patient's condition and the proposed treatment must always be disclosed. The nature and probability of the material risks must also be described, along with information regarding the reasonably expected benefits to the patient. At the same time, the physician needs to be clear about his inability to predict results with certainty. If the procedure or treatment the physician is proposing is irreversible, the physician must so inform the patient. Finally, the physician must explain to the patient the expected result of no treatment and alternative treatments, along with the risks and benefits of each. Courts generally agree that risks that are common knowledge and should already be known to the patient need not be disclosed. Similarly, the physician has no duty to disclose risks that she could not reasonably be expected to know.

The vast majority of risks fall into the middle ground between the minor and the life-threatening, and it is here that two different standards have been developed to measure the physician's obligation, the professional practice standard and the reasonability standard.

Professional Practice Standard

The standard adopted in the early cases, and the one that is still the law in the majority of states, requires the physician to make such disclosure as a reasonable medical practitioner in similar circumstances would make. The Kansas Supreme Court, for example, after reviewing the risk of radiation treatment for cancer, concluded that the question of how disclosure should be made was primarily one of medical judgment and that the duty of the physician should be limited to "those disclosures which a reasonable medical practitioner would make under the same or similar circumstances."[15]

The professional practice standard follows the approach used in medical malpractice cases and looks to the medical community to set the standards for physician performance. The extent of disclosure appropriate to a patient is viewed as a medical question requiring the physician's special skill and training to answer. As in malpractice litigation, when the professional practice standard is applied, the plaintiff must prove the practice of the community by the testimony of medical experts. Whether a patient should be advised of the risks of Demerol, for example, depends on the customary practice in that medical community, which can only be proven at trial through testimony by a medical expert witness.

The Reasonable Patient, or Materiality, Standard

The alternative to the professional practice standard is the materiality rule, which requires the physician to disclose the information that a reasonable person in the patient's position would consider material in deciding whether to undergo the proposed treatment. Under this standard, the practice of other physicians in the community is irrelevant. The issue is what a reasonable patient would want to know. The extent of disclosure is not considered a matter of professional expertise, but one for the judge and jury to decide based on their lay perceptions of what a reasonable patient would want. Because no expert witness is required, the plaintiff in a state with the materiality rule finds it easier to establish a case.

Three leading cases, each decided in 1972, established the materiality rule. In *Canterbury v Spence,* the Court of Appeals for the District of Columbia took issue with the professional practice standard on a number of grounds. First, the court questioned whether in fact any discernible community practice existed, and it expressed concern that what was in fact no custom at all might be might be misinterpreted as a custom to maintain silence. Second, the court noted that each patient's situation was so different that generalized standards were inappropriate. Finally, and most important, the court stated that, unlike medical malpractice situations, the issues involved in deciding how much information to disclose to patients did not require medical skills to resolve. The standard should be what is reasonable under the circumstances, and a reasonable disclosure is governed by the materiality of the information to the patient's decision. Whether a particular risk was material, said the court, depended on its incidence and seriousness. The more likely or more serious the risk, the greater its materiality. The standard, said the court, was an objective one. The issue was not what this particular patient would want to know, but what a reasonable patient would want to know. [16]

Likewise, in *Cobbs v Grant,* the California Supreme Court also discussed the shortcomings of the professional practice approach. Even if community standards for disclosure exist, said the court, they are so nebulous that the physician in effect is given absolute discretion. This result is inconsistent with the patient's right to make an informed decision. As far as the appropriate disclosure is concerned, the court continued, there is no need for the physician to give a "mini-course in medical science." The scope of the physician's communications must be measured by the patient's need. [17] Finally, in *Wilkinson v Vesey,* a Rhode Island appeals court summed up the limitations of the professional practice rule by stating,

"The patient's right to make up his mind should not be delegated to a local medical group—many of whom have no idea as to his informational needs."[18]

The difficulty with the materiality standard, however, is that it does not provide a great deal of guidance to the physician. What a reasonable patient would want to know is not always easy to discern. Physicians who have made judgments about what information to provide have later found that their decisions do not coincide with a jury's evaluation. One of the main reasons for such variance is that the jury reaches its decision after the patient has been injured by the very risk that was not disclosed. A risk of serious injury will likely appear to be far more material after the patient has suffered the injury than before. For that reason, courts in Maine and Virginia, among others, have explicitly rejected the materiality standard.

Causation and Injury

That a physician has failed to disclose information when legally required to do so does not automatically give the patient a right to recover damages based on a lack of informed consent. Instead, as a negligence action, the elements of causation and injury must be established by the patient:

(i) The patient must have been injured by the procedure or treatment in question (or, in the case of "informed refusal," by his failure to undergo the treatment or procedure). Even the most inadequate explanation will not result in liability to the physician if the patient comes through the procedure or treatment without harm.

(ii) When the element of disclosure that was not provided was information as to a risk of the treatment, the patient must have been injured by that particular risk; and

(iii) The patient must show that, but for the failure to disclose, he would not have consented to the procedure or treatment.[19]

The final requirement is sometimes called "but for" causation. The plaintiff must show that the injury would not have occurred but for the plaintiff's wrongful act. If consent would have been given in any event, there is no liability. In dealing with the issue of causation in the context of informed consent, courts have applied either what is called an objective test requiring the plaintiff to prove that a reasonably prudent person would not have consented to the procedure had he known the risks or a subjective test, requiring the patient to prove that he himself would not have consented. The vast majority of courts have chosen to follow the objective test, indicating that the focus should be on the reasonably prudent person rather than on the particular patient in the case at hand because the patient's statements cannot be considered reliable.

Whichever test is used, the requirement of but for causation, if correctly applied, should prevent recovery against physicians in many cases. For the medically indicated treatment, reasonable patients are likely to consent even if the risks are explained in great detail. For example, in a study reported in the *Journal of the American Medical Association*, patients at the Cleveland Clinic who were about to undergo angiography were given consent forms that mentioned such risks as death and loss of an organ, yet 228 of the 232 patients consented to the procedure.[20]

The causation requirement does tend to limit informed consent suits to diagnostic or elective procedures. It is hard for the patient who has undergone a lifesaving treatment to persuade even the most sympathetic jury that he would not have consented had he known there was a risk of minor injury. Further, if a more serious risk is mentioned and a minor one omitted, the causation requirement may create difficulties for the plaintiff.[21]

Consent Exceptions

The law does not require a patient's express consent to be obtained in every situation. Instead, consent will be waived or implied under certain limited circumstances.

Emergencies

If the delay in treatment necessary to obtain a patient's consent would result in significant harm to the patient, the physician may proceed to treat the patient. Similarly, if the patient is unconscious or otherwise unable to consent and treatment must be given immediately, the physician need not wait until the family or guardian has been contacted. Most recent cases have held that the treatment in question need not be lifesaving or necessary to prevent permanent harm so long as time is of the essence and the possible harm to the patient is more than trivial. If there is time to speak with the patient or if the patient's family is readily available, then the physician may not rely on the emergency exception.

The most difficult situations involving the emergency exception to consent arise when the patient is objecting to the proposed treatment. The implied consent in an emergency does not override the patient's right to refuse treatment. However, for the refusal to be effective, it must be based on a full informed consent, which may not be possible under some emergency conditions,

particularly if the treatment in question is lifesaving. In the words of one court, "where there is an emergency calling for an immediate decision, nothing less than a fully conscious contemporaneous decision by the patient will be sufficient to override evidence of medical necessity."[22]

Unanticipated Conditions during Surgery

When a physician performs a procedure on a patient under general anesthesia and discovers an unanticipated condition that in her professional judgment requires attention, she may proceed to treat that condition rather than require the patient to face the risks and inconvenience of a second surgical procedure. In one North Carolina case, a surgeon performing an appendectomy had discovered enlarged ovarian cysts, which he proceeded to puncture. When the patient brought a lawsuit alleging that she had never consented to treatment of the cysts, the court found for the physician, holding that good surgical practice required that he treat the patient's cysts. In the absence of express direction from the patient to the contrary, the court found, a physician performing a major internal operation "may extend the operation to remedy any abnormal or diseased condition in the area of the original incision whenever . . . correct surgical procedure dictates and requires such an extension of the operation originally contemplated."[23]

For the exception to apply, the condition need not be life-threatening, but it must be unanticipated. Courts are generally less willing to permit the physician to rely on the unanticipated condition exception if the procedure involves removal of an organ, affects reproductive capacity, or significantly increases the risks of the operation. In these situations, the patient's right to consent is considered particularly important. Of course, no condition can be considered unanticipated by the physician if the patient has expressly indicated that he does not wish it treated if discovered.

The physician's ability to rely on the unanticipated-condition exception is enhanced if he discusses the possibility of additional procedures with the patient before surgery and obtains authorization to proceed. In one notable case, a surgeon performing pelvic surgery removed the patient's Fallopian tubes when he discovered that they were infected. Since the consent form authorized pelvic surgery and "other operations which are considered necessary during the course of the operation," the appellate court affirmed a judgment for the physician.[24]

Therapeutic Privilege

There may be circumstances in which full disclosure by the physician is thought to be detrimental to the patient. The therapeutic privilege permits the physician to withhold information if she reasonably believes that the patient's mental or physical well-being would suffer as a result of learning the information. The fact that the patient might be upset by information is not sufficient to permit reliance on the therapeutic privilege. Disclosure must pose a serious threat to the patient's health to the point where it is contraindicated medically. When consent is obtained from a third party rather than from the patient, the therapeutic privilege does not apply.

The therapeutic privilege, which is invoked only rarely, has met with resistance from many legal scholars, who view it as paternalistic and contend that it could become an excuse for dispensing with informed consent in some circumstances. Although many courts have affirmed the existence of the therapeutic privilege, it has only rarely been successful as a defense in litigation. Courts and juries tend to view with some skepticism claims by physicians that their failure to disclose was the result of a desire to protect the patient's welfare. The therapeutic privilege is not recognized in many states because of its uncertain parameters and the difficulty of justifying its use since it cannot be used solely to overcome the patient's refusal to follow the physician's treatment agenda. It also cannot be used with third-party authorizers such as guardians.

Waiver

There is no legal obligation for the physician to disclose information to the patient that the patient does not wish to hear. If the physician begins to offer his explanation and is asked by the patient to stop, the physician is not obligated to continue. However, the physician can rely on waiver by a patient only when the patient has clearly expressed a preference not to receive an explanation. When this happens, it is advisable for the physician to discuss with the patient the reasons for the decision and to see whether, with appropriate reassurance and support, the patient may be willing to receive the information. This is a rarely used exception.[25]

Proxy

An additional exception, also fading from legal view, is that of proxy or good faith consent, usually obtained from family members on behalf of a patient who has not been adjudicated incompetent. This kind of consent is most frequently obtained in hallway conversations between clinicians and spouses, siblings, or adult children of patients who the clinician or family suspect are not competent or would be upset by the physician's findings or recommendations.

Treatment Review Boards

Treatment review boards are most often involved in research projects. Their role is not necessarily to substitute consent but to ensure that researchers follow relevant informed consent procedures. Statutes in a few states may allow spouses to substitute consent in certain circumstances. Courts in some states follow a doctrine of making a decision themselves on a patient's behalf based on what they consider to be the patient's best interest.

Advance Directives

A last exception to the requirement of informed consent occurs in the case of advance directives. These include legal instruments such as the living will, the health care proxy, and the durable power of attorney. These and other similar arrangements allow a competent person to authorize another to make decisions on his behalf when and if he is no longer able to make them for himself.

Consent Forms

Except in a few circumstances, such as sterilization or participation in federally funded medical research, there is no legal requirement that consent to treatment be in writing. Yet when a patient sues for lack of informed consent, it may be hard for the physician to show that proper consent was obtained if there is no document or record

to support it. Published studies indicate that patient recall of consent discussions is minimal at best and that patients may claim that no consent was given despite the most elaborate explanation by the physician.[26] For this reason, it has become common practice for health care providers to require patients to sign consent forms for any treatment or procedure involving more than minimal risk. If a question later arises as to whether the patient gave proper consent, the forms can be used as evidence that consent was in fact given.

The signature of the patient on a piece of paper alone does not constitute consent. If the patient can show that the language on the form was too technical for him to be reasonably expected to understand or that his signature was obtained when he was not competent or under circumstances indicating duress, the form is irrelevant. Courts are particularly unimpressed by general consent forms that make no mention of the specific procedure involved or particular risks. Moreover, the fact that a patient has signed a general consent form does not authorize the physician to perform a procedure that the patient expressly refused to permit in a conversation with the physician. If a patient later orally revokes written consent, he is not bound by the signed form.

The language in which consent forms are written often hinders rather than helps their acceptance by the courts. Consent forms often contain terms that are too technical for some patients to understand. One study of surgical consent forms at five major medical facilities concluded that the forms were on the same reading level as texts intended for upper-division undergraduates or graduate students.[27] Further, many health personnel do not understand the purpose of the forms. Forms are often wrongly viewed as a substitute for, rather than as evidence of, the consent process. Consent is considered to take place when the patient signs the paper, regardless of whether a proper explanation has been given. Often, patients are asked to sign forms after they have been sedated or in the middle of the night after they have been awakened from sleep.

To bring some clarity to the issue, many state legislatures, at the behest of physicians' lobbies, have adopted informed consent laws to codify when and what consent is required. The applicable laws vary significantly from state to state. Perhaps the most comprehensive statute is that of Texas, which established a Texas Medical Disclosure Panel charged with developing lists of those medical and surgical procedures that do or do not require disclosure. For those requiring disclosure, the panel was directed to determine the degree of disclosure required and the form in which the disclosure should be made. If a physician or health care provider complies with the requirements of the panel, a presumption is created that informed consent was properly obtained.[28]

Competence

Competence is another essential element of informed consent, like voluntariness and disclosure of adequate information. Competence is a legal conclusion that attempts to define and describe the elastic and ever-changing set of circumstances within which a person is considered to be able or unable to manage any one or more of life's tasks. It is best understood as a process rather than as an event. In this way, we can more readily understand how a person can be competent to perform one task but not another. Similarly, we can see how a person

may be competent to perform a task at 9:00am but incompetent at 2:00pm. Competence can be influenced by emotion, such as depression, mania, or grief; physiological changes such as hypoglycemia, Alzheimer's disease, or high fever; or by cognitive ability.

In general, all adults are presumed to be competent and must be treated as such unless and until a court has found them incompetent. This includes persons diagnosed as having major mental illness or developmental disabilities, whether institutionalized or living in the community.

Four Elements of Competence

Competence includes four basic and interrelated parts. First, the person in question must have a factual understanding of the situation that involves the relevant needs and alternatives. For example, to establish competence, a thirty-year-old woman with bipolar disorder and cervical cancer must understand what the cervix is and the role it plays in reproduction.

The second element requires an appreciation of the seriousness of the condition and the consequences of accepting or rejecting treatment. "Appreciation" includes an emotional as well as a cognitive component. In the case of a psychiatric patient, using our example, appreciation would appear to call for some expression of trepidation or apprehension regarding the possible inability to bear children if treatment is accepted or the possibility of death if the treatment is rejected.

The third element is the requirement that the patient express a preference. This preference does not have to be consistent with the clinician's preference or with what the clinician thinks would be in the patient's best interest. Using our example, the patient may express a preference to preserve her reproductive ability even at the risk of her own life, or she may say that preserving her own life is paramount. Both are indications of competence. If she simply indicated she did not care, however, or could not decide, concerns would be raised about her competence.

The fourth and final element of competence demands that the patient be capable of working rationally with the information disclosed by the clinician. In our example, that means being able to keep the information grounded in reality and separate from whatever delusional material or psychotic thinking may be present at various times as a result of the bipolar disorder.[29]

Competence and the Involuntarily Committed Individual

Involuntarily committed competent patients have an absolute right to refuse not only medical treatment but treatment with antipsychotic medications. This important point is often a source of confusion for clinicians. The reason for the confusion is a blurring of the distinction between competence, which is presumed of any adult, and the standard for involuntary commitment, which is always some variation of inability to care for oneself or danger to oneself or others. Involuntary commitment does not negate the presumption of competence, in part because the standard for involuntary commitment is more of a snapshot of a moment in time, while competence is a dynamic process.[30]

In many states, involuntary commitment does not require judicial intervention. In all states, a judgment of incompetence, whether narrowly or broadly defined, does

require a judicial proceeding. In addition, all states require a judicial proceeding to continue an involuntary commitment beyond its initial stages. Even if granted, this long-term involuntary commitment does not negate the presumption of competence or constitute the equivalent of a competency proceeding, which mandates a separate request to the court for a judgment of incompetence and appointment of a guardian.[31]

When an involuntarily committed patient is found by a court to be incompetent to decide whether or not to consent to treatment with antipsychotic medication, a number of states require a judge to make a decision after a full adversarial hearing. The judge is required in most jurisdictions to reach a decision by using what is referred to as a substituted-judgment analysis. The judge must figure out what the patient would want if he were competent and in the same situation. The judge must not substitute her own judgment for that of the patient or make a judgment of what she considers to be in the patient's best interest. The same procedure and the same standards are used in most jurisdictions to make medical decisions for persons who have been found incompetent to make those decisions for themselves. All of the elements of informed consent apply to the judge, who then adds the substituted-judgment element to her decision-making process.[32]

Children

Contrary to the general rule for adults, children are presumed to be incompetent to consent to treatment. Their parents exercise that right for them. This doctrine is known as substituted consent, and its rationale is twofold, to protect children from their own immaturity and to protect the interests of their parents who are financially responsible for them. The law realizes that in certain situations the interests of parents and children may not coincide. Most states have statutes that authorize courts to substitute their own consent for parental consent when doing so would be in the children's best interest. These cases usually involve young children and arise when parents have religious beliefs that prohibit certain medical procedures such as blood transfusion, surgery, or medication.

According to some views, parents' and children's interests may diverge in the adolescent years as well. Cases involving teenagers may raise issues of consent to testing for pregnancy and venereal disease or to treatment for drug dependence. The law in some states takes the position that without being shielded from parental knowledge, minors might be reluctant to seek testing or treatment. This view is highly controversial, however, as it expands the role of the government at the expense of the family. Critics argue forcefully that it is absurd that a minor can abort a child without her parent's knowledge while she cannot have a wart removed without parental consent.

Two other legal doctrines permit courts to allow minors to make their own informed-consent decisions. The first is the doctrine of the emancipated minor, which applies to children who are no longer receiving parental guidance or financial support. Children can achieve this status through marriage, enlistment in the armed forces, failure of their parents to support them, or judicial decree based on a wide variety of fact patterns. A similar doctrine is that of the mature minor, which allows minors of sufficient maturity and intelligence to make their own medical treatment decisions. These are subjective decisions that may leave clinicians open to liability and in which parental involvement, if at all possible, may be the safer course.

No discussion of informed consent involving children would be complete without some mention of children whose parents are separated or divorced. The parents of children from intact families have equal rights to substitute consent for their children. Separated or divorced parents may have the same equal rights either under state law or pursuant to a court order. It is increasingly rare for one parent to have the entire right and the other parent to have none, but the laws vary from state to state. It is always wise to be clear about this. Many separated or divorced parents are able to put aside their differences in medical situations involving their children, but many are also unable to keep their child's health and treatment needs from becoming entangled in their own feelings and behavior. These situations can be extremely trying for all concerned, including clinicians. Legal advice and even judicial intervention are sometimes necessary to obtain a clear mandate for treatment. Unless an emergency presents itself, examination and treatment of a minor should not proceed without the consent of a parent or a judicial order.[33]

Tips for the Practitioner

Obtaining the patient's consent is the responsibility of the patient's treating physician, who should explain the proposed procedure or treatment to the patient and, if necessary, obtain the patient's signature on any written forms. In teaching hospitals, interns and residents should obtain consent only from those patients who do not have a private physician. If a procedure such as angiography or radiotherapy is to be performed by a specialist, the physician performing the procedure should obtain the consent since he is the most familiar with the risks and benefits of the procedure. The risks of surgery should be presented by the surgeon and the risks of anesthesia by the anesthesiologist.

Some physicians delegate their consent obligations to the nursing or house staff. Doing so is unwise, as the physician remains responsible for the explanation. Yet if a patient indicates to his nurse or another physician that he has questions about the proposed procedure that have not been satisfactorily answered, they should take steps to see that the patient's concerns are resolved.

If possible, consent should be obtained long enough before the proposed treatment or procedure to provide the patient with adequate time to deliberate. If the patient is being admitted to the hospital for elective treatment, consent should be obtained in the physician's office before admission. The consent remains valid unless the patient changes his mind or the facts on which the explanation was based change, but if more than a few weeks elapse from the time consent is given, it is advisable to obtain a new consent as a precaution. If a patient is to undergo a series of treatments, consent may be obtained at the beginning for the entire series so long as the facts on which the consent is based do not change.[34]

1. Marilyn Berner, "Informed Consent" in *The Mental Health Practitioner and the Law* at 23 (Cambridge, Mass: Harvard University Press, 1998).

2. *Schloendorff v Society of New York Hospital,* 211 NY 125, 105 NE 92 (1914).

3. *See Canterbury v Spence,* 464 F2d 772 (DC Cir 1972).

4. Fay A. Rozovsky, *Consent to Treatment: A Practical Guide* § 1.3.2 (Gaithersburg, Md: Aspen Publishers, 1998).

5. *Dries v Gregor,* 72 AD2d 231, 424 NYS2d 561 (4th Dept 1980).

6. *Fanny v Berman,* 72 AD2d 575, 421 NYS2d 30 (2d Dept 1979).

7. *Salis v United States,* 522 F2d 989 (Md 1981).

8. *Siegel v Mt. Sinai Hospital of Cleveland,* 62 Ohio App2d 12, 403 N2d 202 (1978).

9. *Douthitt v. United States,* 491 F Supp 891 (ED Mo 1980).

10. *Klink v G.D. Searle & Co,* 26 Wash App 951, 614 P2d 701 (1980).

11. *McPherson v Ellis,* 305 NC 266, 287 SE2d 892 (1982).

12. *Holt v Nelson,* 11 Wash App 230, 523 P2d 211 (1974).

13. *Russell v Harwick,* 166 So2d 904 (Fla Dist Ct App 1964), *cert dismissed,* 182 So2d 241 (Fla 1966).

14. *Truman v Thomas,* 27 Cal 3d 285, 611 P2d 902, 165 Cal Rptr 308 (1980).

15. *Natanson v Kline,* 186 Kan 393, 409, 350 P2d 1093, 1106 (1960). *See generally* Scott Becker, *Health Care Law* § 18.02 [2] (New York: Matthew Bender, 1998).

16. *See supra* note 3.

17. 8 Cal 3d 229, 502 P2d 1, 104 Cal Rptr 505 (1972).

18. 110 RI 606, 625, 295 A2d 676, 688 (1972).

19. *See supra* note 4.

20. Alfidi, "Informed Consent: A Study of Patient Reaction," 216 Journal of the American Medical Association 1325 (1971).

21. Becker, *supra* note 15, at § 18.02 [2].

22. *In re Estate of Dorone,* 534 A2d 452, 455 (Pa 1987).

23. *Kennedy v Parrott,* 243 NC 355, 362, 90 SE2d 754, 759 (1956). *See* Becker, *supra* note 15, at § 18.02[3][b].

24. *Watson v Worthy,* 151 Ga App 131, 259 SE2d 138 (1979).

25. *Becker, supra* note 15, at § 18.02[4].

26. *See, eg,* Robinson & Merav, "Informed Consent: Recall by Patients Tested Postoperatively," 22 Annals of Thoracic

Surgery 209 (1976); Cassileth, "Informed Consent—Why Are Its Goals Imperfectly Realized?" 302 New England Journal of Medicine 896 (1980).

27. Grunder, "On the Reliability of Surgical Consent Forms," 302 New England Journal of Medicine 900 (1980).

28. Tex Rev Civ Stat Ann, article 4590; Becker, *supra* note 15, at § 18.02[5].

29. Berner, *supra* note 1, at 36–37.

30. *Id* at 39.

31. *Id.*

32. *Id.*

33. *Id* at 41–43.

34. Becker, *supra* note 15, at § 18.03[2].

Resources for Further Research

The literature on informed consent is voluminous. The reader seeking additional information on the topic is encouraged to examine the following texts:

Paul S. Applebaum et al, *Informed Consent: Legal Theory and Clinical Practice* (New York: Oxford University Press, 1987).

Thomas Grisso et al, *Assessing Competence to Consent to Treatment: A Guide for Physicians and Other Health Professionals* (New York: Oxford University Press, 1998).

Deborah Norris, *Glossary of Lay Language Synonyms for Common Terms Used in Informed Consent Documents for Clinical Studies: A Handbook for Clinical Researchers* (Austin, Tex: Plexus Publishing, 1996).

Claire C. Obade, *Patient Care Decision-Making: A Legal Guide for Providers* (St Paul: West Publishing Group, 1991).

Patrick O'Neill, *Negotiating Consent in Psychotherapy* (New York: New York University Press, 1998).

R. Reisner and C. Slobogin, *Law and the Mental Health System* (St Paul: West Publishing Group, 1990).

Lainie Friedman Ross, *Children, Families and Health Care Decision Making* (New York: Oxford University Press, 1998).

R. Simon, *Clinical Psychiatry and the Law,* 2nd ed. (Washington, DC: American Psychiatric Press, 1992).

Jonathan P. Tomes, *Informed Consent: A Guide for the Healthcare Professional* (Chicago: Healthcare Financial Management Educational Foundation, 1993).

Stephen Wear, *Informed Consent: Patient Autonomy and Physician Beneficence within Clinical Medicine* (New York: Kluwer Academic Publishers, 1993).

Becky Cox White, *Competence to Consent* (Washington, DC: Georgetown University Press, 1994).

Section 3

Employment-related issues

Chapter 7

Options for structuring a medical practice

The critical concepts describing the business of American medicine in recent decades are consolidation, integration, and managed care. Indeed, the very concept of medicine as a business is new. Since at least the turn of the twentieth century, physicians had thought of themselves as highly trained professionals who viewed issues of remuneration as a mere sidelight to the goal of relieving sickness and misery. Today, the medical arena—for better or worse—is characterized by competition among health plans, physician groups, and hospitals, all of which do battle in the marketplace for covered lives. It is an arena in which patients will switch their physician, their hospital system, and even their health plan each year to save several dollars a month in premiums.[1]

In view of the trends in health care and their resulting complexity, an understanding of key organizational practice models available to physicians is critical, especially their individual attributes and the requisite tradeoffs of each compared to the others.

Each option has strengths and weaknesses. Only the individual physician can weigh these factors and arrive at the best individual outcome. The most widely used models are described below in order from those that provide the most physician independence to those that provide the greatest integration with other physicians, hospitals, and insurers.

Solo Practice

The dominant form of business structure until recently within the field of medicine was solo practice. Solo practitioners generally open new offices or purchase established practices of retiring physicians. They operate independently and manage their day-to-day operations independently of other providers. Call coverage is usually established informally with other solo practitioners or groups. The solo practitioner has full responsibility for the management of the practice, including financial and operational oversight, marketing, and patient care. Solo practitioners are often sole proprietors, but incorporation in many states affords access to both legal and tax advantages.[2]

The main disadvantages of solo practice include the inability to obtain the advantages of scale available to physicians practicing in groups, such as purchasing supplies in bulk at a discount and spreading overhead costs across a number of physicians. An additional disadvantage is the difficulty of keeping up with the increasingly complex coding requirements and the escalating costs of information technology necessary to comply with billing and other matters.

Independent Practice Association

In most cases, an independent practice association (IPA) is created to permit affiliation of practitioners and physician groups as a means for payer contracting. Through this broad, loose affiliation, physicians can access managed care contracts without sacrificing their independence. IPAs have become prevalent in today's marketplace, given the need to pool contracting and the leverage to achieve competitive reimbursement rates and to provide physician access to managed care patients. IPAs are generally shareholder organizations governed by their members. They range in size from a few physicians to a thousand or more members. Originally, IPAs were viewed as a substandard model with limited purpose and effectiveness. More recently, however, many well-managed IPAs in advanced markets have proven their value through the effective handling of capitation and managed care.[3]

An IPA does not require a physician to integrate his or her practice operations. Instead, members maintain business independence while agreeing to join together for payer contracting. Each physician signs an agreement (which may be either exclusive or nonexclusive, depending on the IPA bylaws). In the case of exclusivity, the physician member can participate in only one IPA and must take all payer contracts through that organization. In less exclusive settings, the physician may be a member of multiple IPAs and take contracts by a number of association channels. IPA proponents contend that this structure preserves the small, entrepreneurial, and efficient practice of care delivery while providing the necessary business and infrastructure to function as a unit. IPAs can take almost any legal form, but they are usually organized as professional organizations. IPAs are usually not for profit, although that is not an absolute requirement.[4]

In its common form, the IPA negotiates with the HMO for a capitation rate inclusive of all physician services. The IPA in turn reimburses the member physicians, although not necessarily using capitation. The IPA and its member physicians are at risk for at least some part of medical costs in that if the capitation payment is lower than the required reimbursement to the physician, the member physicians must accept lower income. This risk sharing sets the IPA apart from a negotiating vehicle that does not bear risk. It is also the reason that true IPAs generally are not subject to antitrust problems unless the IPA was formed solely or primarily to keep out competition. The usual form of an IPA is an umbrella organization for physicians of all specialties to participate in managed care. IPAs that represent only a single specialty have also developed.[5]

The IPA may operate simply as a negotiating instrument, with the HMO providing all administrative support, or it may take on some of the duties of an HMO, such as utilization management and network development. The hospital usually has no role in the traditional IPA, although some hospitals have begun sponsoring IPA development as an alternative to a physician hospital organization (PHO).

The IPA has its advantages. First, it is a model that is well understood and accepted by many managed care executives, a traditional lot who are generally dubious of less conventional structures. Second, in contrast to other models, IPAs require much less capital to start up and operate. Third, some managers believe that IPAs provide physicians more incentive than do models that compensate primarily by means of salary. However, IPAs are not without their problems. They can be unwieldy because they are usually made up of a large number of independent physicians whose only commonality is the contracting vehicle of the IPA. The IPA's ability to preserve independent private practice also means it is unable to maximize its bargaining position for resources or change behavior of nonperforming physicians. An IPA that accepts a high degree of risk for medical costs may be found by the state insurance commissioner to be an HMO and be required to become licensed, with all the complexity of being a licensed health plan. Finally, many IPAs contain a surplus of specialists, resulting in upward pressure on resource consumption.[6]

The early history of IPAs as they initially developed during the 1970s was rocky, with some going out of business. More recently, however, IPAs have enjoyed success, particularly in the western states. Today's IPA generally has stop-loss reinsurance, or the HMO provides such stop-loss coverage, to prevent the IPA from going bankrupt.[7]

Group Practice without Walls

American physicians by and large have historically worked at arm's length and have not generally developed business capabilities or operations with their colleagues. In the last few years, however, a new model known as the Group Practice without Walls (GPWW) has emerged as a hybrid between a solo and a group practice. Also known as a clinic without walls, this arrangement permits physician members to maintain separate offices while agreeing to share components of the office practice, including billing, management of accounts receivable, and other key fiscal operations. This kind of relationship provides a high level of independence for the individual physician, as well as a mechanism for containing costs and for achieving consolidation benefits. Often, consolidation is impelled by the burdensome costs of computer systems necessary to support billing and accounts-receivable functions. Targeted integration is achieved, yet the individual practitioner maintains a high level of independence. GPWWs can take many legal forms, including partnerships, limited liability companies, and professional corporations.[8]

The GPWW is composed of private practice physicians who agree to aggregate their practices into a single legal entity, but the physicians continue to practice medicine in their independent locations. In other words, the physicians appear to be independent from the point of view of their patients, but from the point of view of a contracting entity (such as a health plan or other vendor) they are a single group. The GPWW is owned solely by the member physicians and not by outside investors. Additionally, the GPWW is a legal merging of all assets of the physicians' practices rather than the acquisition only of the tangible assets.

The GPWW is owned by the member physicians, and governance is by the physicians. The GPWW does not require the participation of a hospital and, indeed, is often formed as a vehicle for physicians to organize without being dependent on a hospital for services or support. The GPWW may, however, contract with an outside organization to provide business support services. Office support services are generally provided through the group, although as a practical matter the practicing physician may notice little difference from what he or she is used to receiving. Employees of each of the practices become employees of the GPWW.

The GPWW enjoys an advantage over some other models because it has the legal ability to negotiate and commit on behalf of all the members of the group. The GPWW also has the ability to achieve some modest economies of scale. The most common subset of these services includes centralized billing, centralized scheduling, group purchasing, and data sharing. Less frequently, the GPWW centralizes recruiting and can help with employee leasing. The GPWW is free of hospital influence (at least theoretically) and therefore has great flexibility.

Perhaps the main advantage of the GPWW is that income is affected by the performance of the group as a whole. Therefore, the GPWW has some ability to influence practice behavior. If a member physician is practicing in a manner that adversely affects the group as a whole, considerable peer pressure can be brought to bear. The group can even expel a physician if the problems are serious and are not rectified.

From a management point of view, the main disadvantage of the GPWW is that

the physicians essentially remain in independent practice. Except for obvious practice behavior, the physicians continue to practice in the manner to which they have become accustomed. The ability of the group actually to manage practice behavior is thus seriously limited only to those elements that are gross outliers (for example, exceptionally long hospital stays). Thus, optimal efficiencies are not achieved. Although there is some alignment of incentives, disparate goals continue to exist.

The ability of a GPWW to accept risk-based reimbursement (such as capitation) is enhanced but is not optimal. The GPWW is potentially capable of negotiating with health plans for such contracts, but distribution of income and risk favor other practice options. The very feature that attracts many physicians to a GPWW's potential independence from a distrusted hospital is also a source of weakness. In other words, alternative sources of capital, information systems, and management expertise must be explored.

From the individual physician's point of view, the GPWW structure has weaknesses as well. First, it does not have leadership as strong as in a true medical group. This, along with the other disadvantages noted, may lead to structural instability. The lack of a single office location inhibits the development of a group culture. Further, it permits easy exit for physicians from the structure. The attenuated decision making that is characteristic of GPWWs can result in an inability to respond quickly in a managed care environment. A GPWW can nonetheless offer some benefit to physicians—as long as the physicians recognize it as a transitional entity.[9]

As GPWWs were formed, federal and state regulators became concerned that physicians were using this structure to legitimize otherwise questionable referrals between medical practices for physician, lab, and other ancillary services. Accordingly, the group-practice exception under the Ethics in Patient Referrals Act (better known as the Stark I Act)[10] limits the ability of a GPWW to qualify as a group practice under which referrals for physician services and in-office ancillary services are permitted. As an example, the exception requires that ancillary services be located within the same building as the group practice or consolidated in a single location.[11] Although the GPWW structure is useful in integrating practices and as a precursor to full practice merger, its utility has been reduced by the provisions of Stark I by various announcements of the Office of the Inspector General under the Medicare Fraud and Abuse Anti-kickback Statute. Development of a GPWW requires careful attention to avoid violation or risk of challenge under these statutes. In addition, some states have passed statutes restricting or prohibiting self-referral that must be examined in connection with a GPWW.

Physician Practice Management Organization

The physician practice management (PPM) organization is a relatively new beast in the health care organizational zoo. In a melding of Wall Street and the physician's office, entrepreneurs have capitalized for-profit PPMs operating independently of hospitals. Most often, these PPMs have purchased physician practices, beginning with primary care groups but including some large specialty groups as well, and have multiyear contracts with those physicians. The physicians may be given varying degrees of equity participation in the PPM and a voice in governance.

In some cases, the PPM may offer equity in exchange for the value of the acquired practice but not if it pays cash for the practice.

These entities may be attractive to practitioners who, exasperated by the business pressures of a practice, would prefer selling to an entity specializing in managing physician practices as opposed to a distrusted hospital, or those who feel that a PPM has more capability to manage a practice than a hospital does. As these entities become publicly traded, a further attraction to physicians is the possibility of seeing their equity grow.

Typically, the PPM provides management for all support functions (such as billing and collections, purchasing, negotiating contracts, and so forth) but remains relatively uninvolved with the clinical aspects of the practice. In many cases, the physician remains an independent practitioner, although the PPM owns all the tangible assets of the practice. The PPM usually takes a percentage of the practice revenue, often at a rate equal to or slightly below what the physician was already paying for overhead. The physician agrees to a long-term commitment as well as to noncompete covenants.[12]

The primary advantage of a PPM is that its sole purpose is to manage physicians' practices. This means that it will either have or will obtain expertise that does not usually reside in either a hospital or a payer. Also, the PPM has the ability to bring substantial purchasing power to bear by combining the purchasing needs of several hundred (or potentially more) physicians. The PPM can also provide a greater sense of ownership to the participating physicians in an equity model, thus helping align incentives and goals.

The principal disadvantage of the PPM is that it may not achieve sufficient mass in the market to influence events substantially or to negotiate favorable terms. In addition, physicians may resist the terms usually required under their contracts and may not change their practice habits sufficiently to be truly effective in managed care; this last issue becomes especially critical if the PPM is seen more as a vehicle to negotiate fees than as a system to improve quality and lower costs. PPMs often lack strong physician leadership. Business leadership often comes from non-physicians. Moreover, investor-owned PPMs are expected to return a profit. If that profit is not forthcoming, investors will demand changes, many of which may be unpalatable to participating physicians. Finally, a number of widely publicized PPM insolvencies have soured many physicians on the idea of turning over the management of their practices to a third party.[13]

Single-Specialty Group Practice

A single-specialty group practice is most succinctly described as the consolidation of two or more specialists in the same field to create a group. Many single-specialty groups originated as solo practices that shared call coverage. Over the years, they grew closer and ultimately merged their practices and operations. The number of single-specialty groups has risen sharply during recent years as a consequence of the growing complexity of operating a medical practice. Now one of the more popular organizational models, single-specialty groups range in size from two to more than a hundred physicians. Initially impelled by similar interests and call coverage, the further development of single-specialty groups can be attributed to the growth of managed care, the desire to cut

costs, and the leverage provided to a specialty discipline by consolidation. As single-specialty group practices grow, many of the financial and operational aspects of the practice integrate to form a more centralized structure.[14]

Unlike the GPWW, in which the physicians combine certain assets and risks but remain in their own offices, practicing medicine as they always have, single-specialty groups are located in a few sites and function in a group setting. Because the physicians occupy the same facility or facilities, there is a high degree of interaction among the members of the group, ideally fostering common goals and objectives for group success. These groups are independent of the hospital, yet it is common for a group to identify strongly with one or more hospitals. Although this is advantageous for the physicians so long as relations are good, it can be devastating to the group if relations with the hospital sour.

The single-specialty group is usually a partnership or professional corporation, although other forms are possible. Typically, the more senior members of the group enjoy more fruits of the group's success (for example, higher income, better call schedules, and so forth). New members of an existing group who pass a probationary period often are required to pay in a substantial capital contribution to join, which can sometimes create an entry barrier to growth. Other groups employ new physicians for a lengthy period to control the finances of the group as well as to give all parties the opportunity to see whether the relationship is a good fit. In any case, it is common for the group to require physicians to sign a non-competition agreement as a condition of their employment to protect the group from a physician's defecting and taking patients away from the group.[15]

Single-specialty groups have significant structural advantages over other arrangements. They have the ability to achieve significant economies of scale, have strong negotiating leverage, and, from a management perspective, have the ability to influence physician behavior. They are attractive to health plans because they not only deliver a large block of physicians with one contract but they also have the ability to manage their own resources. The group can also effect changes (such as switching hospitals) that can have a rapid and positive effect on managed care. Although the capital investment required of partners can be an entry barrier, it is also an exit barrier, thereby promoting greater stability, an attractive quality in the eyes of health plans.

Single-specialty groups are not without their disadvantages. These include political infighting, uncontrolled overhead, and poor utilization patterns. If the group has markedly disproportionate compensation between senior members and new physicians, the turnover of new members can lead to instability. While groups are able to develop specific cultures that allow them to cohere, they also have a tendency to resist change, which can be an Achilles heel in a dynamic marketplace.

Multispecialty Groups

Some of the groups with the most burnished reputations in the United States are multispecialty group practices founded early in the twentieth century, such as the Mayo Clinic, the Cleveland Clinic, the Scripps Clinic, and others of similar reputation and heritage. While these are large and attract patients from throughout the world, most multispecialty groups are smaller and have a less comprehensive representation. The size

of a multispecialty group ranges from two to well over one thousand physicians. The trend in some cities has been the consolidation of groups to form large multispecialty groups. Driving this trend has been the need for greater efficiency, the impact of competitive markets, the effect of financing health care through large managed care contracts, and the relative stability afforded by larger organizations. Most multispecialty groups are organized as professional corporations or partnerships.[16]

Multispecialty groups share many of the same advantages and disadvantages as single-specialty groups. Multispecialty groups, like their single-specialty brethren, are able to recruit new physicians more easily because of their stable cash flow and their strong bargaining position with vendors and health plans. Their compensation and benefit packages generally are quite favorable compared with smaller, less integrated physician structures. However, multispecialty groups can become calcified in their ways and become less able to change than individual physicians. This is a serious problem if the group is also top-heavy with subspecialists who treat primary care physicians as second-class citizens. If the group is unwilling to consider redistributing the rewards to the primary care physicians, it may suffer defections of those physicians, which will make the group less desirable from a managed care standpoint.[17]

The Physician-Hospital Organization

Physician hospital organizations (PHOs) are legal entities (most often corporations) structured to include physicians and hospitals as members. The physician component might be a group practice, an IPA, or individual practitioners. Each PHO is unique. The PHO is structured to be separate and distinct from the hospital and physician members but is designed to represent both parties in key insurance company negotiations and contracts. Governance of the PHO usually includes representatives of both entities and is often structured so that each has equal board representation. Hospitals have been especially interested in the development of PHOs as a mechanism to link physicians to their organizations. Some physicians see PHOs as a mechanism to gain access to capital and contracts, as well as to align their interests with those of one or more of the hospitals in the marketplace.[18] Approximately one-third of all groups nationwide participate in a PHO, with single-specialty groups being the most likely to participate, according to an AMA survey. Almost three-fourths of groups participate in PHOs to negotiate managed care contracts with health care payers. Approximately one-half of the groups that participate in a PHO are involved in the actual provision of health care services.[19]

PHOs are the first step of the evolutionary ladder in vertical integration with respect to practitioners and facilities. They often form as a reaction to market forces from managed care. PHOs are among the simplest types of vertically integrated systems to develop. They are also a vehicle to provide some integration while preserving the independence and autonomy of the physicians. For hospitals, PHOs offer opportunities to form a more unified medical staff, more effectively market medical services to payers, and enhance physician relationships overall.

Initial capitalization and ownership occur with varying formulas, but most attempt to achieve equal ownership between physicians and the hospital. The hospital may put up the majority of the cash. For the sake of practitioner motivation, some commentators view physician equity as a favorable feature.[20] Governance can evolve over time. Hospital administrators can manage the entity in its simplest form. However, most PHOs eventually establish formal governing boards.[21]

PHOs may be divided into two broad categories, open and closed. These are described separately because health plans often view them this way.

Open PHOs

The open PHO is one that is open to virtually any member of the medical staff of the hospital. Although there are usually minimum credentialing requirements, this is not always the case. Open PHOs are almost always specialty dominated. The creators of the open PHO are often specialists themselves who have become concerned that health plans are selectively contracting, thereby reducing the amount of business that the specialists collectively are doing. The medical staff then approaches the hospital administration to form the PHO, mainly to allow all the members of the medical staff to participate with health plans. In this scenario, primary care physicians are usually courted but may still be relegated to second-class status, even if unintentionally.

Some open PHOs claim that although their genesis is an open format, the ultimate goal will be to manage the membership and remove the physicians who are unable to practice cost effectively. Health plans view such claims with skepticism, although it is certainly possible. The political reality of an open PHO is that it is quite difficult to bring sufficient discipline to bear on medical staff members who wield a high level of influence. This is complicated by the dichotomy of payment mechanisms, in which a certain portion of reimbursement to the hospital rewards cost effectiveness (for example, prospective payment, capitation, and package or bundled pricing), whereas other forms of reimbursement reward the opposite (for example, fee-for-service and simple discounts on services).[22]

Closed PHOs

The primary distinction between a closed PHO and an open one is simply the decision to limit physician membership in the PHO. While a closed PHO presents more thorny political issues than an open PHO, it carries a greater potential for success. The two general approaches to limiting membership are by specialty type and by practice profiling.

Limitations by practice type are more common and more easily accomplished. The most common limitation is the number of specialists, to address the frequent imbalance between primary care physicians and specialists found in open PHOs. Indeed, it is not uncommon to find closed PHOs having a disproportionate number of primary care physicians on the governing board as well as in the membership of the PHO. The limitation on the number of specialists is most often accomplished by projecting the enrollment (or covered lives) that the PHO is expected to cover over the next several years and then recruiting specialists according to predetermined ratios of specialists required for that enrollment.

The second type of limitation involves practice profiling and, for technical reasons, is more difficult to carry out. This type of limitation requires the PHO to adopt some objective yardstick of performance to evaluate each physician's practice. Based on that

yardstick, physicians with satisfactory statistics would be invited to join the PHO. This analysis is difficult to perform unless the PHO has access to adequate data, which is rarely the case.[23]

The primary advantage of the PHO is its ability to negotiate on behalf of a large group of physicians allied with a hospital. This advantage may be nonexistent if no health plan wishes to negotiate, but it may be quite valuable if the hospital and key members of the medical staff are attractive to health plans and are not already under some exclusive contract. Once again, closed PHOs, given their exclusive nature, are more attractive to health plans than open ones are. PHOs are often willing to provide performance guarantees to the health plan. Additionally, physicians may view the PHO as a facilitator to landing direct contracts with self-insured employers, with the Health Care Financing Administration for Medicare risk contracts, and with the state for managed Medicaid contracts.

A second advantage of a PHO is its theoretical ability to monitor and analyze data and to administer the delivery system, at least from the standpoints of quality and utilization management. Again, this advantage is more likely to be found in a closed PHO than in an open one, primarily because a closed PHO has a greater ability to centralize tasks in the hands of fewer physicians. The third advantage of a PHO, at least from a managerial viewpoint, is that it is the first step to greater integration between a hospital and its medical staff. While a PHO may by itself yield better relations, those relations can quickly sour if the PHO consumes time, energy, and money but fails to produce results. If the PHO does result in a better ability to contract, then its mission is successful, at least for the near term.

If the PHO does not succeed, or if success appears to be short lived, then the PHO may be the base from which a more integrated model may be built.[24]

The primary disadvantage of the generic PHO is that it often fails to result in any meaningful improvement in contracting ability. Often, health plans already have provider contracts in place and see little value in going through the PHO. Moreover, health plans may also view the PHO as merely a gambit for physicians to keep their reimbursement high. Again, open PHOs are at a significant disadvantage if the health plan does not want all the physicians in the PHO to be participating in the health plan. Health plans often want the right to select the providers and are generally unwilling to relinquish that leverage. Even closed PHOs may suffer from this problem if health plans specifically refuse to contract with certain physicians who are members of the PHO.

Health plans may view the PHO as a barrier to effective communication with the physicians and a hindrance to utilization management. Unless the PHO has a compelling story to tell concerning its ability to manage utilization, the health plan may conclude that it can do a better job without the PHO's interference. On the other hand, if the health plan has relatively unsophisticated utilization-review capabilities, or if the plan is too small to be able to devote adequate resources to utilization management, the PHO may represent an attractive working partner.[25]

The Management Service Organization

The management service organization (MSO), a relatively new type of structure, represents the evolution of the PHO into an entity that provides more services for physicians. These include administrative services such as practice management, marketing, managed care contracting, recruiting, management information service (MIS) development, purchasing, facilities development, accounting, billing, and personnel management. The MSO can be hospital affiliated, a hospital-physician joint venture, physician owned, or investor owned. The physician usually remains an independent private practitioner, under no legal obligation to use the services of the MSO exclusively. The reasons for MSOs' creation are usually the same as for the PHO, and ownership and governance issues are similar to those described above.[26]

The MSO may be considerably broader in scope. Besides providing all of the services described above, the MSO may actually purchase many of the assets of the physician's practice. For example, the MSO may purchase the physician's office space or office equipment and then lease them back to him (at fair market value). The MSO can employ the office support staff of the physician as well. MSOs can further incorporate functions such as quality management, utilization management, provider relations, and even claims processing.[27]

The primary advantage of the MSO over a PHO is the ability of the MSO to bring economies of scale and professional management to the physician's office services, thus potentially reducing overhead costs. The MSO may also have the potential ability to capture data concerning practice behavior, which may be used to help the physicians practice more cost effectively. Such efficiency develops when the MSO contains more advanced functions, such as utilization management and claims processing. The disadvantages of the MSO are similar to those of a PHO in that the MSO may fail to reduce overhead as promised.

Integrated Delivery System

An integrated delivery system (IDS) is a local or regional health care network that provides a full range of services for patients in a geographical area. The services may include wellness programs, preventive care, ambulatory clinics, outpatient diagnostic and laboratory services, emergency care, general hospital services, rehabilitation, long-term care, congregate living, psychiatric care, home health, and hospice care. Typically, an IDS establishes alliances and contractual relationships with other providers for those services not offered by the IDS.[28] There are three types of integrated delivery systems, each of which will be discussed separately.

Foundation-Model IDS

A foundation-model IDS is one in which a hospital creates a not-for-profit foundation and actually purchases physicians' practices (both tangible and intangible assets) and puts those practices into the foundation. This model usually occurs when for some legal reason the hospital cannot employ the physicians directly or use hospital funds to purchase the practices directly. (For example, the hospital is a not-for-profit entity that cannot own a for-profit subsidiary, or there is a state law against the corporate practice of medicine.) It is important to note that to qualify for and maintain its not-for-profit status, the foundation must prove that it provides substantial community benefit.

The foundation itself is governed by a board that is not dominated by either the hospital or the physicians (indeed, physi-

cians may not represent more than 20 percent of the board) and includes lay members as well. The foundation owns and manages the practices, but the physicians become members of a medical group that, in turn, has an exclusive contract for services with the foundation. In other words, the foundation is the only source of revenue for the medical group. The physicians have long-term contracts with the medical group, the contracts containing noncompetition clauses. Although the physicians are in an independent group and the foundation is also independent from the hospital, the relationship is close among all members of the three entities. The medical group, however, retains a significant measure of autonomy in its own business affairs, and the foundation has no control over certain issues, such as individual physician compensation.[29]

The primary advantages of the foundation model concern legal constraints that require the foundation's creation in the first place. Because the construction of this entity is unwieldy, it is best suited to those states in which it is required, so that a not-for-profit hospital can proceed with a fully integrated model. That said, the foundation-model IDS provides for a greater level of structural integration than any other model discussed up to this point. A not-for-profit foundation may also be better able to access the bond market for capital advantageously.

Because the foundation clearly controls the revenue that the medical group will get, it has considerable influence over that group. The foundation also has the ability to ration the clinical and administrative resources required to meet obligations under managed care contracts and can achieve greater economies of scale. If the foundation consolidates medical office locations, these economies are improved, as is the foundation's ability to provide more comprehensive services to enrolled members. A foundation also has the ability to invest required capital to expand services and to recruit primary care physicians.[30]

From a management standpoint, the primary disadvantage of a foundation-model IDS is that the physicians in the medical group are linked only indirectly to the foundation and the business goals of that foundation. Although the indirect link is quite strong, the medical group remains an intermediate organization that can operate in ways that are potentially inconsistent with the overall goals of managed care. An example would be a group that is dominated by specialists and in which primary care physicians are treated as second-class citizens. Another example would be a group that compensated member physicians based on fee-for-service or other measures that are easily manipulated, producing a less than optimal control of quality and utilization.

Related to this issue is the inherent potential for conflicts between the governing boards of the hospital and the medical group. Should the priorities of the two organizations diverge (and they often do), serious disputes may arise, potentially leading to litigation. The last main disadvantage is the not-for-profit status of the hospital and foundation. Because of that status, the foundation must continually demonstrate that it provides a community benefit to maintain its status. The risk of private inurement is also increased.

Staff-Model IDS

A staff-model IDS refers to a health system that employs the physicians directly. Physicians are integrated into the system ei-

ther through the purchase of their practices or direct hiring. The system is often more than a hospital, being instead a larger, more comprehensive organization for the delivery of health care. Because the physicians are employees, the legal issues that attend to an IDS using private physicians are diminished.

The staff model IDS is theoretically in a good position to be able to rationalize resources and to align goals of all the actors in the delivery system. Physicians are almost always paid based on a salary, and incentive programs can be designed to reward the physicians in parallel with the goals and objectives of the system. Significantly increased economies of scale are attainable, and capital resources can be applied more efficiently. Staff models also have a greater ability to recruit new physicians because the income stream to the new physician begins immediately upon employment, no small consideration to the young physician burdened with student debt. The problems of taxable status, private inurement, and fraud and abuse are also greatly reduced. Health plans usually regard a staff-model IDS as an attractive business partner, assuming that cost, quality, and access are acceptable.

A significant problem with the staff model occurs when management assumes that simply because the physicians are employees, they can be managed like other employees of the system. This assumption will quickly undermine the organization. Physicians are a highly trained, highly intelligent, and sometimes highly independent lot who operate clinically with considerable autonomy. Any medical system that does not recognize this will face problems with its medical staff.

Nevertheless, staff models often run into problems with physician productivity.

Salaried physicians are no longer motivated to see large numbers of patients, as they are under a fee-for-service regime. The staff-model IDS may be most attractive to physicians who do not wish to practice full-time or who wish to limit their hours. Some staff-model organizations have had such problems with low productivity that they have at least partially eroded the economies of scale that are the underlying rationale for a tightly integrated system. Physicians in staff models often feel little loyalty and are more easily recruited away than physicians who have an investment in a group.

The last disadvantage is the high capital requirement to build and operate the system. Once adequate patient volume is coming through, staff models can have excellent financial performance. Until this point, however, they are often highly leveraged. Furthermore, expansion of an existing system similarly requires large amounts of capital.[31]

The Physician-Ownership IDS Model

The physician-ownership model refers to a vertically integrated system in which the physicians hold a significant portion of ownership interest. In some cases, the physicians own the entire system. In others, the physicians own a smaller percentage but over 51 percent. The physicians' interest is through their medical group, as physicians holding equity themselves as simple shareholders could raise questions of Medicare/Medicaid fraud and abuse.

The advantages of the physician-ownership model are similar to those described for the staff model above. Unlike the staff model, however, the physician-ownership model enjoys a powerful advantage by virtue of physician ownership: total alignment of goals of the medical group and of the health system. Because the physician-owners' success is linked directly to the overall success of the entire organization, there is far less problem with setting objectives. As a result of this alignment, strong physician leadership usually results, with improved loyalty and diminished turnover among members. Finally, this model can choose either to contract with or to own the hospital rather than be dominated by it.

The most salient disadvantage of the physician-ownership IDS model is the high level of resources required to build and operate it. Significant capital is necessary to acquire the personnel, facilities, and practices necessary to provide comprehensive medical services, an appropriate level of managerial support, and the required infrastructure. The source of this capital is mainly the physicians' practices, although outside access to capital is possible as well. Consequently, the buy-in cost to new physician partners will be high, creating a barrier to some physicians joining the group other than as employees.[32]

Traditional Employment

Another practice option is employment by corporations or hospitals. Corporations and hospitals may employ physicians if they are not limited by laws governing the corporate practice of medicine. The existence of such legislation varies from state to state and will dictate whether this option is available in a given area.

As an employee, the physician is generally salaried and receives a benefit package that includes a defined-contribution retirement plan—such as a 401(k) or 403(b)—and malpractice coverage. Although considered restrictive by some, employment may be less risky than other work options and provides a modicum of protection from a dynamic marketplace. Employment usually includes established working hours and specific productivity expectations. A negative aspect of employment, however, is that salaried physicians do not attain the potential benefits (income and otherwise) of incorporation.

Hospitalists

Facing pressures from managed care companies to decrease hospital stays, cut costs, and increase the volume of patients whom physicians see in their offices, some hospitals are turning to the "hospitalist," usually an internist or family physician, who focuses his or her practice solely on managing the care of the hospital patient. Hospitalists are usually salaried by the hospital, managed care company, or private practice and bill the patient's insurer directly. More than three thousand hospitalists are in practice nationwide, according to the National Association of Inpatient Physicians, and it is likely that hospitalists will soon become part of the fabric of a changing health care system in the United States. Preliminary studies indicate that putting a hospital-based physician in charge of delivering inpatient care can shave a full day off the average patient stay. Other advantages cited include lower cost of medical care since the hospitalist knows the hospital intimately and can presumably use its resources more efficiently.[33]

Large HMOs are among the most enthusiastic users of inpatient specialists, as hospitalists are also known, for these reasons. HMOs contend that the hospitalists free office-based physicians to see their full quota of outpatients on time. But hospitalists are also among the most controversial figures in medicine today. Internists in particular argue that while hospitalists may promote efficiency and lower costs, their role threatens to undermine the traditional relationship between patient and physician. If a physician abandons a longtime patient at the hospital door just when the patient needs the doctor most, they argue, trust begins to crumble. Other critics also argue that valuable information about a patient's life and illnesses—ranging from allergies to blood tests to preferences for end-of-life care—may be lost as care is transferred from one physician to another.[34]

Advocates of inpatient physicians counter these criticisms. The Norman Rockwell physician who takes care of patients from womb to tomb has become a myth, they assert. Group practice already fragments a patient's care, while computerized databases and e-mail can ensure that details about a patient's health are never lost. Further, statistics indicate that physicians admit far fewer patients to the hospital than they once did, and hospitalized patients are sicker than they used to be, forcing office physicians to maintain the difficult technical skills of caring for acutely ill patients even though they use those skills less and less. Finally, sicker hospitalized patients have conditions that can change from minute to minute, which warrant frequent monitoring that office-based physicians can no longer provide.[35]

The patient handoff is fundamental to the hospitalist model. In fact, the discontinuity of care created by the handoff is the source of one of the strengths of the hospitalist model, the presence of a physician in the hospital throughout the day who can coordinate inpatient care and react to clinical data in real time. Yet this discontinuity leads to the two greatest potential drawbacks of the model: (1) an information "voltage drop" caused by the movement of information from the office to the hospital ward and back to the office and (2) potential patient dissatisfaction caused by assignment of a new physician—often a stranger—to care for patients at their time of greatest need. Hospitalists themselves express concern about discontinuity of care. In a survey of 372 US hospitalists, only 1 percent thought that communication "always suffered" under the hospitalist model, but 88 percent stated that it "occasionally" (80 percent) or "regularly" (8 percent) suffered.[36]

All hospitalists manage medical patients in the hospital. Other potential roles for these physicians include providing triage in the emergency department, transferring out-of-network patients, managing patients in the intensive care unit, managing preoperative and postoperative treatment of surgical patients, and providing leadership in hospital quality improvement and regulatory work. A variety of models of care are needed to meet the clinical, organizational, financial, and political demands of diverse health care systems.[37]

The growing reliance on hospitalists in the United States has implications for several areas of internal medicine, including patient care, administration, clinical practice, and medical education. The new hospitalist practice highlights the long-standing tensions about the role and direction of internal medicine, tensions that affect general and specialty care in both outpatient and hospital settings. The careers of hospitalists will depend on whether burnout is a problem and whether hospitalists will be able to compete effectively with subspecialists, such as cardiologists and physicians specializing in AIDS.[38]

1. Gail P. Bender, "Solo Practice," 5 in *The Business of Medicine* (Julie K. Silver, ed, Philadelphia: Hanley and Belfus, 1998). *See generally* Paul Starr, *The Social Transformation of American Medicine* (New York: Basic Books, 1982).

2. Kenneth H. Paulus, "Organizational Options Available to Physicians" in Silver, *supra* note 1, at 17–18 (1998).

3. Peter R. Kongsvedt, *The Managed Health Care Handbook,* 3d ed, 46–62 (Gaithersburg, Md: Aspen Publishers, 1996).

4. *Id. See also* Paulus, *supra* note 2, at 19.

5. Kongsvedt, *supra* note 3, at 46–62.

6. *Id.*

7. *Id.*

8. Paulus, *supra* note 2, at 18. *See also* Keith M. Korenchuk, *Transforming the Delivery of Health Care: The Integration Process,* 2d ed (Englewood, Colo: Medical Group Management Association, 1994). *See also* "Physician Group Practices" in *Health Care Corporate Law, Facilities and Transactions,* chap 8 (Gaithersburg, Md: Aspen Publishers, 1994).

9. Donald H. Caldwell, Jr, *U.S. Health Law and Policy 1999: A Guide to the Current Literature* 62 (Chicago: AHA Press, 1999).

10. 42 USC § 1395nn. *See also* "The Rapidly Changing World of Clinics Without Walls," 130 Medical Economics 72 (May 8, 1995).

11. 42 USC § 1395nn-(h)(4)(A). *See also* "The Critics Rip into GPWWs," 137 Medical Economics 72 (May 8, 1995).

12. Kongsvedt, *supra* note 3, at 46–62.

13. *Id.* More than a few PPMs have failed to attain their expected level of profitability and have spawned shareholder lawsuits alleging they misled investors. *See* "MedPartners Settles Suit by Investors," The Wall Street Journal, Southeast Journal page S1 (July 28, 1999). Some have filed for bankruptcy protection from their creditors. *See* "The PPM Meltdown: How FPA's Implosion Buried Its Doctors," 140 Medical Economics 76 (Jan 25, 1999).

14. Paulus, *supra* note 2, at 19.

15. Kongsvedt, *supra* note 3, at 46–62.

16. Paulus, *supra* note 2, at 19–20.

17. Kongsvedt, *supra* note 3, at 51–52.

18. Paulus, *supra* note 2, at 20.

19. *Medical Groups in the US, A Survey of Practice Characteristics,* 1996 ed (Chicago: American Medical Association) *quoted in Medical Group Practice: Legal and Administrative Guide* 1:13 (Gaithersburg, Md: Aspen Publishers 1998). *See also* Paulus, *supra* note 2, at 20.

20. Kongsvedt, *supra* note 3, at 53–56.

21. *Id.*

22. *Id.*

23. *Id.*

24. *Id.*

25. *Id. See also* Paulus, *supra* note 2, at 20.

26. *Medical Group Practice supra* note 2, at page 1:13. *See generally* Marianne F. Fazen, *Managed Care Desk Reference* (Reston, Va: St Anthony Publishing, 1996).

27. Kongsvedt, *supra* note 3, at 57.

28. Marianne F. Fazen, *Managed Care Desk Reference* 151 (Reston, Va: St Anthony Publishing, 1996).

29. Kongsvedt, *supra* note 3, at 57–58.

30. *Id* at 58.

31. *Id* at 59.

32. *Id. See also* D.C. Coddington, K.D. Moore, & E.A. Fisher, *Integrated Health Care: Reorganizing the Physician, Hospital, and Health Plan Relationship* (Englewood, Colo: Center for Research in Ambulatory Health Care Administration/MGMA, 1994).

33. Donna Kutt Nahas, "A New Breed in Medicine: The 'Hospitalist,'" The New York Times page A1 (Jan 11, 1998); Robert M. Wachter, "The Emerging Role of 'Hospitalists' in the American Health Care System," 335 New England Journal of Medicine 514–517 (1996); J.D. Moore, Jr, "The Inpatient's Best Friend. Hospitalists Specialize in Managing Care of the Very Ill." 27 Modern Healthcare 54–62 (1997).

34. Abigail Zucker, "At the Hospital, a New Doctor Is In," *The New York Times* page E7 (March 24, 1998).

35. *Id. See also* Marilyn Chase, "New Breed of Doctors Is Taking Full Charge of Stays in the Hospital," *The Wall Street Journal* page B1 (March 8, 1999). *See also* The Annals of Internal Medicine, vol 130, no 4 (part 2), (Feb 16, 1999), which is a special issue devoted to the hospitalist movement.

36. Robert M. Wachter, "An Introduction to the Hospitalist Model," 130 Annals of Internal Medicine 338–342 (1999).

37. *Id. See also* "When Hospitals Takes Over . . . Who Wins? Who Loses?" 75 Medical Economics 100 (Dec 28, 1998).

38. Steven A. Schroeder & Renie Schapiro, "The Hospitalist: New Boon for Internal Medicine or Retreat from Primary Care?" Annals of Internal Medicine, 382–387 (vol 130, no 4 [part 2]) (Feb 16, 1999).

Chapter 8

Hospital medical staff issues

The medical staff is by far the most important component of any hospital. The physicians admit the facility's patients and administer the proper medical care. In properly selecting and monitoring the hospital's physicians, the hospital can foster good patient care along with efficient hospital operations. Yet in doing so, the hospital may take actions that restrict the physician's ability to practice her profession how and where she chooses. Because the stakes are high for both sides, disputes between the staff and the hospital arise with some frequency.

This tension between the hospital and its medical staff has grown in recent years as a consequence of several factors. First, the hospital must take an active role in examining the qualifications of its physicians. A long line of judicial rulings makes it clear that a hospital will be held liable for the negligence of a medical staff member if it has not adequately reviewed her qualifications and monitored her performance. The hospital, therefore, must create and enforce a system for evaluating the quality of care being rendered to its patients and taking

timely action against any physician whose performance is unsatisfactory. Changes in the reimbursement system have created another source of pressure on hospitals to monitor their medical staff, this time from a financial perspective of efficient use of hospital resources.

Meanwhile, changes in the practice of medicine have increased pressure on physicians to seek hospital medical staff appointments. Unlike the general practitioners of the mid-twentieth century, who conducted the bulk of their practice in an office, many physicians now practice almost exclusively as specialists within a hospital. Moreover, physicians who are not based within a hospital require access to new technology and procedures available only in a hospital. Magnifying the effect of this change in medical practice has been a significant increase in recent years in the number of physicians, producing a surplus in many parts of the nation. While hospitals in the past competed for physicians to serve their patients, physicians are now competing for limited openings on hospital staffs. Nonphysician health practitioners have also grown in number and are pressing for access to hospitals.[1]

Despite the high number of suits brought against hospitals by dissatisfied physicians, the hospital typically has less to lose in a medical staff controversy than the physician. Often, the very procedures designed to protect the staff member's rights work against her. The high legal costs involved in pursuing an appointment through the hospital's due-process mechanisms and then in court can be more burdensome for an individual than an institution. The resulting publicity can also be damaging to the physician, no matter what the outcome, and may inevitably brand the physician as a troublemaker. Finally, courts heavily favor hospitals in these sorts of disputes. If hospitals have a reasonable basis for their actions and carefully follow procedures, they will win the vast majority of cases brought against them.

Organization of the Medical Staff

In any hospital accredited by the Joint Commission on the Accreditation of Healthcare Organizations (JCAHO), the members of the medical staff are organized as a group. The critical document for the organization of the medical staff is the medical staff bylaws. Under JCAHO guidelines, the bylaws are adopted by the medical staff, subject to the governing body approval. JCAHO guidelines mandate that bylaws cover a variety of issues, including (1) the organizational structure of the medical staff, its departments, officers, and committees, including an executive committee to act for the medical staff between meetings; (2) the criteria for medical staff appointments; (3) the procedures that will be used in reviewing applicants for medical staff posi-

tions, in delineating privileges, and in taking disciplinary action against staff members; (4) a mechanism for communication among the medical staff, the administration, and the governing body; and (5) a procedure for amending the bylaws.

The medical staff as an organization has two responsibilities for which it is accountable to the hospital's governing body, monitoring the quality of all medical care provided to patients and reviewing the ethical conduct and professional practices of its members. The main ways the medical staff meets these responsibilities is through its role in reviewing appointments, assessing staff performance, and restricting or terminating privileges.

Failure to meet these responsibilities can jeopardize the hospital's accreditation. Moreover, courts have repeatedly held that negligence by the hospital or its medical staff in failing to review the qualifications of applicants or to monitor the ongoing performance of staff members will subject the hospital to liability to patients injured by such physicians. Finally, in some states, detailed credentialing responsibilities have been imposed on hospitals through state statutes or hospital codes in an effort to improve the quality of medical care.[2]

Medical staff appointments are for a fixed term, which under the JCAHO rules cannot exceed two years. The first term, or some portion of it, is required by the JCAHO to be provisional. During this period, the new physician must be subject to extra scrutiny to determine her fitness for staff appointment. At the end of each appointment term, all staff members must be reevaluated based on their performance and their compliance with the criteria for staff membership and, if appropriate, be reappointed by the governing body.[3]

The medical staff also has monitoring mechanisms for physicians already on staff. Based on information generated by the medical staff or from other sources such as patients, nurses, or other hospital employees, the hospital must determine whether to extend a physician's appointment, or to reduce her privileges, deny her reappointment, or terminate her appointment during its term. As with the initial appointment, the final decision is made by the governing body after a recommendation by the medical staff.

Denial of Medical Staff Privileges

Despite the deference granted by courts to hospitals, an unlawful denial of privileges can generate a litany of claims from a spurned applicant. Hospitals and members of their medical staffs can be exposed to liability for a denial of due process and interference with a physician's property interests. Additionally, hospitals and members of their medical staffs are not exempt from antitrust claims if there is (1) an agreement among two or more persons; (2) an intent to harm or unreasonably restrain competition; and (3) an actual injury to competition.[4] Failure to comply with the statutes and regulations that require a review of applications can also jeopardize a hospital's continued participation in the Medicare program. Given these concerns, practitioners should recognize some of the issues surrounding the grant or denial of medical staff privileges.

A physician does not have an unqualified right to practice, even in a public hospital.[5] Instead, a physician has a liberty interest, which includes the right to engage in any of the common occupations in the practice of medicine at a public hospital.[6] A physician's liberty interest in engaging in

the profession cannot be abridged without adequate procedural due process. In addition, there must be a rational basis that furthers a legitimate state interest before interfering with a liberty interest.[7] If a public hospital acts arbitrarily or unreasonably, a physician might successfully contend that she has been deprived of her Fourteenth Amendment due-process rights.[8] Given the nature of private hospitals and their growing importance, however, it should not surprise any observers that the same principles governing public hospitals have been applied to require nongovernmental facilities to provide a physician with an opportunity to be heard and present contrary evidence when that physician is denied medical staff privileges.

In a public hospital, once a physician is admitted to the medical staff, he may have a property interest in retaining privileges.[9] Several courts have emphasized that, to establish a protected property interest, the deprived physician must demonstrate that the existing rules, regulations, or understandings, including the hospital's bylaws or applicable provisions of state law, result in an entitlement to medical staff privileges.[10] In cases that have addressed claims raised following a hospital's failure to renew a physician's medical staff privileges, the physicians have generally failed to demonstrate a protected property interest. In *Lim v Central Hospital,* the court addressed claims by a physician against a hospital that denied his application for a renewal of staff privileges. The court rejected the physician's claim and noted that the bylaws did not imply an entitlement to reappointment. Consequently, the physician did not have a protected property interest. The court noted, however, that if the physician's privileges had been terminated during any period, the physician might be able to argue that he had been deprived of a property right without the necessary due process.[11]

Historically, private hospitals have had absolute discretion in selecting medical staff physicians. Although a private hospital may receive government funds and is licensed under government statutes, the required state action may not be present that would give a physician due-process rights. Plaintiffs have sometimes argued, however, that the hospital's receipt of government funds provides sufficient government involvement with the hospital to create state action. In addition to the receipt of government funds, other courts have noted a hospital's fund-raising efforts and provision of facilities to the public as grounds to justify the requirement of due process.[12]

Due Process

Despite the murkiness of the term, courts have determined that *procedural* due process includes adequate notice, adequate opportunity for a hearing, the right to introduce evidence, and the right to confront and cross-examine witnesses. The touchstone of procedural due process is a sense of fair play. Fair procedures are common-law rights that protect individuals from arbitrary exclusion or expulsion from private organizations that control an important economic interest. Courts have held that a physician may be entitled to representation by an attorney, but courts have not universally held that physicians are entitled to representation at the hearing. The physician may also be entitled to access to records that are essential to the physician's defense.[13]

Although the procedural due process requirements can be cumbersome, the substantive due process requirements are

significantly less rigorous. Substantive due process merely requires that the grounds for dismissal not be arbitrary, capricious, discriminatory, or unreasonable. In *Sosa v Board of Managers of Val Verde Memorial Hospital,* a physician claimed violation of his due process and equal protection rights when his application for medical staff privileges was denied. Rejecting the physician's claim, the court announced a standard that has been adopted by many courts across the nation:

The court is charged with the narrow responsibility of assuring that the qualifications imposed by the Board are reasonably related to the operation of the hospital and fairly administered. In short, so long as staff selections are administered with fairness, geared by a rationale compatible with hospital responsibility, and unencumbered with irrelevant considerations, a court should not interfere.[14]

The hospital is faced with a two-edged sword in defining standards to evaluate physicians' applications for medical staff privileges. If the standard is too broad, courts may determine that it is void for reasons of vagueness. Yet if it requires specific certification or membership in professional societies, it can be held to be illegal, arbitrary, or capricious. Required membership in or certification by a particular society or professional group, for example, has been deemed an excessive limitation by some courts.

Justifiable Exclusions

Despite the requirements of due process, there are still circumstances when courts have found that a physician may be properly removed from a medical staff:

Failure to Obtain or Maintain Insurance

As the cost of malpractice insurance premiums has increased, some physicians have let their policies lapse. In a landmark case, *Holmes v Hoemako Hospital,* an Arizona court held that a rule mandating professional liability coverage was not unlawful, arbitrary, or capricious. Recognizing the economic realities of malpractice suits and noting that the hospital is almost always joined as a codefendant, the requirement was held to have a rational relationship to the health and welfare of the citizens served by the hospital.[15]

"The Disruptive Doctor"

As modern medicine has required treatment to be administered by an increasing number of physicians, the ability to work well with others has become more important. Conduct that disrupts and adversely affects the care provided to patients in a hospital can justify the revocation of a physician's medical staff privileges. In *Mahmoodian v United Hospital Center, Inc,* the West Virginia Supreme Court upheld a termination due to a physician's refusal to give verbal orders to nurses, interference with procedures, and failure to respond to a physician's request for assistance in the evaluation of a patient.[16] Similarly, in *Bryan v James E. Holmes Regional Medical Center,* where the plaintiff physician had a history of abusive treatment of nurses, technicians, and fellow physicians, the US Court of Appeals for the Eleventh Circuit determined that the hospital's revocation of plaintiff's medical staff privileges was done "in the reasonable belief that the action was taken in the furtherance of quality health care."[17] Responding to one physician's assertions that an ability to work with others was un-

related to medical competence, the Oregon Supreme Court ruled:

Most other courts have found that the factor of ability to work smoothly with others is reasonably related to the hospital's object of ensuring patient welfare. This conclusion seems justified, for, in the modern hospital, staff members are frequently required to work together or in teams, and a member, who, because of personality or otherwise, is incapable of getting along, could severely hinder the effective treatment of patients. . . . Hospitals uniformly consider cooperativeness an important factor, and in these circumstances, it seems questionable whether this court should gainsay the hospital's experience and judgment in this matter.[18]

The failure of a physician to follow written orders or established procedures has also been held to be adequate grounds for dismissal.[19] Unreasonable criticism of coworkers can also be sufficiently objectionable to support the denial of medical staff privileges. In *Sussman v Overlook Hospital Association,* the court stated, "Constructive criticism properly expressed can be salutary and lead to a betterment of conditions. Destructive criticism can become obnoxious and disruptive of morale and good public relations. To be critical is one thing; to be hypercritical is quite another."[20]

In summary, although courts have recognized that a physician's personality can affect the quality of patient care, courts generally will uphold the governing body's decision to remove a physician from the medical staff whose disruptive personality poses a risk to high-quality patient care only if: (1) the medical staff bylaws provide that the ability to work with others is a criterion for medical staff membership; (2) there is clear evidence that the physician has been disruptive; (3) the physician is given due process; and (4) the physician's behavior could be detrimental to patient care.

Impairment

In general, impaired physicians may be justifiably excluded from the medical staff or group practice. Consistent with this view, the American Hospital Association has adopted a management advisory that cautions hospitals to implement drug screening for all applicants for privileges, including physicians, regardless of a particular job description. State statutes are the primary source of definition for the term *impaired physician*. The statutes vary in level of specificity and, consequently, in terms of what conditions are included. Commonly, state statutory definitions of impairment include both substance abuse and mental illness or mental deterioration. Several states also include deterioration, impairment, or disabilities of a physical nature in the definition. Typically, these statutes require that the condition or disease pose a risk to patients before it can be characterized as an impairment. Physicians with contagious diseases such as AIDS or hepatitis are often regulated under separate state statutes that specify under what conditions they can practice medicine.

When a medical staff or group practice terminates or disciplines a physician because of impairment, it must also determine whether it has a duty to report the physician to a state entity. State laws and regulations may specify a group practice's reporting obligations with regard to impaired providers. For example, some states, such as Indiana, mandate that a practitioner, upon a reasonable belief that a practitioner with the same license is incompetent, report the colleague to a peer-review body with jurisdiction over the colleague. In other states, where the medical board has responsibility for issuing reporting requirements, the medical staff or medical group must be familiar with the board's rules concerning impaired practitioners. State law, however, may insulate impaired practitioners from disciplinary action, including peer-review and medical board reporting, unless the impairment becomes habitual or poses a danger to patients. If an impaired practitioner has enrolled in a treatment program but has not suffered any disciplinary or peer-review action, the impairment is not reportable. Finally, although the terms and requirements of the Americans with Disabilities Act and the Rehabilitation Act of 1973 are beyond the scope of this book, physicians, hospitals, medical groups, and the attorneys who represent them should recognize that these statutes may apply under certain circumstances.

Medical Society Membership

Membership in the local medical society cannot serve as a precondition to medical staff privileges. If a physician loses membership in a local medical society for ethical reasons, however, a hospital may deny privileges if the misconduct has been the object of hearings by the hospital and the medical society.

Peer Review

Background

Beginning in the early 1960s, many state legislatures enacted statutes that prevented the pretrial discovery or admission into evidence of the records of peer-review committees. Immunity from civil liability was also granted to individual members of peer-review committees. These protections were intended to enhance the effectiveness of peer-review committees by assuring participants of confidentiality. Health care professionals contend that without these safeguards, committee members would not speak freely. Without free and honest discussion, the committee would be unable to serve its function of monitoring and improving the quality of care provided by physicians on a medical staff. Peer-review protections are based on the premise that physicians are best able to evaluate each other, and the evaluation process has been insulated to encourage self-regulation by accommodating existing human foibles reflected in the profession, most notably the infamous conspiracy of silence, rather than with an eye toward judicial oversight.

All fifty states, the District of Columbia, and the federal government have enacted some form of legislation to protect the peer-review process. As one might suspect, no two statutes are exactly alike. However, most statutes share two common features: Almost all provide some form of immunity to peer-review committee members, and almost all prohibit discovery and admission of peer-review records to some degree.

The Health Care Quality Improvement Act

Congress enacted the Health Care Quality Improvement Act of 1986 (HCQIA) in partial response to federal court judgments against physicians who served on peer-review committees. The specific impetus for the act came from the widespread outcry against the federal court judgment in *Patrick v Burget,* where a jury awarded sig-

nificant damages in an antitrust suit against a group of Oregon physicians engaged in peer-review activity.[21]

The stated purpose of the act is to improve the quality of medical care in the United States by protecting physicians and hospitals who perform peer-review activities from the threat of liability and by requiring the reporting of information about adverse medical staff decisions to a central information bank. The immunity provisions of the statute are critical for medical staff decision making since they have the potential to eliminate many of the types of liability. The immunity extends to actions by professional review bodies, which are defined as health care entities (hospitals, health maintenance organizations, group medical practices, and professional societies) and the governing body or any committee of a health care entity. To qualify for immunity, the review body must be taking action against a physician based on her competence or professional conduct. The action must be taken in the reasonable belief that it was in furtherance of high-quality health care, after a reasonable effort to obtain the facts, after adequate notice and hearing procedures, and with reasonable belief that the action was warranted. Although the act does not require specific notice and hearing procedures, it does describe, in very detailed language, procedures that, if followed, will be deemed to satisfy the act's requirements.

If the prerequisites for immunity are satisfied, the professional review body and its members cannot be held liable for damages under federal or state law, with the exception of liability for violation of the civil rights laws. This protection extends to federal antitrust liability with its threat of treble damages, as well as to civil actions under state law for denial of fair procedure.

The act will not eliminate all legal disputes involving medical staff appointments, however. It is limited to actions based on the physician's competence or professional conduct, which could be interpreted not to include such issues, for example, as whether to award an exclusive contract to a particular group of physicians or to close the staff. Actions taken for economic reasons are specifically not protected by the act, which means, for example, that it is unlikely that the physicians' action in *Patrick v Burget* would have been protected, since the courts found that the physicians were misusing the peer-review process for anticompetitive reasons. The act is also limited to protection from suits for damages, so that an aggrieved physician would still be able to seek an injunction, and actions by nonphysician practitioners (other than dentists) are not covered.

When a physician is dissatisfied with a hospital decision concerning medical staff appointment, he may make other legal claims as well. As an example, allegations of defamation frequently accompany suits against hospitals in this area, and they may give rise to significant damages. A hospital will be liable for defamation only if the statements made about the physician were untrue and damaging. In addition, there is generally a qualified privilege for statements made in connection with peer review, which means that the plaintiff must show that they were made out of malice toward the physician (that is, with the knowledge that they were untrue or with reckless disregard for their truth or falsity). State immunity statutes and the Health Care Quality Improvement Act provide some protection against these types of suits. Other similar claims include tortious interference with contract, which requires a showing that the

hospital's action disrupted the physician's relationship with her patients, and intentional infliction of emotional distress.

Physicians have charged from time to time that the hospital decisions regarding appointment violated the provisions of Title VII of the federal civil rights act. Because Title VII applies to discrimination affecting employment, a nonsalaried physician may have trouble proceeding on this basis. State statutes regarding discrimination based on race, sex, age, or disability may apply as well, and the Health Care Quality Improvement Act provides no protection from violation of state or federal civil rights laws.

The National Practitioner Data Bank

HCQIA also requires the reporting of information to the National Practitioner Data Bank (NPDB) maintained by the Department of Health and Human Services. To reduce the occurrence of medical malpractice, the NPDB is intended to restrict the ability of incompetent physicians to move from state to state. Health care organizations are required to report to the state licensing board professional-review actions that adversely affect a physician's medical staff privileges for more than thirty days and a physician's surrender of his or her clinical privileges, either while that physician is under investigation by the entity for possible incompetence or unprofessional conduct or as a sanction for not conducting such an investigation or proceeding.

To constitute a professional-review action, the health care organization's action must be taken in the course of professional-review activity, be based on the physician's competence or professional conduct, and adversely affect the physician's medical staff privileges or membership in a medical society. All reports of adverse actions must be made within fifteen days of the date the adverse action was taken or clinical privileges were voluntarily suspended.[22]

In addition to adverse actions affecting clinical privileges, a health care entity that is also a self-insurer must report medical malpractice payments of any amount on behalf of all licensed health care practitioners, not only physicians, within one month of payment. Payments that must be reported include those in satisfaction of a legal judgment as well as those made under a settlement or partial settlement agreement. A health care entity that fails to report such payments may be fined up to $10,000 for each failure.[23] Health care entities need not report claims that are based mainly on association or lack of association with a professional society or association; fees, advertising, or other competitive acts intended to solicit or retain business; participation in prepaid group health plans, salaried employment, or any other manner of delivering health services; association with a member or members of a particular class of health care practitioners; or any other matter that does not relate to competence or professional conduct of the health care practitioner.[24]

The HCQIA reporting requirement refers to final actions only. Therefore, if the time to appeal an action has not expired, the action is not yet final. In addition, if an appeal is requested, the action does not become final until appeal measures are exhausted in most cases. A practitioner who is reported receives a copy of the report and an opportunity to submit comments that will later be sent out with the report when the data bank is queried.[25]

Other health care entities must also report to the NPDB. Medical-malpractice insurers must report all malpractice payments on behalf of a health care practitioner, regardless of the amount. State licensing boards must report all adverse actions against physicians' and dentists' licenses, and they may report adverse actions against the licenses of other health care practitioners. Professional societies may report disciplinary actions to the NPDB also but are not required to do so.[26]

Information reported to the NPDB is confidential and may not be disclosed, except in connection with peer review and as necessary to carry out the requirements of HCQIA. Entities that receive information directly from the NPDB may disclose it to others only for the purpose of professional-review activity within that entity. According to federal regulations, those who receive NPDB information indirectly may use the information only for the purpose for which it was provided, presumably professional peer-review activity.[27] Further, a lawyer who receives information from the NPDB in connection with a malpractice suit may use the information only within the context of that suit.

When a physician applies for medical staff privileges, the hospital must obtain a report of the information on file with the NPDB concerning the applicant. After granting staff privileges, the hospital must obtain reports every two years on each physician for whom it has granted privileges. The hospital's reliance upon information provided by the NPDB will not result in liability unless it is known that the information provided is false. Upon request, other health care entities and the board also may obtain reports on physicians from the NPDB. However, the information on file with the

NPDB is confidential and may be disclosed by such hospitals and other health care organizations receiving it only in connection with a professional-review activity by the hospital or other health care organization.

There are a number of steps that a hospital can take to ease staff anxieties in this matter. First, it can arrange for insurance coverage that will defend and indemnify those who participate in the appointment process in the event of litigation. Second, it can require all applicants and members of the medical staff to release all participants in the appointment process from civil liability. The JCAHO requires applicants for staff appointments to acknowledge and agree to provisions in the medical staff bylaws for release and immunity from civil liability. Such releases should be obtained at the time the staff member applies, rather than when a dispute arises, by which time the physician is unlikely to be willing to sign. Finally, the hospital should adhere as closely as possible to the requirements set forth in HCQIA.

Health care organizations sometimes have difficulty determining under what circumstances actions against a practitioner's medical staff privileges must be reported to the NPDB. The NPDB has established a help line, 800 767-6732, to which such questions can be addressed. In addition, callers to the help line may request a copy of the current guidebook, which contains examples of actions that are or are not reportable. For example, a restriction or denial of clinical privileges that occurs solely because a physician fails to meet an entity's established threshold eligibility criteria for that particular privilege is not reportable to the NPDB, nor are investigations that do not result in the surrender or restriction of clinical privileges reportable.

Emergency Strategies

Hospitals are under pressure to improve their financial performance and marketability as lower hospitalization rates and shorter lengths of stay under managed care will cause at least some hospitals to go out of business. In order to improve performance, hospitals are engaging in internal medical staff strategic planning to determine the ideal level of various types of services. Based on these projections, the hospital may expand some services, limit or close others, or outsource certain services to subcontractors. After evaluating the optional number of specialists in different service areas, the hospital may choose to close the staff to new applicants in certain departments and enter into exclusive contracts with a physician or physician group in others. In addition to internal strategic planning, the hospital may also seek to gain market share by entering into joint ventures with other hospitals, physician groups, and managed care organizations. These joint ventures may also result in realignment of services and medical staff positions within the hospital.[28]

Medical Staff Strategic Planning

Some hospitals are scrutinizing the medical staff composition against market demands to determine which clinical practice areas are understaffed. The hospital then crafts a development plan and targets recruitment in those areas. It may go further and close the staff except to applicants for which there is an identified need.

In general, courts have upheld the closing of select departments to new applicants if the hospital has documented legitimate reasons.[29] However, a hospital may not close a department in order to exclude a particular physician or to protect a group of physicians from competition. The medical staff should have ample input and involvement in the decision-making process, with appropriate safeguards to ensure that anticompetitive motives are not driving the medical staff's position.

A new and related issue involves the creation of specialized services within the hospital. Many hospitals are creating innovative and highly specialized units, similar to a "center of excellence" concept but on a smaller scale. With consultation from the medical staff, the hospital may design these specialized units with state-of-the-art equipment and capability. In most cases, physicians on the medical staff invest significant time and effort in helping the hospital establish these specialized units. Potential conflicts can arise in those situations where the hospital has an opportunity to further its own interests to the detriment of physicians on the medical staff, who devoted their time and expertise to the project. For instance, in one situation a hospital developed a special pediatric unit with the support and assistance of pediatricians on the medical staff. The hospital then advertised the pediatric unit and, as part of that advertisement, the pediatricians employed by the hospital. Independent pediatricians on the medical staff benefit from the improved facility, but their work in helping the hospital create the specialized unit may also end up steering patients to competitors who are employed by the hospital. This can be particularly troublesome if the hospital later decides to limit privileges for the unit to physicians with specialized training, as established by the hospital, thus excluding physicians who contributed to the unit's design and implementation.[30]

Exclusive Contracting

Hospitals may contract with a physician or a group of physicians to provide certain services within the hospital on an exclusive basis. As managed care drives hospitals to move from open staff, fee-for-service systems to vertically integrated systems capable of accepting risk payment, exclusive contracts will likely become more prevalent. As long ago as 1989, a survey by the American Hospital Association Hospital Data Center and Division of Medical Affairs reported that over 73 percent of hospitals had entered into one or more exclusive contracts.[31] Although the survey indicated that exclusive contracting was not confined to hospital-based physicians, they were involved in the majority of exclusive contracts: pathology (59.5 percent), radiology (58.8 percent), emergency medicine (52.4 percent), and anesthesiology (35.2 percent).[32] Courts have tended to uphold exclusive contracting.[33] When the hospital enters into an exclusive contract, the privileges of the physicians who had been practicing in that area are terminated. In some cases, terminated physicians have filed suit, but they have been largely unsuccessful. Courts have tended to hold that the hospital can enter into exclusive contracts, which then restrict physicians who are otherwise qualified from practicing in the hospital.[34]

Integration/Joint Ventures

In response to managed care pressures, hospitals are entering into a variety of joint ventures and other transactions in order to strengthen their market share and to expand their outpatient focus. These strategies include vertical integration and joint ventures with physicians as well as horizontal integration and joint ventures with other hospitals.

Hospital administrators often urge their medical staffs to integrate with the hospital system in order to develop the infrastructure and negotiate leverage to succeed in managed care. The form of integration may be as limited as collaboration on managed care contracting (perhaps through a physician hospital organization) or as extensive as acquisition of physician practices to form large hospital-owned group practices. Hospitals are also investing in the formation of management services organizations, which provide administrative services to physician practices. For hospitals, these strategies are necessary for survival. In evolved managed care systems, hospital inpatient utilization easily goes from 450 days per thousand covered lives to less than 250, sometimes as low as 150. Some experts have estimated that more than 80 percent of the nation's hospitals will be forced to significantly downsize, merge or, in some cases, close within a matter of years.[35]

Hospital integration and joint venture activities will have a significant impact on the medical staff. The Indiana State Medical Association, with sponsorship from the AMA and other state medical societies, studied the effect of physician hospital organizations (PHOs) on the medical staff. The study concluded that, regardless of medical staff leadership involvement in the PHO, there will be significant long-term issues, including possible duplication of effort and conflict between the medical staff and the PHO. This is particularly true if the PHO begins to take on some of the medical staff's responsibilities in such areas as credentialing and quality assurance.[36] Although there is currently a fairly clear distinction between the medical staff and the physician component of the PHO (which may or may not be an organized physician organization),

this study anticipates that there may eventually be a formal merger of the medical staff and the physician component of the PHO, or at least a consolidation of overlapping functions.[37]

To illustrate the potential for conflict, consider a situation in which a hospital and select physicians on the medical staff form a PHO. The PHO is a separate legal entity contracting on behalf of the hospital and those physicians. The hospital and medical staff physicians participating in the PHO will have an incentive to attract as much of the available managed care business as they can (assuming that the PHO is able to negotiate profitable contracts). This creates an opportunity to use the hospital credentialing process to limit the privileges of physicians who do not participate in the PHO in order to steer more business to the PHO. Hospital credentialing however, is designed to ensure the competence of medical staff members and the quality of care in the hospital. It should not be used to further the interests of the PHO. Under these circumstances, excluded physicians may have more success in bringing antitrust and other legal claims than they have had in the past. For the medical staff, this further illustrates the need for medical staff bylaws, which clearly establish the medical staff's role and responsibilities and which ensure the proper functioning of the credentialing process.[38]

Managed Care Contracting

Managed care contracting relationships are creating conflicts for hospitals and medical staffs. Managed care organizations (MCOs) seek to contract selectively with hospitals and physicians to negotiate the best possible terms. This leads to situations in which the MCO may negotiate a contract with the hospital but fails to negotiate a contract with any physicians from certain specialties at that hospital, or vice versa. In addition, MCOs sometimes use leverage with the hospital to negotiate better terms in their physician contracts. If hospitals and medical staffs do not resolve these issues, they will adversely affect patient care, as well as the viability of the institution.

Hospital Access for MCO Plan Physicians

MCOs typically contract selectively with hospitals and physicians. As a result, situations arise in which the MCO contracts with physicians who do not have staff privileges at the MCO's contracted hospital. To address these situations, MCOs may attempt to negotiate with the hospital to include a provision in the hospital participation agreement that will allow the MCO's participating physicians to gain access to the hospital. If the hospital has a closed medical staff or has closed select departments, the MCO may negotiate a provision requiring the hospital to maintain an open medical staff. Alternatively, the MCO may negotiate a provision that requires the hospital to grant temporary privileges to the MCO's participating physicians.[39]

All physicians applying for staff membership, including the MCO's participating physicians, must be subject to the same medical staff membership criteria and credentialing process as are generally required. Any agreement must comply with the medical staff bylaws. If the hospital agrees to contract provisions that allow the MCO's participating physicians to obtain staff privileges even though they do not meet the criteria for membership that have been established by the medical staff and the hospital board, this will usurp the medical

staff's role in the credentialing process, which may adversely affect patient care.

Physician networks and groups may face similar dilemmas in their managed care contracting arrangements. Independent practice associations (IPAs) and physician organizations (POs) are contracting on behalf of a large number of physicians, often on a regional basis. In some managed care contracts there will be IPA/PO physicians who do not have staff privileges at the MCO's participating hospitals. The IPA/PO should negotiate with the MCO to provide that physicians will refer patients to participating hospitals, if feasible. This avoids forcing physicians to obtain staff privileges at another hospital, which can be particularly important when the IPA/PO includes physicians in rural areas. This example underlines the importance of medical staffs giving particular consideration to the use of institutional (or "loyalty") criteria for medical staff membership. Hospitals want to impose these criteria to encourage physicians to concentrate their practice at that hospital's facilities. Yet, depending on market conditions, physicians are often wise to maintain privileges and a significant practice at more than one hospital.[40]

Hospital-Based Physicians

In some cases, the MCO will present the hospital-based physicians with a standard "take it or leave it" contract. If they reject the contract, the MCO may then pressure hospital administration to induce the physicians to sign. One particularly aggressive MCO has even reduced payments if less than a specified percentage of hospital-based physicians agree to participate in the MCO's panel.[41] In another situation, the MCO threatened to terminate its agreement

with the three hospitals at which an anesthesiologist group provided services unless
the group signed the MCO's participation
contracts without modification. The group
signed the participation contracts but then
filed suit alleging that the MCO violated
antitrust laws by reducing competition and
quality of care. The court dismissed the lawsuit.[42]

Even if the physician's contract with the
hospital does not require it to contract with
an MCO, other physicians on the medical
staff may exert pressure on the physicians.
For example, surgeons have pressured anesthesiologists by moving their surgical cases
to hospitals where the anesthesiologists participate in the same managed care plans.
Other physicians on staff may engage in
similar conduct. Physicians evaluating managed care agreements should consider their
goals, options, leverage, and political factors.
Is the contract one they want? Does the
physicians' contract with the hospital require them to contract with the MCO? Is
the MCO an important one to the hospital,
requiring that physicians reach an agreement quickly?

The hospital's occupancy rate will also
influence how aggressive it is in contracting.
Similarly, the number of other hospital contracting options in the market for the MCO
will affect negotiations. If the hospital is
particularly strong in the service area, it may
have greater leverage with the MCO in negotiations because the MCO needs it.[43]

Conclusion

The market and the government are insist-
ing that health care providers contain medical costs without sacrificing quality. Under
managed care, the efforts to control costs
are directed heavily toward hospital services.

These pressures are causing hospitals to
react aggressively, in part by exercising
greater control over the medical staff. This
may involve economic credentialing, exclusive contracting, managed care contracting,
and other strategies. Yet, the tactic of hospital control will not succeed. Physician leaders on the medical staff must understand
their role and work to ensure that it is
clearly established within the hospital.

1. Scott Becker, *Health Care Law: A Practical
    Guide,* 2d ed. (New York: Matthew Bender,
    1998). *See also* Donald H. Caldwell, Jr, *U.S.
    Health Law and Policy 1999: A Guide to the
    Current Literature* (Chicago: American
    Hospital Publishing, 1998), chap. 11. *See gen-
    erally,* Marcia J. Pollard & Grace J. Wigal,
    *Hospital Staff Privileges: What Every Health
    Care Practitioner and Lawyer Needs to Know*
    (Chicago: Hospital Administration Press,
    1996); Stephen M. Shortell, *Effective
    Hospital-Physician Relationships* (Ann Arbor,
    Mich: Health Administration Press, 1991).

2. Becker, *supra* note 1, at § 15.02[3]. *See also*
    Tom Curtis, "The Medical Staff," in Michael
    G. MacDonald et al, eds, *Treatise on Health
    Care Law* § 6.01 (New York: Matthew
    Bender 1995); Fay A. Rozovsky, et al,
    Medical Staff Credentialing: A Practical Guide
    (Chicago: American Hospital Publishing,
    1994; Horty, "The Legal Status of the
    Hospital Medical Staff," 22 St. Louis
    University Law Journal 485 (1978).

3. Joint Commission on the Accreditation of
    Healthcare Organizations, *1997 Hospital
    Accreditation Standards* MS.5 (1996).

4. 15 USC § 1 (1997); *Patrick v Burget,* 486 US
    94 (1988); *Arizona v Maricopa County
    Medical Society,* 457 US 332 (1982).

5. *Hyman v Galveston,* 273 US 414 (1927).

6. *Meyer v Nebraska,* 262 US 390 (1923).

7. *Shapiro v Thompson,* 394 US 618 (1969).

8. *Woodbury v McKinnon,* 447 F2d 839 (5th Cir
    1971).

9. *Perry v Sindermann,* 408 US 593 (1972);
    Board of Regents v Roth, 408 US 546 (1972).

10. *See Shahawy v Harrison,* 875 F2d 1529 (11th Cir 1989); *Hannon v Turnage,* 842 F2d 653 (7th Cir 1990) (noting that continued employment assurances may result in property interest); *Ezekwo v NYC Health & Hospitals Corp,* 940 F2d 775 (2d Cir 1991) (holding property interest in becoming chief resident of department and requiring due process prior to denial). *But see Lowe v Scott,* 959 F2d 323 (1st Cir 1992) (holding no property interest in staff privileges at private hospital); *Sosa v Board of Managers of Val Verde Mem Hosp,* 437 F2d 173 (5th Cir 1971).

11. 871 F2d 644, 647 (7th Cir 1989).

12. *See generally, Modaber v Culpeper Mem Hosp,* 674 F2d 1023 (4th Cir 1982); *Simkins v Moses H. Cone Mem Hosp,* 323 F2d 959 (4th Cir 1963); *O'Neill v Grayson County War Mem Hosp,* 472 F2d 1140 (6th Cir 1973); *Applebaum v Bd of Directors of Barton Mem Hosp,* 163 Cal Rptr 831 (Ct App 1980); *Crowder v Conlan,* 740 F2d 447 (6th Cir 1984); *Aschermann v San Francisco Med Society,* 114 Cal Rptr 681 (1974).

13. *Garrow v Elizabeth Gen Hosp & Dispensary,* 382 A2d 393 (NJ Super Ct 1977), *modified,* 401 A2d 533 (NJ 1979); *Christhilf v Annapolis Emergency Hosp Ass'n,* 496 F2d 174 (4th Cir 1974).

14. *See Sosa v Board of Managers, supra* note 10.

15. 373 P2d 477 (Ariz 1977). *See also Courtney v Shore Mem Hosp,* 584 A2d 817 (NJ Super Ct 1990).

16. 404 SE2d 750 (W Va 1991).

17. 33 F3d 1318 (11th Cir 1994), *cert denied,* 115 S Ct 1363, 131 L Ed2d 220 (1995).

18. *Huffaker v Bailey,* 273 Or 273, 540 P2d 1398 (1975) at 1401–1402.

19. *Laje v R. E. Thomason Gen Hosp,* 564 F2d 1159 (5th Cir 1977), *reh'g denied,* 568 F2d 1367 (5th Cir 1978), *cert denied,* 437 US 905, *on remand,* 665 F2d 724, *reh'g denied,* 670 F2d 181 (5th Cir 1982). *See contra, McElhinney v Wm Booth Mem Hosp,* 544 SW2d 216 (Ky 1976); *Miller v Eisenhower Med Cent'r,* 166 Cal Rptr 826, 27 Cal3d 614, 614 P2d 258 (1980).

20. 231 A2d 389 (NJ Super 1967).

21. *Patrick v Burget,* 800 F2d 1498 (9th Cir 1986) *rev'd and remanded,* 486 US 94, *reh'g denied,* 487 US 1243 (1988).

22. Department of Health and Human Services, *National Practitioner Data Bank Guidebook,* at E-14 (1996). A copy of this approximately 200-page guidebook may be obtained from the Health Resources and Service Administration, Bureau of Health Professions, Division of Quality Assurance, Parklawn Building, Room 8-A-55, 5600 Fishers Lane, Rockville, MD 20857.

23. 42 USC §§ 11131 and 11134.

24. 42 USC § 11151.

25. Aspen Health Law Center, *Medical Group Practice: Legal and Administrative Guide* § 4:9 (Gaithersburg, Md: Aspen Publishers, 1998).

26. 42 USC §§ 11131-11133.

27. 45 CFR § 60.13.

28. Sandra Dillard van der Vaart, "Managed Care and Medical Staff Issues," 18. Washington, DC: American Health Lawyers Association [Report No MC97-0034], 1997.

29. *See Desai v St Barnabas Medical Center,* 103 NJ 79, 510 A2d 662 (1985); *Guerrero v Burlington County Memorial Hospital,* 70 NJ 344, 360 A2d 334 (1976).

30. van der Vaart, *supra* note 28, at 19.

31. American Hospital Association, Division of Medical Affairs, Medical Staff Survey Report (May 1991).

32. *Id.*

33. van der Vaart, *supra* note 28, at 20.

34. *Healow v Anesthesia Partners, Inc,* 92 F3d 1192 (9th Cir 1996); *Coffey v Healthtrust, Inc,* 955 F2d 1388 (10th Cir 1992); *Morgan, Strand, Wheeler and Biggs v Radiology, Ltd,* 924 F2d 1484 (9th Cir 1991); *Sandcrest Outpatient Services v Cumberland County Hospital System, Inc,* 853 F2d 1139 (4th Cir 1988); *Collins v Associated Pathologists, Ltd,* 844 F2d 473 (7th Cir), *cert denied,* 102 LEd 2d 110 (1988); *White v Rockingham Radiologists, Ltd,* 820 F2d 98 (4th Cir 1987); *Bloom v Hennepin County,* 783 F Supp 418 (D Minn 1992); *Castelli v Meadville Medical Center,* 702 F Supp 1201 (WD Pa 1988).

35. van der Vaart, *supra* note 28, at 23.

36. Indiana State Medical Association, *Case Study Analysis of Physician Hospital Organizations* (1994).

37. van der Vaart, *supra* note 28, at 23.

38. *Id.*

39. *Id* at 24.

40. *Id* at 25.

41. *Id* at 27.

42. *Ambroze v Aetna Health Plans of New York, Inc,* 95 Civ 6631 (SDNY 1996), *appeal docketed,* No 96-7778 (2d Cir Sept 13, 1996).

43. American Society of Anesthesiologists, *Managed Care Contracting: Considerations for Anesthesiologists,* 9–14 (1996).

Chapter 9

A primer on employment discrimination law:

What you don't know *can* hurt you

Most physicians would prefer to practice their healing art without having to worry about the hassles of running a business. Practically speaking, however, rare is the physician who needs no staff—nurses, receptionists, office administrators, billing clerks, or custodians—to practice medicine. Once she hires such persons, like it or not, a physician necessarily dons another hat—that of employer, a role that brings with it an entirely new set of rights and responsibilities imposed by numerous levels of government. While the day-to-day management of a practice can to some extent be delegated to office administrators and support staff, the physician-owners of a practice nevertheless bear the final responsibility. At the end of the day, they bear the headaches of pending litigation, they endure the wrath of disgruntled employees or ex-employees, and they write the checks to pay legal fees, settlements, or adverse verdicts. Thus, no matter how far removed a physician is from the day-to-day management of staff, he cannot afford to be ignorant of the requirements imposed on employers by federal and state employment laws.

With the proliferation of statutes regulating the workplace and the dramatic increase in litigation in American society, employment discrimination claims have become an increasing burden on employers, with physicians being no exception. New federal statutes (and modifications to existing ones) enacted in the last decade have expanded the types of potential liability and expanded the types of monetary damages for which an employer may ultimately be held liable. As a result, employment-related claims look even more attractive to a plaintiff's attorney and to disgruntled employees and ex-employees. They cost little to file and have a greater likelihood of recovery than they did in the recent past. Thus, in addition to protecting against instances of discrimination that do occur, employment-related lawsuits have increasingly become a vehicle for terminated workers to exact a measure of revenge from their former employers.

Given the current economic climate in the health care industry, employment-related claims will undoubtedly increase. The President's Advisory Committee on Consumer Protection and Quality in the Health Care Industry had this somewhat grim outlook on the hospital labor market in March 1998:

While employment in all sectors of the health care industry is expected to grow substantially over the next decade, the outlook for a large number of hospitals is unclear because of the substantial number of excess beds that exist in many markets. . . . A 1997 survey of hospital human resource managers by Deloitte and Touche found that 21 percent intended to eliminate positions in 1997, as compared to 28 percent in 1996 and 36 percent in 1995. . . .

Data from the Bureau of Labor Statistics suggest that hospital restructuring already has had a significant labor market impact, with 163,000 hospital workers losing their jobs between January 1993 and December 1995. While 74 percent of these workers were reemployed by February 1996, their median weekly earnings were 12 percent lower. Seventeen percent of the laid-off hospital workers remained unemployed and 10 percent had dropped out of the labor force. . . . While it may be possible for displaced hospital workers to move into jobs in expanding sectors of the industry, those jobs often require different skills than hospital workers currently possess. . . .[1]

Unfortunately, as many physicians have learned from experience, any nonconsensual termination of an employee—no matter how justified—can be fodder for a lawsuit. Disgruntled ex-employees without legiti-

mate claims may for a variety of reasons initiate costly litigation, alleging sexual harassment, racial discrimination, or other supervisory mistreatment heretofore unknown to the physicians running the practice. Less frequently, current employees may also allege claims of unlawful workplace treatment or conditions.

But employment-related claims are not only increasing in frequency, they are also becoming more costly to employers. In fact, between 1990 and 1995, the average monetary award in sexual harassment claims more than tripled, from $16,480 to $53,030.[2] This figure does not even include costs incurred *regardless* of the outcome, such as defense attorney's fees and any lost revenue associated with the defendant's or its representatives' missed time from work during the litigation process. For a physician, the latter cost alone can be extremely significant.

As a result, when wearing their "employer" hats, physicians have to be careful about when, how, and under what circumstances employees are hired, terminated, and disciplined in the workplace. Thus, it is important for physician-employers to know what the pertinent employment discrimination statutes say, when they apply, and how the investigation of a claim of discrimination will proceed from initial reporting through discovery, settlement negotiations, and, if it gets that far, trial.

The following overview of the federal employment discrimination statutes is designed to help the busy clinician know his rights and responsibilities under the various laws, understand how employment discrimination claims will be handled or litigated once they are filed, and, most important, learn practical ways to prevent claims or claim-engendering events from ever happening. While this chapter is no substitute for consultation with an experienced attorney in specific situations, it should serve as a useful starting place for any discussion of prevention, litigation, and resolution of employment discrimination claims in the health care workplace.

Federal Civil Liability for Race or Gender Discrimination

Claims for unlawful discrimination on the basis of race or gender are governed by both federal and state laws (state laws are addressed briefly later in this chapter). The primary authority under which race and gender discrimination claims are brought is a federal statute, Title VII of the Civil Rights Act of 1964[3] (known colloquially as Title VII), which makes it an unlawful employment practice for an employer:

to fail or refuse to hire or to discharge any individual, or otherwise to discriminate against any individual with respect to his compensation, terms, conditions, or privileges of employment, *because of such individual's race, color, religion, sex, or national origin.* (Emphasis added.)

The Equal Pay Act of 1963 (EPA), which prohibits gender discrimination in payment of salary or wages to women and men performing substantially equal work for the same employer, is another, less frequently invoked statute governing women's rights in the workplace.

It should be noted from the outset that Title VII is worded broadly enough to protect both genders and all races, religions, or nationalities, regardless of majority or minority status in a particular workplace or the community at large. If the employee or applicant can show that a prohibited characteristic was even a factor in the challenged

employment decision, he may be able to recover damages from the employer.

The language of Title VII expressly prohibits discharge or discriminatory treatment on the overt basis of race, gender, or the other listed characteristics. In addition, the law recognizes claims alleging that a job requirement, promotional criterion, or benefit prerequisite that appears race and gender-neutral on its face, in fact, has a "disparate impact" on a particular gender or racial group. The statute has also been held to prohibit workplace harassment or the maintenance of a "hostile work environment."

The evidence an employee is required to show varies with the type of claim. Familiarity with each type of claim can help an employer prevent them, deal with situations that could result in claims as they occur, and be prepared to participate in an Equal Employment Opportunity Commission (EEOC) administrative investigation or lawsuit if a claim is ultimately filed. Also, since Title VII is the paradigmatic employment discrimination statute, many of the principles applicable to claims brought under it are also applicable to claims for other types of discrimination.

Intentional Discrimination Cases

Allegations of intentional discrimination are conceptually the most straightforward because the employee typically claims that she was not hired, was fired, was denied a promotion, was disciplined, or was denied some other benefit of employment on the basis of one of the prohibited classifications. In some cases, the employee may be able to demonstrate overt evidence of racial or gender bias, such as direct statements of the motivation for a particular decision (for example, "We only hire male doctors") or more general racially or sexually derogatory remarks made by the decision maker. Of course, it is fairly easy for a disgruntled employee to make up this type of allegation, and such cases often boil down to a swearing contest between the employee and the decision maker or supervisor. Cases in which such allegations can be substantiated can be tough to win, however, and many settle out of court to avoid increased litigation costs as well as collateral damage to the practice's reputation.

More often, however, the employee has very little direct evidence and must rely instead on statistical or comparative evidence to prove that she was treated differently from other employees or applicants solely because of race or gender. This type of case is commonly referred to as one of disparate treatment. For example, a male applicant for a nurse position may attempt to allege that he was rejected for an open position because he is a man. If he cannot point to any particular statements by the hiring physician or office manager that only females would be considered for nursing positions, he may try to establish that the employer has such a policy by arguing that the employer has hired very few male nurses, or none at all, despite having had qualified applicants. To prove such a claim, the applicant will seek—and in most cases will be entitled—to delve into the employer's application and hiring procedures and records. This can be a time-consuming and expensive process, even if the claim is ultimately found meritless.

Before allowing an employee to argue a claim of non-overt discrimination before a jury, however, a court will require the employee to establish what is known as a prima facie case of discrimination, that is, enough evidence to establish circumstances giving rise to an inference of wrongful discrimina-

tion. The idea is to require the employee to come forward with enough evidence to permit a jury to conclude that illegal discrimination is afoot, that is, more than "mere speculation" or "conjecture."[4] The establishment of a prima facie case does not mean that an employee automatically prevails, only that the case can go forward. Often, claims are dismissed administratively or by a court when the employee is unable to establish one of the basic elements of a case, such as qualification for the job or satisfactory performance.[5]

The elements of the prima facie case differ slightly based on the type of underlying claim. Basically, the employee or applicant will have to demonstrate membership in a class protected in the statute; qualification for the job or promotion applied for (or satisfactory job performance in the current position); an adverse employment action (such as termination, demotion, or failure to hire or promote); and that the position or promotion remained open to, or was filled by, a similarly qualified applicant or employee outside the protected class. In the context of employee discipline, the elements are slightly different. To establish a prima facie case of disparate treatment, a plaintiff must generally show that similarly situated employees outside the protected class engaged in acts of comparable seriousness but were treated less severely.[6]

An employee does not necessarily have to be fired by the employer to have a claim for wrongful discharge in violation of Title VII or any other employment statute. Rather, a plaintiff may allege "constructive discharge," meaning that the employer altered the working conditions for the worse or purposefully allowed them to become so intolerable that the employee was forced to resign. A plaintiff alleging constructive discharge must prove both that the employer's action (or inaction) was deliberate and that the working conditions were intolerable.[7] Working conditions are generally considered intolerable if a "reasonable person" in the plaintiff's position would have felt compelled to resign.

Once the plaintiff establishes a prima facie case of discriminatory treatment, a presumption of discrimination arises. The burden then shifts to the employer to articulate a "legitimate, nondiscriminatory" reason for the challenged employment action.[8] Typical legitimate reasons offered by employers include economic concerns, reduction in workload, another applicant's higher qualifications or greater experience, or the plaintiff's poor performance, attitude, or disciplinary record.

If the employer can establish a legitimate reason for the challenged action, the presumption of illegal discrimination "drops out of the picture," and the employee bears the ultimate burden of proving both that the employer's asserted reason was disingenuous and that bias against the plaintiff's protected characteristic was the true reason for the adverse employment action. The ultimate burden of persuading the judge or jury that the defendant intentionally discriminated against the plaintiff remains at all times with the plaintiff.[9]

Disparate-Impact Cases

In a second type of claim, less common than the straightforward intentional discrimination claim, a rejected applicant alleges that a neutral hiring or promotional criterion is illegal because it has a "disparate impact" on members of the applicant's protected class. Typical examples from case law include height and weight minimums for prison

guards (argued to have a disparate impact on women) and standardized tests (argued to have a disparate impact on some racial minorities). Employers remain free to impose job-related testing and competency requirements on their employees. Such criteria are more likely to survive a legal challenge, though, if the employer can show that they are necessary to perform the essential functions of the job and if administered as but one factor in a broad application and evaluation process. The plaintiff trying to establish such a case faces a difficult hurdle. As a result, these cases are not very common, especially in health care, where particularized skills and training are often required.

Harassment

The Title VII cases that are often the most troubling to employers are cases of sexual or racial harassment. According to the EEOC, the federal agency that initially receives and investigates all charges of employment discrimination, "the number of sexual harassment claims . . . filed with the EEOC more than doubled during the first half of the 1990s."[10] Such claims permit employees to sue for general workplace conditions not necessarily related to the denial of a promotion, a termination, or any other explicit management decision. Since supervisory employees are almost inevitably involved in hiring, termination, and promotion decisions, they have a more obvious connection to the challenged events when an intentional discrimination suit is filed. In contrast, allegations of sexual or racial harassment by an employee's coworkers, and even subordinates, can subject the company to liability under certain circumstances.

There are two general types of sexual harassment claims for which an employer may be held liable under Title VII. The first is known as "quid pro quo" harassment, in which an employee alleges that a supervisor made (or threatened to make) the employee's continued employment, promotions, or other working conditions contingent upon engaging in sexual activity with the supervisor. Such claims may involve overt propositions, for example, "The promotion is yours if you sleep with me." More typically, plaintiff alleges that subtle comments or conduct left an employee with the impression that sexual favors can be traded for advancement or benefits. It is generally agreed that this type of sexual harassment—making job advancement or benefits explicitly or implicitly contingent on sexual conduct—was an intended target when Title VII was passed.

A large percentage of Title VII litigation involves the second type of claim, one alleging that the employee's terms or conditions of employment were altered because she was subjected to a "hostile work environment." To establish a sexual harassment claim based on a hostile work environment, the employee must show that she was subjected to unwelcome comments or conduct based on her sex. The comments or conduct must have been "sufficiently severe or pervasive to alter the plaintiff's conditions of employment and to create an abusive work environment." She must also show some factual basis for holding the employer liable.[11]

Each of these elements of a sexual harassment claim based on a hostile work environment has been subjected to thorough dissection and analysis by the courts. The judge or jury must find that the comments or conduct would have been unwelcome to a "reasonable person" or a "reasonable woman." In other words, conduct that would only be offensive to an idiosyncratic person of especially heightened sensitivity does not ordinar-

ily give rise to liability. Obviously, the greater the degree to which the plaintiff participated in, invited, or acquiesced to the conduct in question, the harder time he will have proving that the conduct was unwelcome. As a result, the offending employee and/or employer will often contest the case on this particular element.

Typical fact patterns supporting liability on this type of claim include undesired sexual advances and requests for sexual favors (even if unconnected to any threats of adverse employment consequences), unconsented sexual touching or other physical contact, the posting of lewd or offensive materials in the workplace, and improper inquiries into an employee's personal or sex life. The US Supreme Court recently ruled that same-sex harassment (in that case, males who taunted and propositioned a male coworker) is prohibited by the statute as well.[12]

It should also be noted that an employee may raise a claim of hostile-work-environment workplace harassment based on his or her race, religion, or national origin as well. Such claims may arise, for instance, when a minority employee is subjected to racial epithets, racist materials or displays, or offensive jokes.

Courts often rely on the requirement that the conduct be "sufficiently severe or pervasive" to distinguish between typical jocular workplace banter and conduct that crosses the line into harassment. To judge whether a work environment is hostile or abusive, the courts look at "the totality of the circumstances," including "the frequency of the discriminatory conduct; its severity; whether it is physically threatening or humiliating, or a mere offensive utterance; and whether it unreasonably interferes with an employee's work performance."[13]

Nevertheless, the line between mere offensive conduct and harassment is by no means clearly established. In any event, the parties involved tend to present widely divergent accounts of the relevant facts. Especially troubling is the fact that both kinds of sexual harassment claims can arise from consensual relationships among employees or, more typically, from relationships that began as consensual but deteriorated along the way.

Unless a practice or health care provider has a well-enforced rule prohibiting consensual relationships altogether (which the astute reader may by now be thinking is a good idea), it is very difficult to guard against this type of claim being alleged at some point. However, to avoid liability for this type of claim, an employer should have policies in place aimed at preventing potentially actionable conduct, a means for addressing legitimate grievances once they arise, and adequate disciplinary measures if a claim is shown to have arguable merit. Later in this chapter there are some helpful hints for avoiding these types of claims and, at a minimum, reducing or eliminating employer liability once they arise.

Religious Discrimination

Discrimination on the basis of religion also falls within the purview of Title VII. It is governed by many of the same general principles, including the requirements that the employee establish qualification for the job and otherwise satisfactory job performance. However, the statute covers "all aspects of religious observance and practice, as well as belief, unless an employer demonstrates that he is unable to reasonably accommodate to an employee's . . . religious observance or practice without undue hardship on the con-

duct of the employer's business."[14] As a practical matter, this means that in addition to claims for disparate treatment or harassment based on religion (for example, disciplining an evangelical Christian for "witnessing" to patients or other employees, while allowing other employees to proselytize their secular causes or hobbies), an employee may also make a claim for an employer's failure to make reasonable accommodation for his or her religious beliefs.[15] For example, an employee may file such a claim following denial of time off for a religious holiday or challenging an employer's policy or requests of this kind generally.

To establish a prima facie religious accommodation claim, a plaintiff must establish that he or she has a bona fide religious belief that conflicts with an employment requirement, has informed the employer of this belief (or, in some states, that the employer had reasonable notice of the beliefs and the potential conflict), and was disciplined or terminated for failure to comply with the conflicting employment requirement.[16] The employer must then establish that it could not provide the requested accommodation, or any reasonable accommodation, without imposing an undue hardship on the company or other workers.

The statute does not define "undue hardship"; thus the precise reach of the employer's obligation to its employee must be determined case by case. However, the concept embraces more than mere financial hardship and must be "real" rather than speculative or hypothetical. Moreover, the Supreme Court has held that compliance with Title VII does not require an employer to give an employee a choice among several accommodations, nor is the employer required to demonstrate that alternative accommodations proposed by the employee constitute undue hardship. Rather, the employer must show merely that some reasonable accommodation was offered the employee, regardless of whether that accommodation is the one requested by the employee.[17]

Age Discrimination

Claims of age discrimination are governed by the federal Age Discrimination in Employment Act (ADEA)[18] enacted in 1988, which makes it unlawful for an employer to "refuse to hire, to discharge, or otherwise to discriminate against any individual with respect to his compensation, terms, conditions, or privileges of employment, because of such individual's age." The statute affords this protection only to workers over forty years of age, however, as its purpose is to combat bias and stereotypes that an employee's productivity and competence decline with age. Employers remain free to consider factors such as performance and competency, but they may not rely solely on age as a measurement of those factors during hiring, firing, or other employment actions.

Most often, the plaintiff presents a straightforward claim that he was treated differently—for example, discharged or denied a promotion—because of his age. The law is somewhat unclear as to whether or not a claim for age-based harassment or a hostile work environment may be brought under the ADEA.[19] Furthermore, the Supreme Court has not determined whether an age discrimination plaintiff can use a disparate-impact theory, arguing that a facially neutral criterion has a disproportionate impact on older workers.[20]

As in race and gender discrimination claims under Title VII, a plaintiff-employee

advancing a disparate-treatment claim under the ADEA may rely on either direct evidence of age bias in the employer's decision making (for example, comments like, "That Simpson is too old to cut the mustard any more," made by a decision maker or supervisor near the time of the challenged action) or circumstantial evidence raising an inference of bias.[21] Once again, in the latter type of case, courts require the employee to establish a prima facie case of age discrimination. Under this statute, they are required to show (1) that the employee was over forty years old and thus protected by the ADEA; (2) that he was discharged, demoted, or suffered some other adverse employment action; (3) that at the time of the adverse action, he was performing his job at a level that met his employer's legitimate expectations; and (4) that the adverse action "occurred under circumstances that raise a reasonable inference of unlawful age discrimination."[22] Although the employee's replacement need not be a person under forty for the claim to pass muster, evidence that the replacement was substantially younger than the fired or demoted employee-plaintiff often implies that age discrimination is afoot.

When a protected older employee is terminated as part of an overall reduction in the employer's workforce, a slightly different set of standards applies. In a so-called reduction-in-force case, the salient question "is not why members of the group were discharged or whether they were meeting performance expectations, but whether the particular employees were selected for inclusion on the list for discharge because of their age."[23] The fact "that employees substantially younger than the plaintiff, whose performance was inferior to the plaintiff's, were not subject to the same adverse action as the plaintiff" will be considered relevant but not conclusive. In one reduction-in-force case, a hospital was held liable for $100,000 in damages for termination of a fifty-three-year-old director of admissions as part of a larger elimination of sixty-one full-time positions. However, in that case, the decision makers had explicitly expressed an intention to lay off "older employees" or "those old people." Also, some employees were asked to come back after the layoffs, the plaintiff was not rehired for a clinical nurse position, and the hospital had subsequently hired more persons than were initially laid off.[24]

As in other employment discrimination claims, once the plaintiff has come forward with this initial showing, the burden shifts to the employer to provide a legitimate, nondiscriminatory reason for taking the challenged action (while the overall burden remains on the employee to prove that age was a motivating factor). However, employers are allowed to impose some age-related restrictions on employment or on certain positions or duties, so long as the age requirement can be considered a "bona fide occupational qualification reasonably necessary to the normal operation of the business."[25] These kinds of restrictions are most often upheld in occupations requiring physical strength and agility or those that have an impact on the safety of the general public (such as police work).

The ADEA also expressly permits an employer to take otherwise prohibited actions where necessary either "to observe the terms of a bona fide seniority system that is not intended to evade the purposes of [the ADEA]" or to observe the terms of a neutral bona fide employee benefit plan.[26] Practically speaking, this portion of the statute makes an exception for different benefits or work assignments based on seniority and longevity, so long as these factors are not used as a subterfuge for age discrimination. Employers may continue, for example, to have minimum age limits for vesting of or distribution of pension benefits.

Finally, the ADEA does not prohibit compulsory retirement of an employee aged sixty-five or over who "for the two-year period immediately before retirement, is employed in a bona fide executive or a high policymaking position, if such employee is entitled to an immediate nonforfeitable annual retirement benefit from a pension, profit-sharing, savings, or deferred compensation plan . . . which equals, in the aggregate, at least $44,000."[27] This provision may come into play if a practice group wants to impose early retirement on a senior physician in the group.

Hospitals and large practices that find themselves considering a reduction in force must be careful in documenting how they selected candidates for termination. Likewise, a physician-employer should make certain to thoroughly research and document the necessity of any proposed age restriction on particular job classifications or on the performance of certain medical procedures. Such documentation is absolutely crucial to avoid any inference that an employer is trying to weed out older employees by some other means. As always, an attorney versed in employment law should be consulted for advice about any questionable or emotionally charged situations.

Discrimination against Persons with Disabilities

Persons with disabilities are protected primarily by two federal statutes. The first, Section 504 of the Rehabilitation Act of

1973, prohibits employment discrimination against federal government employees with disabilities and imposes similar obligations on some facilities that receive federal funds.[28] Workers in the private sector are governed by the much broader and more recently enacted Americans with Disabilities Act (ADA), passed by Congress in 1990. Although cases involving ADA claims draw from older Rehabilitation Act cases for guidance and have incorporated some of the same legal principles, the substantive provisions of the ADA are much broader and more intricate.

The ADA is especially important for physicians to understand not only because it covers discrimination against the disabled in employment matters but also because it requires health care facilities to provide equal access to treatment for the disabled and businesses to take measures to guarantee physical access to the disabled. Further, physicians should understand the ADA because even if their practice or hospital is never a named defendant in an ADA claim, they may nevertheless be called as expert witnesses regarding the disabled status (or lack thereof) of a patient attempting to establish an ADA claim against his or her employer.

Employment Discrimination under the ADA: Physicians as Employers

The ADA serves as the statutory basis for a wide variety of claims against employers. ADA cases employ many of the same general principles applicable in other types of employment discrimination cases (as previously discussed). Because of its nexus with medical determinations of who is disabled and a worker's ability to perform a job, however, the ADA has its own unique set of standards and definitions.

The ADA's basic substantive provision provides that [n]o covered entity shall discriminate against a qualified individual with a disability because of the disability of such individual in regard to job application procedures, the hiring, advancement, or discharge of employees, employee compensation, job training, and other terms, conditions, and privileges of employment.[29]

The ADA also prohibits discrimination against a nondisabled applicant or employee "because of that individual's family, business, social, or other relationship or association with an individual with a disability." A "covered entity" is defined as "an employer, employment agency, labor organization, or joint labor-management committee."[30] It should also be noted that any employment-related liability under the ADA belongs to the practice or group employing the plaintiff, not to a physician personally.[31]

Employment claims under the ADA generally fall into two broad, yet often overlapping categories, wrongful discharge and failure to provide "reasonable accommodation" to a person covered under the statute. Like the ADEA, the ADA is somewhat unclear as to whether an employee can bring an action for a hostile work environment based on harassment because of a disability, although there have been few, if any, successful such cases reported.[32] The disparate-impact approach to liability is available under the ADA, however. Employers have been held liable based on a facially neutral and objective hiring or benefit criterion found to have an unreasonably disproportionate effect on disabled persons.[33] A disparate impact claim in this context focuses on the business necessity and reasonableness of the objective criterion at issue. For example, rules requiring a pilot to have good vision or a truck driver to have a valid commercial driver's license may work more disadvantage to the disabled than to the able-bodied, but such rules are reasonably related to the essential functions of the job and therefore are permitted.

To prove wrongful discharge in violation of the ADA, a plaintiff must establish "(1) that he was disabled, (2) that he was otherwise qualified for his position, and (3) that he was fired solely on the basis of disability."[34] An accommodation claim similarly requires the employee to prove that he was a qualified person with a disability, that the employer knew about his disability, and, additionally, that the employer failed to make a "reasonable accommodation" for that disability. These two types of claims raise similar issues of determining the existence of a disability, its impact on the employee's ability to do the job, and the availability of reasonable accommodations for the disability, the primary difference being that one also involves a termination.

No matter the type of claim, an employee suing under the ADA must first establish that at the time of the alleged adverse employment decision he was "disabled" as defined in the statute. A physician—whether encountering the definition in her role as an employer or an expert witness—should note from the outset that the ADA definition of disability is different from that which physicians might ordinarily use as a medical determination of disability and from that used by the Social Security Administration in determining eligibility for disability insurance benefits. The term *disability* is defined in the ADA as:

(A) a physical or mental impairment that substantially limits one or more of the major life activities of [an] individual;
(B) a *record of* such an impairment; or

(C) *being regarded as having* such an impairment.[35] (Emphasis added.)

This expansive definition of an individual with a disability was adopted to "combat the effects of erroneous but nevertheless prevalent perceptions about the handicapped."[36]

The first area of inquiry is thus whether the employee has a physical or mental impairment that substantially limits a major life activity. The physical or mental impairment is usually established fairly easily, as it has been defined broadly to mean:

any physiological disorder or condition, cosmetic disfigurement, or anatomical loss affecting one or more of the following body systems: neurological; musculoskeletal; special sense organs; respiratory, including speech organs; cardiovascular; reproductive, digestive, genito-urinary; hemic and lymphatic; skin; and endocrine; or . . . any mental or psychological disorder, such as mental retardation, organic brain syndrome, emotional or mental illness, and specific learning disabilities.[37]

Relying on this broad definition, the US Supreme Court ruled in 1998 that infection with the HIV virus is, for purposes of the ADA, a physical impairment from the moment of infection and during every stage of the disease, even before it develops into AIDS.[38] However, the term *disability* does not include temporary medical conditions, even if those conditions require extended leaves of absence from work.[39] As one court has summarized:

The ADA simply was not designed to protect the public from all adverse effects of ill-health and misfortune. Rather, the ADA was designed to "assure[] that truly disabled, but genuinely capable, individuals will not face discrimination in employment because of stereotypes about the insurmountability of their handicaps." Extending the statutory protections available under the ADA to individuals with broken bones, sprained joints, sore muscles, infectious diseases, or other ailments that temporarily limit an individual's ability to work would trivialize this lofty objective.[40]

The statute and accompanying regulations list the following as major life activities: "caring for oneself, performing manual tasks, walking, seeing, hearing, speaking, breathing, learning, working . . . sitting, standing, lifting and reaching."[41] In the Supreme Court case referred to above, the court determined that reproduction also qualifies as a major life activity for purposes of the ADA. Therefore, plaintiffs whose ability to carry on reproductive activity is hindered by asymptomatic HIV are permitted to bring claims against employers and health care providers for discrimination based on their HIV-positive status.[42]

Finally, to determine whether an employee is disabled under the ADA, a court must evaluate not just whether an employee is restricted but whether he or she is "[s]ubstantially limited" in performing a major life activity "as compared to the condition, manner, or duration under which the average person in the general population can perform that same major life activity."[43] A court may also consider the "nature and severity of the impairment," its "duration or expected duration," and any "permanent or long term impact."[44] When the major life activity at issue is working, the "inability to perform a single, particular job does not constitute a substantial limitation." In this circumstance, the phrase "substantially limited" means "significantly restricted in the

ability to perform either a class of jobs or a broad range of jobs in various classes. . . ."[45] Due to this requirement, and also because an employee must demonstrate that she is "otherwise qualified" for the job in question, plaintiffs asserting ADA claims will typically try to argue that they are impaired in some major life activity besides working.

In some cases, even when an employee or applicant is determined not to actually have a physical impairment substantially limiting a major life activity, he may nevertheless fit the statutory definition because he has a record of such a condition or is regarded as having such a condition. Thus, employers are required by the statute to avoid discriminating not only against actually disabled persons but also against persons whom it regards as disabled or who may have been disabled in the past. The breadth of this definition provides plaintiffs an even wider path to reach federal court with allegations of job discrimination and suggests that employers must be especially careful in dealing with applicants or employees who make any reference to or exhibit any outward signs of physical or mental impairment.

If the plaintiff can establish that he is a person with a disability as defined in the ADA, he must next demonstrate that he is "otherwise qualified" for the position or promotion in question. Under the ADA, an individual is otherwise qualified if he or she "with or without reasonable accommodation, can perform the essential functions of the employment position that such individual holds or desires."[46] As the Supreme Court has stated, an individual is otherwise qualified only if "able to meet all of a program's requirements in spite of his handicap."[47] Several courts have included an employee's ability and willingness to show up for work as part of being otherwise qualified and have thus dismissed ADA claims made by plaintiffs with records of excessive absenteeism.[48]

Finally, the employee also has to prove a causal connection between the disability and the adverse employment action. In other words, if an otherwise qualified employee is fired, demoted, or disciplined for any reason other than his disability, there is no valid ADA claim. As a practical matter, this inquiry often overlaps with the employer's presentation of a "legitimate, nondiscriminatory" reason for the challenged action, which is the next step in the litigation of an ADA claim, as it is in a Title VII claim. Again, examples of legitimate reasons include poor job performance (unrelated to the disability), excessive absenteeism (for nonmedical reasons), lack of cooperation with coworkers, insubordination, or economic downturns (as long as disabled persons were not specifically targeted for termination).

In almost any ADA employment case, the plaintiff must establish that the employer failed to consider or to provide reasonable accommodation for the disability in question. The EEOC defines a reasonable accommodation as "any change or adjustment to a job or work environment that permits a qualified applicant or employee with a disability to participate in the job application process, to perform the essential functions of a job, or to enjoy benefits and privileges of employment equal to those enjoyed by employees without disabilities."[49] For example, according to the EEOC, reasonable accommodation may include: acquiring or modifying equipment or devices; job restructuring; part-time or modified work schedules; reassignment to a vacant position; adjusting or modifying examinations, training materials, or policies; providing readers and interpreters; and making the workplace readily accessible to and usable by people with disabilities.[50]

As in the context of religious accommodation claims, the employer is not required to provide an accommodation that would impose an undue hardship on the operation of the business. Undue hardship means that an accommodation would be unduly costly, extensive, substantial, or disruptive, or would fundamentally alter the nature or operation of the business. In evaluating whether an accommodation is an undue hardship, the EEOC or a court will evaluate such factors as the cost of the accommodation, the employer's size and financial resources, and the nature and structure of its operation.

Many of these issues that the courts consider as separate elements in an ADA case are, as a practical matter, inextricably intertwined. The important lessons for physicians as employers are (1) that any employment decision regarding a person with a real or perceived disability should be well documented; (2) that legitimate, nondiscriminatory reasons for any decision should be clearly communicated to the employee-applicant and documented in the application or personnel file; and (3) that the possibility of reasonable accommodation be actually considered and such consideration (and all related communications) be well documented in case a future claim is filed.

Medical Examinations and Inquiries

The ADA also prohibits an employer from requiring a medical examination or making inquiries of an employee as to whether he is an "individual with a disability or as to the nature or severity of the disability unless such examination or inquiry is shown to be job-related and consistent with business necessity."[51] What this means is that a physician as employer should not inquire about whether an applicant is disabled except to the extent necessary to determine his or her ability to perform the essential functions of the job, with or without reasonable accommodation.

To help determine whether a medical examination is permissible under this standard, the EEOC has promulgated various explanatory regulations. Specifically, agency regulations state that an employer is permitted "to make inquiries or require medical examinations (fitness-for-duty exams) when there is a need to determine whether an employee is still able to perform the essential functions of his or her job."[52] Section 9.4 of the *EEOC Technical Assistance Manual on the Employment Provisions of the ADA* states, "If a worker has an on-the-job injury which appears to affect his/her ability to do essential job functions, a medical examination or inquiry is job-related and consistent with business necessity." Therefore, generally speaking, courts will consider an employer's request for a fitness-for-duty exam after an on-the-job injury to be job related and a business necessity under the pertinent regulations.[53] Similarly, according to interpretive guidelines issued by the EEOC, screening for illegal drugs is not considered a medical exam under the ADA and thus is perfectly legitimate, even without a showing that it is job related.[54]

The ADA's provisions governing medical exams for applicants may affect a physician not only in the role of employer, however, but also in his or her role as a medical evaluator. Under the ADA, "the term 'employer' means a person engaged in an industry affecting commerce who has 15 or more employees for each working day in each of 20 or more calendar weeks in the current or preceding calendar year, and any agent of such person."[55] An independent physician may frequently be enlisted to perform a medical fitness-for-duty or return-to-work physical exam. An open question is whether the physician himself can be held liable for performing such an exam—as the employer's agent—if the exam turns out to have been illegal under the ADA and was relied on by the employer in its discrimination against the plaintiff. This novel theory of physician liability has been asserted—although it has not yet prevailed—in at least one case in North Carolina by an employee of a shipping company who injured her eye and was required by her employer to have an eye exam before returning to work as a package driver. The plaintiff in that case contended that the physician was an agent of the employer because the employer referred the plaintiff to him for a return-to-work physical and then relied on the physician's opinion in refusing to allow her to return to work.[56]

Fortunately, for now, there is no case law in support of such a claim, and the agent language in the definition of *employer* under the employment discrimination statutes has been interpreted as "an unremarkable expression . . . that discriminatory personnel actions taken by an employer's agent may create liability for the employer."[57] In fact, the majority of federal appellate courts have refused to hold any individual personally liable under the similar definitions of employer contained in Title VII, the ADEA, and the ADA.[58]

While physicians ought not to be too worried about engendering this type of claim, any arrangements, relationships, or practices that might raise suspicions of collusion with a requesting employer should be avoided. To be insulated from this type of claim, a physician should maintain both independence from the employer and objective medical judgment.

Liability for Equal Access to Public Accommodations

One other main aspect of the ADA is worth mentioning here, although it is not related to employment discrimination claims. The ADA also prohibits discrimination in services provided by public accommodations (including the professional offices of health care providers).[59] As a result, it has been used as the basis for claims against a physician or hospital for failure to provide medical treatment for persons with infectious diseases such as AIDS.[60] Although physicians' offices, like other public accommodations, are not permitted to discriminate in the access they provide to persons with disabilities, the statute does allow a doctor to refuse to provide treatment if the infectious condition "poses a direct threat to the health or safety of others." However, this direct-threat exception will only apply if there is "a significant risk to the health or safety of others that cannot be eliminated by a modification of policies, practices, or procedures or by the provision of auxiliary aids or services."[61]

A discrimination claim under this portion of the statute does not open a physician, clinic, or hospital to liability for monetary damages. Rather, at the present time, "the only type of enforcement that Congress has made available to a private plaintiff [as opposed to the relief available in a suit for enforcement brought by the attorney general]—is specifically limited to providing injunctive relief, ie, an order to cease and desist the illegally discriminatory practice."[62]

The Family and Medical Leave Act of 1993

The Family and Medical Leave Act of 1993 (FMLA) entitles "eligible employee[s]" to up to twelve weeks of unpaid leave during any twelve-month period for the birth or adoption of a child; to care for a spouse, child, or parent with a serious health condition; or because of an employee's own serious health condition that renders the employee unable to work.[63] The statute defines an "eligible employee" as an employee "who has been employed . . . for at least twelve months by the employer with respect to whom leave is requested" under the statute and "for at least 1,250 hours of service with such employer during the previous twelve-month period."[64] A "serious health condition" is any "illness, injury, impairment, or physical or mental condition that involves . . . inpatient care in a hospital, hospice, or residential medical care facility or continuing treatment by a health care provider."[65]

The employee may elect—or may be required by the employer—to use up paid sick leave or vacation time before taking the leave guaranteed by the FMLA. The employer is free to pay the employee for FMLA-mandated leave if desired but is under no obligation to do so. The statute also requires an employee to give thirty days' advance notice if the reason for which leave will be requested is foreseeable (such as the birth of a child or a prearranged surgical procedure).

The statute allows employees to bring individual suits for alleged violations of their FMLA rights. It also prohibits an employer from terminating, punishing, or otherwise penalizing an employee for asserting rights under the FMLA. In particular, EEOC regulations provide that "[E]mployers cannot use the taking of FMLA leave as a negative factor in employment actions, such as hiring, promotions or disciplinary actions. . . ."[66] Employers are also required to post or distribute written guidelines informing employees of their rights under the FMLA.

Retaliation Claims

In addition to prohibiting harassment or discrimination in the workplace on the basis of sex, race, religion, gender, age, or disability, federal employment discrimination statutes also prohibit employers from retaliating against employees who oppose unlawful practices or assert their rights under these statutes. Title VII's antiretaliation provision, which serves as the model for each of the others, specifically makes it unlawful:

. . . for an employer to discriminate against any of his employees or applicants for employment . . . to discriminate against any individual . . . because he has opposed any practice made an unlawful employment practice by this subchapter, or because he has made a charge, testified, assisted, or participated in any manner in an investigation, proceeding, or hearing under this subchapter.[67]

Similar language is found in the ADA, ADEA, and FMLA as well.[68]

To establish a prima facie case of retaliatory discharge (or other adverse employment action) in violation of one of these statutes, an employee must generally prove that the employee engaged in "protected activity"; the employer took adverse employment action against the employee; and some causal connection existed between the protected activity and the employer's adverse action.[69]

The employee will usually be able to point to some sort of adverse employment action, such as termination, denial of a promotion, or disciplinary action.[70] Therefore, the success of a claim ordinarily depends on whether the employee engaged in "protected activity" and, if so, whether there was a causal link between the protected activity and the adverse action.

The pertinent language of Title VII, which also applies in retaliation cases under other employment discrimination statutes, characterizes two broad categories of activities as protected for the purposes of a retaliation claim. An employer may not retaliate against an employee for participating in an ongoing investigation or proceeding under Title VII or for opposing discriminatory practices in the workplace.[71] The statute specifically defines participating as "(1) making a charge; (2) testifying; (3) assisting; or (4) participating in any manner in an investigation, proceeding, or hearing under Title VII."[72]

"Opposition activity" does not require the official filing of an EEOC charge and may include "utilizing informal grievance procedures as well as staging informal protests and voicing one's opinions in order to bring attention to an employer's discriminatory activities."[73] Activities such as "complaining to the employer" and "participating in an employer's informal grievance procedures," when done in a manner that is "not disruptive or disorderly," have been held to be opposition activities protected under Title VII.[74] As a practical matter, however, the less formal an employee's activity allegedly in opposition to discriminatory practices, the less likely that it will be deemed protected.[75]

Most important, to recover for retaliation, the plaintiff is not required to establish the validity of the underlying allegations of a Title VII or other statutory violation. Rather, the plaintiff must simply have a reasonable belief in the validity of the claim.[76] Therefore, employers have to be careful that they do not help create a claim where once there was none by taking adverse employment actions against an employee who has raised a question about illegal discrimination. Although the underlying claim may ultimately prove invalid, liability can arise just as swiftly from an allegation of retaliatory discharge or demotion.

To defend against a retaliation claim, an employer will often deny any causal relationship between the allegedly protected activity and the challenged employment decision *and* seek to establish legitimate, nonretaliatory grounds for the decision. Such grounds may include poor job performance or disciplinary records. An employer should be careful, however, to avoid discharge or demotion based on vague notations such as poor attitude, uncooperative, or not a team player. These reasons, when combined with the employer's knowledge of protected activity, may in the court's hindsight smack of retaliation in disguise.

Litigation of Federal Employment Discrimination Claims: What Can an Employer Expect?

Once an EEOC charge is filed, an attorney should assist a physician or practice group to determine exactly what law or laws govern plaintiff's claim, to make sure that all procedural requirements have been or will be met by the plaintiff, and to evaluate the employer's likelihood of success or potential financial exposure. This evaluation process will require the physician or her agent to be informed about what to expect in the investigation and litigation of an employment discrimination claim.

Jurisdictional Thresholds

First, all physician-employers should be aware that the federal employment discrimination statutes discussed in this chapter do not apply to all employers. Rather, each of them has what is called a *jurisdictional threshold*, meaning that the statute has no jurisdiction over employers with fewer than a certain number of employees. Practically speaking, this means that the smallest practices or clinics may not have to worry about compliance with federal employment discrimination law at all.

Specifically, Title VII applies to employers with fifteen or more employees. The ADA likewise applies to employers with fifteen or more employees but also requires that the employees counted have been on the payroll "for each working day in each of 20 or more calendar weeks in the current or preceding calendar year." The ADEA applies to employers with twenty or more employees, and the FMLA applies only to employers with over fifty employees "for each working day during each of 20 or more calendar workweeks in the current or preceding calendar year. . . ."[77]

The case law is somewhat unsettled as to whether and under what circumstances part-time employees are counted in determining whether a particular jurisdictional threshold has been met. Courts may also consider related corporations, partnerships, or other business entities in deciding who is the employer in a particular case. Thus, small physicians' groups that are part of larger provider networks may satisfy the jurisdictional threshold in question, depending on the level of control that the parent entity exercises on employment policies and decisions.

The EEOC Pre-Suit Investigation and Evaluation

Fortunately, although the myriad federal and state employment discrimination laws can be burdensome and confusing, many of the statutes have built-in measures to encourage speedy (that is, pre-lawsuit) resolution of meritorious cases, disposition of frivolous ones, and thoughtful negotiation of the harder ones. Each of these statutes requires a potential claimant to file a charge of discrimination with the local branch office of the EEOC or an equivalent state agency before filing a lawsuit. The "EEOC charge," as it is known, must be filed within 180 days of the alleged discriminatory activity and before filing an action in federal court.[78]

This administrative filing requirement serves two main purposes, to give the employer (aka "the charged party") notice of the claim and to give the EEOC an opportunity to investigate and possibly settle the grievance.[79] Upon receiving a charge of discrimination, the EEOC will notify the employer that a charge has been filed and will conduct its own investigation of the circumstances of the claim. This investigation may impose no burden on the employer, as in cases where the charge is procedurally deficient or invalid on its face or, in some cases, may result in a full-blown administrative investigation if the EEOC is concerned that serious violations have occurred. The employer is required to cooperate with the EEOC investigation, whatever its scope, and will be given an opportunity to provide the EEOC with any documentation or testimony in defense of the challenged actions.

It is wise at this point for a practice group or hospital to enlist an employment law attorney (if one is not already involved) to help navigate the investigation process and keep a bad situation from becoming any worse.

If the EEOC determines that there is reasonable cause to believe that illegal discrimination has occurred, it will then seek to conciliate the charge, that is, to reach a voluntary resolution between the charging party and the employer. If this effort is not successful, the EEOC may bring a suit in its own name in federal court. In such a case, EEOC attorneys will prosecute the case on behalf of the charging employee at government expense.

If the EEOC determines that there is no reasonable cause to believe that a violation has occurred (which has been the result in approximately 60 percent of all claims filed for the last three fiscal years, 1996 to 1998),[80] that it is unable to make a reasonable-cause determination, or that there is reasonable cause but it is unwilling or unable to bring the case itself, the EEOC will issue a notice of right to sue that permits the charging party to file an individual lawsuit. Upon receipt of such a right-to-sue letter, the employee-applicant will have only ninety days to file a federal complaint either on his own or with the assistance of a privately retained attorney. Complaints filed outside that ninety-day period will be barred from further litigation.

If a lawsuit is filed, whether by the EEOC or the individual employee, the EEOC's determination of reasonable cause—whether affirmative or negative—will have no impact on the decision of the court reviewing the case. The district court will consider all procedural defenses raised by the employer (now called the defendant), including those arising out of noncompliance with the administrative filing procedures. The court will also oversee and coordinate the parties' discovery efforts, rule on any pretrial motions regarding the employer's legal defenses, and, if necessary, conduct a trial of the case. For a general overview of the litigation process, see the discussion in chapter 5.

The EEOC charge strictly limits the timing of the acts that can be alleged as discriminatory in a subsequent lawsuit. If the last allegedly discriminatory act happened more than 180 days before the filing of the charge, any claim arising out of that act will be barred automatically. No employment actions or conditions before the 180-day period immediately preceding the filing of the charge may be considered by the EEOC (or ultimately by a court) unless they are shown to be related to some discriminatory act occurring within the past 180 days as a "series of separate but related acts amounting to a continuing violation."[81] In attempting to establish a continuing violation, however, the employee must often show that he or she "failed to perceive the alleged discriminatory animus causing the claimed injury prior to the statutory period" and did not realize that the actions were discriminatory or illegal until within the 180-day statutory period.[82] It will often be difficult for a plaintiff to show that certain conduct was so severe and pervasive that it altered the terms and conditions of employment and yet somehow was not perceived as illegal or discriminatory at the time.

The filing of the EEOC charge limits not only the timing of the events that can be considered by the EEOC or a reviewing court but also the scope of the employee's or applicant's claim. Only those discrimination claims actually stated in the initial charge, those reasonably related to the original com-plaint, and those developed by reasonable investigation of the original complaint may be maintained in a subsequent federal lawsuit.[83] For example, if an employee initially complains to the EEOC only about the denial of a particular promotion based on his race, he usually cannot in a later lawsuit raise a claim of hostile work environment never mentioned in the EEOC charge of discrimination.

These procedural and substantive safeguards do not work perfectly, as both frivolous and meritorious lawsuits still find their way into court. The process does serve to resolve or weed out a large number of claims that would otherwise tie parties up in court for a long time. Knowledge of how the administrative charging process works can help a physician or hospital know how to cooperate in the process to head off potentially burdensome litigation.

Remedies Available to the Employee

It is important for a physician to understand the remedies available under the federal employment discrimination statutes so that he or she can both understand the seriousness of the potential hazard from claims and know how to participate and negotiate once a claim has been filed. Various remedies—from reinstatement or transfer, to back pay, to compensatory and punitive damages—will be on the table when the EEOC or a plaintiff's attorney is trying to negotiate a settlement. Recent changes in the remedies available have contributed to the continued increase in claims filed, but they have also afforded parties more creativity in finding amicable routes to settlement.

Title VII and the ADA originally only allowed a successful plaintiff to obtain injunctive relief (that is, an order directing the employer to rehire, promote, or not to engage in any future discrimination against the plaintiff or other employees similarly situated) or to recover back pay (wages for time missed on the job or as a result of not being hired or given a certain promotion). However, with the passage of the Civil Rights Act of 1991, Congress opened the door for Title VII and ADA plaintiffs in certain circumstances to recover compensatory and punitive damages as well. These additional kinds of remedies are available only in cases in which intentional discrimination or a hostile work environment has been proved (not in disparate-impact cases). Further, in ADA cases alleging failure to provide reasonable accommodation, neither compensatory nor punitive damages are available "where the covered entity demonstrates good faith efforts, in consultation with the person with the disability who has informed the covered entity that accommodation is needed, to identify and make a reasonable accommodation . . ." for the employee's disability without imposing "an undue hardship on the operation of the business."[84]

Possible compensatory damages include future lost wages (also known as "front pay"), emotional pain and suffering, inconvenience, mental anguish, and loss of enjoyment of life. To recover these types of damages, a plaintiff must offer testimony regarding the particular damages incurred. Once a plaintiff claims emotional distress, however, he places his mental condition in controversy and opens the door to discovery regarding his psychiatric history. If the employee never saw a psychiatrist or other mental health professional for her alleged condition, her likelihood of obtaining damages is greatly diminished. As a result, such damages are often difficult to prove as a practical matter.

Punitive damages are available under Title VII and the ADA only "if the complaining party demonstrates that the respondent engaged in a discriminatory practice or discriminatory practices with malice or with reckless indifference to the federally protected rights of an aggrieved individual."[85]

Although it opened the door to these new types of damages, the Civil Rights Act of 1991 also placed caps on the total amount of compensatory and punitive damages that could be awarded to any complaining party in a Title VII or ADA case. Congress enacted a sliding scale of caps, increasing the possible award as the number of employees of a liable party increased. The lowest cap is $50,000, "in the case of a respondent who has more than 14 but fewer than 101 employees," and ranges up to $300,000 for an employer with more than 500 employees.[86] Note that this cap does not apply to awards of back pay.

The FMLA provides a somewhat different scheme of available remedies. If a violation of the FMLA is proved, the employee may not only request to be reinstated or promoted but is also entitled to recover damages equal to "the amount of any wages, salary, employment benefits, or other compensation denied or lost to such employee by reason of the violation." If the employee has no lost or denied compensation (for example, because her request for leave was denied), she may recover the amount of actual monetary losses sustained as a direct result of the violation, such as the cost of providing care for the sick relative, up to a sum equal to twelve weeks of wages or salary, plus interest. The sum recovered may also be doubled unless the employer can show that its violation was in good faith and that it "had reasonable grounds for believing that the act or omission was not a violation of the statute."[87] Note that compensatory damages for pain and suffering are not available. Instead, the employee will be awarded double damages unless the employer proves that its violation was a good-faith, reasonable mistake.

Finally, the ADEA does not provide its own remedial scheme for successful plaintiffs. Rather, it incorporates certain provisions of the more generally applicable Fair Labor Standards Act (FLSA).[88] Based on those provisions, an employee who proves an ADEA violation may recover any unpaid wages, and if the employer's discriminatory conduct is found to have been willful, the damages are doubled. Conduct will be considered willful if the employer either knew or showed reckless disregard for whether its conduct was prohibited by the ADEA.[89] Neither the FLSA nor the ADEA permits the recovery of compensatory or punitive damages, however, as the Civil Rights Act of 1991 did not address remedies available for age discrimination claims.

Under each statute, the complaining employee retains a legal obligation to mitigate damages, meaning that in a discharge claim, the claimant must attempt to find suitable alternative work. Any award of lost past or future wages will be reduced by the amount of wages and benefits the employee was otherwise able to obtain or should have been able to obtain with reasonably diligent effort.

All of these statutes permit the court to order the losing side to pay the prevailing party's costs of litigation, including reasonable attorney's fees, which can often be substantial. As a practical matter, attorney's fees are awarded primarily to successful plaintiffs. They may be awarded to a prevailing defendant only upon a showing that the complaint plaintiff filed was "particularly frivolous or wholly lacking in arguable merit."[90]

State Employment Discrimination Statutes

The foregoing discussion has focused on the federal antidiscrimination laws most applicable to physician-employers. Physicians should also be aware, however, that most states have their own set of antidiscrimination laws in some form or another.[91] Frequently, state laws will be similar to their federal counterparts, but they may have a lower jurisdictional threshold (that is, they will apply to smaller employers than the federal laws do) and may be broader in the scope of protection afforded or in the number and types of protected classes. Therefore, it is important for a physician practice group or hospital to have competent local counsel to walk them through any special provisions of a particular state's laws.

Other types of state law claims may also be asserted in conjunction with a Title VII or ADA claim. For example, a plaintiff may allege that the supervisor who sexually harassed her is liable for intentional or negligent infliction of emotional distress or common-law assault or battery. These state law claims are attractive to plaintiffs because they are not governed by as many procedural rules and prerequisites as Title VII and other federal claims, may allow for individual liability, and may not limit recovery to certain amounts or types of damages. The required showings and available remedies for these types of claims vary from state to state. Once again, consultation with local counsel is strongly recommended when dealing with them.

Practical Suggestions for Reducing Exposure to Employment Discrimination Claims

A primary purpose of this book is to suggest practical ways to organize and operate a health care practice with a minimum of legal interference. Following are some suggestions for prevention and handling of potential employment discrimination claims (summarized in the accompanying box). However, as has been noted repeatedly, these practical suggestions are no substitute for consultation with an experienced attorney familiar with all the relevant facts and the needs of a particular practice.

Implement a Meaningful Employee Grievance Procedure

Just because sexual harassment or intentional racial discrimination occurs on the job, an employer does not necessarily have to be held liable. If the employer can show

that it was concerned about harassment in the workplace, informed employees of its intolerance of harassing conduct, and took reasonable steps to prevent it or to deal with potentially troublesome situations, it may still have a good case for avoiding liability.

On the other hand, the mere existence of a general antidiscrimination policy may not be sufficient to protect against liability. For example, in 1986, the US Supreme Court found that an employee's failure to invoke her employer's general nondiscrimination policy in response to sexual harassment by a supervisor did not prevent the employer from being held liable under Title VII. Rather, the Court faulted the policy for making no specific prohibition of sexual harassment and for requiring an employee to lodge general discrimination complaints with her supervisor, who in this case was the alleged harasser. The Court did state that an employer might be better protected from liability if it had a grievance policy "better calculated to encourage victims of harassment to come forward."[92]

KEY POINTS

Tips for Reducing Exposure to Employment Discrimination Claims

1. Implement a meaningful employee grievance procedure.
2. Don't invite a retaliation claim.
3. Publish and enforce general disciplinary rules as consistently as possible.
4. Conduct regular employee evaluations.
5. Document decisions.
6. Conduct in-service training to heighten employee sensitivity.
7. Stay away from taboo topics in interviews.
8. Consider purchasing employment-practices liability insurance.
9. Develop a good relationship with an employment law attorney—and take advantage of it.

In two opinions issued in 1998, the Supreme Court attempted to clarify the standard for when an employer might be held vicariously liable for an employee's sexual harassment of a coworker or subordinate. In a nutshell, the Court stated that an employer can be held liable for a hostile environment "created by a supervisor with immediate (or successively higher) authority over the employee" whenever the "supervisor's harassment culminates in a tangible employment action, such as discharge, demotion, or undesirable reassignment." However, when no such "tangible employment action" is taken (that is, there is no actual employment-related consequence for a victim's refusal to acquiesce), a defending employer may avoid liability if it can prove "by a preponderance of the evidence . . . (a) that the employer exercised reasonable care to prevent and correct promptly any sexually harassing behavior, and (b) that the plaintiff employee unreasonably failed to take advantage of any preventive or corrective opportunities provided by the employer or to avoid harm otherwise."[93]

This standard splits the burden of preventing workplace harassment. Employers are required to make tangible efforts to prevent and correct harassment, and employees are required to use internal grievance policies and procedures to address hostile or abusive situations before filing EEOC charges or lawsuits.

Of course, even this guidance is not altogether clear. It says little about when an employer may be held liable for workplace sexual harassment committed by a nonsupervisory employee. However, it does emphasize the importance of having a meaningful sexual harassment and discrimination policy and grievance procedure. An antidiscrimination policy should therefore be clearly worded to address and provide examples of sexual harassment, state a clear prohibition of such ha-

rassment, inform employees of their rights to have their complaints addressed within the company and to file an EEOC charge if the company is unresponsive or ineffective in dealing with the situation, be published by adequate means to all employees, and be regularly reviewed and updated by management for compliance with the law.

Key elements of an internal grievance procedure most likely to provide protection against liability would include:

1. a means for reporting allegedly harassing incidents to a management-level employee other than the employee's supervisor—preferably to a person somewhat outside the general chain of command;

2. immediate investigation of all claims by neutral management personnel;

3. temporary procedural mechanisms for separating or limiting the contact between victims and their alleged harassers; and

4. resolution of all claims by a finding of no actionable harassment (with documented reasons for such a finding) or of improper conduct followed by appropriate remedial or disciplinary measures—including as possible options suspension, pay reductions, demotion, required attendance at additional antiharassment training, and even termination of the offender.

A practice group might also want to consider adopting a simple process whereby disciplinary actions or negative findings might be reviewed on appeal by the practicing physicians or some other independent review panel in certain circumstances.

A medical practice, by its very nature, can be somewhat hierarchical, with real or perceived differences among physicians, nurses, and other staff concerning status, benefits, duties, and responsibilities. As a result, crafting an effective and meaningful grievance procedure may be especially challenging. Care must be taken to provide all employees with a meaningful opportunity to have their claims reviewed and, where necessary, investigated by persons with authority to remedy any problems or discipline the offending parties. Yet the reviewing persons must not be so entrenched in the authority structure of the practice that the justice and efficacy of the grievance process are compromised. If only the physician-owners of a practice are involved in the review and disciplinary process, nurses and staff may fear that their claims of harassment or discrimination by a physician will not be afforded full and fair review or will be met with reprisal. The grievance procedure should avoid even the appearance of impropriety—perhaps by incorporating some lower-level personnel as part of the review and investigation process.

Many employment law attorneys have experience drafting and implementing these kinds of policies and procedures, and they can take some of the work out of a practice's efforts to comply with the law and protect against liability.

Don't Invite a Retaliation Claim

As noted in the foregoing review of federal employment discrimination law, an employer is prohibited from retaliating in any form against an employee's exercise of the rights afforded by any of these statutes. Thus, once an employee has asserted or raised an issue regarding rights under a particular statute—whether by complaining to a supervisor, calling an attorney, or contacting the EEOC—care should be taken to avoid any adverse employment actions that even hint of retaliation against that employee. The employer should attempt to maintain the status quo for that employee as best as possible under the circumstances until the claim can be fully investigated and resolved in some fashion. One obvious exception is to separate an employee complaining of racial or sexual harassment from the alleged harasser. Remember that the employee need not prove the validity of the underlying Title VII or other statutory violation to prove a retaliation claim. The employee needs only to have had a reasonable belief that a violation had occurred or was occurring when the claim was asserted.

Publish and Enforce General Disciplinary Rules As Consistently As Possible

The focus in most intentional discrimination claims will be on the employer's motives for making particular employment decisions. Therefore, when it comes to terminating or disciplining employees, a well-publicized and consistently enforced disciplinary policy and accompanying procedures can go a long way toward heading off or defending claims. The policy envisioned here is separate from the previously discussed ones dealing with allegations of workplace harassment, although there may be some overlap between the two, and is designed to address issues of job performance in addition to an employee's ability to work with fellow employees.

The development and enforcement of general disciplinary policies and procedures is important for several reasons. First, developing a clear understanding of the conduct and performance standards required for continued employment and advancement will promote good employee morale. If employees are told what it takes to succeed, they can improve their performance accordingly. Happier employees file fewer lawsuits, so it is in a practice group's best interest to provide a clear roadmap for success in the practice. Second, a clear, enforceable code of conduct may help prevent the kind of harmful activities that give rise to hostile work environment claims. Third, and most important, adequate disciplinary records and remedial measures can help an employer document an employee's deficiencies or productivity concerns so that if termination, demotion, or other discipline becomes warranted, the employer's decision will be less vulnerable to challenge.

Thus, in sum, the key elements of an adequate employee disciplinary policy are

1.   clearly written, easily understandable, and well-publicized policies of acceptable and unacceptable workplace behavior, required duties, and/or standard levels of expected performance;

2.   an adequate range of disciplinary measures (with penalties increasing with the frequency or the seriousness of the offense) and a practical means for imposing them impartially; and

3.   proper documentation of each step of the disciplinary process, from initial promulgation of the rules to actual disciplinary action taken against a particular employee.

The idea is not only to improve workplace conditions but to be able to document contemporaneously the performance or conduct-related reasons that a particular employee was disciplined, demoted, or terminated in case a racial, gender, or other bias claim is later asserted.

As with all employment policies and procedures, such as those contained in an employee handbook or posted on bulletin boards, the employer should be careful not to create an employment contract where none exists. Most states have employment at will, meaning that an employment relationship

may be terminated at any time by either party for any reason unless there is an employment contract. Employees have, with some success, sued employers for breach of contract by relying on promises contained in employee handbooks as the basis for their claims. Any policy manual or handbook should therefore contain a disclaimer that the policies stated therein are nothing more than the employer's statements of policy and are not intended to form a contractual relationship.

Conduct Regular Employee Evaluations

As an adjunct to the disciplinary process, which is designed primarily to deal with instances of wrongful behavior or poor performance, it is also wise for an employer to implement a system of regular evaluation of all employees. With regular reviews, each employee's individual performance issues can be identified, and his or her progress (or lack of progress) can be tracked over time. Systemic, regular, and universally applicable employee review and evaluation lessen the likelihood that an employee will later be able to claim that negative disciplinary records were formulated after the fact in support of an employer's effort to cover up discrimination.

The evaluation process will be greatly enhanced by the drafting and publication of written job descriptions delineating the essential functions and qualifications of each job. Such writings can help eliminate controversies over whether an employee alleging an ADA claim was able to perform the essential functions of the job or whether a gender discrimination plaintiff was adequately performing her present position when passed over for a promotion. Administrative and judicial decisions are necessarily rendered in hindsight, and thus the more contemporary evidence an employer can point to in support of its legal defenses, the better the chance of ultimate success.

Document Decisions

The need for adequate documentation of all employment-related decisions—whether companywide or about a specific employee—should again be emphasized. In harassment cases, the key issue is what the employer's management personnel knew about the harassment, when they knew it, and what they did about it. In intentional discrimination cases, the focus may be on whether a particular employee's performance or conduct grew unacceptable, when this happened, what was done to give the employee a chance to improve, and how other employees in similar situations were treated. Many of these claims frequently boil down to a determination of which party is more credible in its account of how the employment decision was made or the employee's claim was responded to. Therefore, in any hiring, firing, promotion, or discipline situation, an employer should document all aspects of its decision-making process.

Many of the principles regarding creation, retention, and disclosure of personnel files and other records discussed in chapter 3 are equally applicable in the employment law context.

Conduct In-Service Training to Heighten Employee Sensitivity

Of course, no employer—physician or otherwise—relishes the thought of micromanaging employee behavior. When the liability stakes and the likelihood of an incident are so high, an employer cannot afford to turn a blind eye to the conduct of employees and supervisors in the workplace. It is not enough for a practice merely to draft and approve some sort of policy regarding workplace discrimination and harassment. The rules and regulations will do no good if they are not understood by the employees who must attempt to live by them. Therefore, a practice group's or hospital's regular training program should include instruction regarding its and its employees' mutual rights and obligations in the workplace. Consider how much stronger a defense against liability can be presented when the employer is able to document that it made regular, meaningful, reasonable efforts to protect against harassment or intentional discrimination in the workplace.

Stay Away from Taboo Topics in Interviews

The EEOC has published literature offering specific guidance regarding hiring and promotion questions that are impermissible under one or more of the federal employment discrimination laws. For example, under the ADA, an employer may not inquire specifically about an applicant's disability, except to the extent it may impair his ability to do the job or may require reasonable accommodation. Questions to a woman about her childbearing or childraising plans may run afoul of Title VII prohibitions of gender and pregnancy discrimination and should therefore be avoided. Any application questions regarding race or ethnicity (if included at all) should make certain to include a disclaimer that such factors are recorded for statistical purposes and will not be factored into the employment decision.

The physicians and staff in a practice responsible for recruiting and hiring should familiarize themselves with these guidelines (which can be obtained by contacting a local EEOC office or visiting the agency's official Website at www.eeoc.gov) to avoid committing unwitting violations of the law. Larger employers that interview and hire frequently may find it beneficial to standardize a list of topics to be covered, and to be avoided, in interviews. Conducting interviews in a respectful, sensitive manner can help a practice to avoid violating the law. It can also set a good example of proper workplace behavior from an employee's initial contact with the practice.

Consider Purchasing Employment Practices Liability Insurance

As the frequency and cost of defending employment claims have grown, so has the burgeoning market for employment practices liability insurance coverage. A number of insurance carriers have begun offering this relatively new kind of coverage through endorsements to general liability and business policies. As with medical malpractice insurance, the policy should provide payment of defense counsel's fees as well as any settlement or judgment. Some insurers may also offer, as an adjunct to the policy, guidelines and training on how to reduce exposure to these types of claims.

Like any other insurance coverage, the terms of an employment practices liability endorsement or policy should be thoroughly reviewed using the guidelines set forth in chapter 4. In particular, the physician will want to ask which of the state and federal statutes and types of claims are covered; whether coverage is provided only for actual lawsuits or includes defense costs and indemnity for claims investigated and resolved at the EEOC charging stage; whether and to what extent the physician will have the

opportunity to participate in selecting counsel and deciding whether or not to settle a case; what, if any, conditions (such as particular grievance procedures) the employer must satisfy to obtain coverage and keep it in force; and whether the insurer and its counsel have a proven track record in handling and covering these or similar types of claims.

Develop a Good Relationship with an Employment Law Attorney—and Take Advantage of It

The usefulness of developing a good working relationship with an attorney specializing in employment law and liability cannot be overemphasized. An experienced attorney can keep a practice abreast of changes in the law and offer regular advice about compliance. Moreover, it is often helpful to consult an attorney when making particular decisions—about either implementing and changing personnel policies or specific hiring, firing, and disciplinary actions—that may raise issues of race, sex, age, disability, or the like. An attorney who knows a practice and its members well can help tailor policies and procedures to fit its particular needs and can also help develop effective responses to potential crises.

Conclusion

The construction, implementation, and operation of all of these policies and procedures certainly sound like a lot of work. The goals, once again, are for the employer to prevent potentially actionable conduct or illegal discrimination from occurring, to be equipped to deal with allegations that such conduct has occurred, to avoid the expense and inconvenience of an EEOC investigation or lawsuit when possible, and to be protected from liability in the event a claim is ultimately filed. As with other types of claims discussed in this book, the amount of time and effort spent on prevention is much less than that incurred in the filing and litigation of an actual claim.

1. President's Advisory Committee on Consumer Protection and Quality in the Health Care Industry, "Final Report," chap 13, p. 205 (March 1998), *citing* James C. Franklin, "Industry Output and Employment Projections to 2005," Monthly Labor Review 118(11):45–59 (November 1995); J.D. Moore, "Downsizing Slows Down," Modern Healthcare 36–40 (December 15, 1997); and Institute of Medicine, *Nursing Staff in Hospitals and Nursing Homes: Is It Adequate?* (Washington, DC: National Academy Press, 1996).

2. Best's Review of Property-Casualty Insurance, December 1, 1996, *cited* in Carol A. Ellington, "Employment Practices Liability in the Physician Office," The Digest, Fall/Winter 1997, St. Paul Medical Services 1998. All references taken from St. Paul Medical Services' publications are reprinted with permission. ©1998 St. Paul Fire and Marine Insurance Co. All rights reserved.

3. 42 USC § 2000e et seq (West 1999).

4. *See, eg, Lovelace v Sherwin Williams,* 681 F2d 230, 241-42 (4th Cir 1982); *Goldberg v B. Green and Company,* 836 F2d 845 (4th Cir 1988)(speculative assertions that defendant's state of mind and motive are in dispute are not enough to withstand summary judgment).

5. *See, eg, Hughes v Bedsole,* 48 F3d 1376, 1383 (4th Cir 1995) (plaintiff "must . . . eliminate concerns that she was fired because of performance or qualifications . . .").

6. *See, eg, Cook v CSX Transportation Corp,* 988 F2d 507, 511 (4th Cir 1993); *Mayberry v Vought Aircraft Co,* 55 F3d 1086, 1990 (5th Cir 1995); *Neuren v Adduci, Mastriani, Meeks & Schill,* 43 F3d 1507, 1514 (DC Cir 1995); *Pierce v Commonwealth Life Ins Co,* 40 F3d 796, 802 (6th Cir 1994).

7. *Bristow v Daily Press, Inc,* 770 F2d 1251, 1255 (4th Cir 1985); *see also Johnson v Shalala,* 991 F2d 126, 131 (4th Cir 1993).

8. *St. Mary's Honor Center v Hicks,* 509 US 502, 506-07 (1993).

9. *Id.*

10. Ellington, *supra* note 2, at 2; *see also* "Sexual Harassment Charges—EEOC & FEPAs Combined: FY 1991-FY 1997" (visited May 17, 1999) <http://www.eeoc.gov/stats/harass.html>.

11. *Wrightson v Pizza Hut of America, Inc,* 99 F3d 138, 142 (4th Cir 1996); *Spicer v Virginia,* 66 F3d 705, 710 (4th Cir 1995) (en banc).

12. *Oncale v Sundowner Offshore Services,* 118 S Ct 998 (1998).

13. *Harris v Forklift Sys,* 510 US 17, 23, 114 S Ct 367, 371 (1993).

14. 42 USC § 2000e(j) (West 1999).

15. *See, eg, Trans World Airlines v Hardison,* 432 US 63 (1977); *EEOC v Ithaca Indus,* 849 F2d 116, 118 (4th Cir 1988) (en banc) (definition of religion under Title VII requires employers to make reasonable accommodations, short of undue hardship).

16. *See, eg, Chalmers v Tulon Company of Richmond,* 101 F3d 1012, 1019 (4th Cir 1996); *Philbrook v Ansonia Bd of Educ,* 757 F2d 476, 481 (2d Cir 1985); *Turpen v Missouri-Kansas-Texas RR Co,* 736 F2d 1022, 1026 (5th Cir 1984), *aff'd on other grounds,* 479 US 60, 65, 107 S Ct 367, 370, 93 LEd 2d 305 (1986).

17. *Ansonia Bd of Educ v Philbrook,* 479 US 60, 68 (1986).

18. 29 USC § 621 et seq (West 1999).

19. *Causey v Balog,* 162 F3d 795, 801 (4th Cir 1998) (assuming without deciding that such a cause of action exists); *EEOC v Massey Yardley Chrysler-Plymouth,* 117 F3d 1244, 1249 (11th Cir 1997) (same); *Crawford v Medina Gen Hosp,* 96 F3d 830, 834 (6th Cir 1996) ["we find it a relatively uncontroversial proposition that such a (hostile environment) theory is viable under the ADEA"].

20. *Hazen Paper Co v Biggins,* 507 US 604, 610 (1993).

21. *See, eg, Burns v AAF-McQuay, Inc,* 96 F3d 728, 731 (4th Cir 1996), *cert denied,* 117 S Ct 1247 (1997) (applying *McDonnell-Douglas* framework in ADEA context).

22. *O'Connor v Consolidated Coin Caterers Corp,* 517 US 308, 310 (1996).

23. *Mitchell v Data Corp,* 12 F3d 1310, 1315 (4th Cir 1993).

24. *Woodhouse v Magnolia Hospital,* 92 F3d 248 (5th Cir 1996).

25. 29 USC § 623(f)(1).

26. 29 USC § 623(f).

27. 29 USC § 631(c).

28. The pertinent portion of that statute provides that "[n]o otherwise qualified individual with a disability in the United States . . . shall, solely by reason of her or his disability, be excluded from the participation in, be denied the benefits of, or be subjected to discrimination under any program or activity receiving Federal financial assistance. . . ." 29 USC § 794(a) (1994).

29. 42 USC § 12112(a).

30. 42 USC § 12111(2).

31. *See, eg, Cohen v Temple Physicians,* 11 F Supp 2d 733 (ED Pa 1998) (doctors, in their individual capacities, could not be held liable to former employee for termination by physician's corporation allegedly on the basis of disability).

32. *Walton v Mental Health Association of Southeastern Pennsylvania,* 168 F3d 661, 667 (3d Cir 1999)(assuming that claim exists but upholding judgment for employer); *Wallin v Minnesota Dept of Corrections,* 153 F3d 681, 687–88 (8th Cir 1998)("We will assume, without deciding, that such a cause of action exists."), *petition for cert filed,* 67 USLW 3410 (US, Dec 21, 1998) (No 98-1007); *Moritz v Frontier Airlines,* 147 F3d 784, 788 (8th Cir 1998) ("Although we are uncertain whether such a cause of action exists, . . . [plaintiff] has failed to establish a prima facie case of discrimination"); *McConathy v Dr Pepper/Seven Up Corp,* 131 F3d 558, 563 (5th Cir 1998) (same); *Keever v City of Middletown,* 145 F3d 809, 813 (6th Cir) (upholding denial of claim with no qualification

as to the certainty of its existence), *cert denied,* 119 S Ct 407 (1998).

33. *See Harding v Winn-Dixie Stores,* 907 F Supp 386, 389 (MD Fla 1995), *citing* 42 USC § 12112(b); 29 CFR §§ 1630.1, 1630.5, and 1630.7. *Cf Crowder v Kitagawa,* 81 F3d 1480 (9th Cir 1996) (disparate impact theory generally available under the ADA).

34. *Porter v United States Alumoweld Corp,* 125 F3d 243, 246-47 (4th Cir 1997), *citing* 42 USCA § 12112 and *Doe v Univ of Maryland Med Sys Corp,* 50 F3d 1261, 1264–65 (4th Cir 1995).

35. 42 USC § 12102(2), *cited in Halperin v Abacus Technology Corp,* 128 F3d 191, 198 (4th Cir 1997).

36. *School Bd of Nassau County v Arline,* 480 US 273, 279 (1987) (citation omitted).

37. 45 CFR § 84.3(j)(2)(i) (1997).

38. *Bragdon v Abbott,* 118 S Ct 2196 (1998).

39. *See* 29 CFR pt 1630, app at 339 (1996) (noting that "temporary, non-chronic impairments of short duration, with little or no long term or permanent impact, are usually not disabilities").

40. *Halperin v Abacus Technology Corp,* 128 F3d 191, 200 (4th Cir 1997).

41. *See* 29 CFR § 1630.2(i) (1996); 29 CFR Pt 1630, App § 1630.2(i) (1996); 45 CFR §84.3(j)(2)(ii) (1997); 28 CFR § 41.31(b)(2) (1997).

42. *Bragdon,* 118 S Ct at 2204–2205.

43. 29 CFR § 1630.2(j)(1)(ii).

44. 29 CFR § 1630.2(j)(2).

45. 29 CFR § 1630.2(j)(3).

46. 42 USCA § 12111(8).

47. *Southeastern Community College v Davis,* 442 US 397, 406 (1979) (decided under the Rehabilitation Act).

48. *See, eg, Carr v Reno,* 23 F3d 525, 529 (DC Cir 1994) (holding "coming to work regularly" to be an "essential function"); *Jackson v Veterans Admin,* 22 F3d 277, 279–80 (11th Cir 1994) (holding that an employee with a history of sporadic unpredictable absences was not "otherwise qualified"); *Law v United*

States Postal Serv, 852 F2d 1278, 1279–80 (Fed Cir 1988) (noting that a regular and reliable level of attendance is a necessary element of most jobs).

49. US Equal Employment Opportunity Commission, "The ADA: Your Responsibilities as an Employer," found at <www.eeoc.gov/facts/ada17.html> (last accessed June 1, 1999).

50. *Id.*

51. 42 USC § 12112(d)(4)(A).

52. 29 CFR pt1630, app § 1630.14(c)

53. *Porter v United States Alumoweld Company,* 125 F3d 243, 246 (4th Cir 1997) (finding fitness-for-duty examination of plaintiff's back proper where his job "required lifting and pulling, and . . . he had encountered problems carrying out his job due to back problems even before surgery"). *See also Grenier v Cyanamid Plastics,* 70 F3d 667, 676 (1st Cir 1995) (finding that if the plaintiff were "treated as an existing employee returning from disability leave, . . . the employer would be able to demand medical certification of ability to return to work") and *Pesterfield v Tennessee Valley Auth,* 941 F2d 437, 438 (6th Cir 1991) (holding that an employee who was hospitalized for psychiatric treatment was required to provide medical certification as to ability to return to work), *cited in Porter,* 125 F3d at 246.

54. US Equal Employment Opportunity Commission, *supra* note 49.

55. 42 USC § 12111(5) (1998).

56. *Robbins v United Parcel Service,* No 5:98CV64-V (WDNC).

57. *Birkbeck v Marvel Lighting Corp,* 30 F3d 507, 510 (4th Cir 1994).

58. *EEOC v AIC Security Investigations,* 55 F3d 1276, 1280–81 (7th Cir 1995) (rejecting individual liability under the ADA).

59. 42 USC § 12182(a).

60. *See, eg, A.R. v Kogan,* 964 F Supp 269 (ND Ill 1997) (patient stated claim for individual liability of physician under ADA for alleged refusal of physician and clinic to treat patient after discovering her HIV-positive status); *Sharrow v Bailey,* 910 F Supp 187 (MD Pa 1995) (allowing claim against doctor and hospital for discrimination on the basis of HIV-positive status); *Howe v Hull,* 873 F Supp 72 (ND Ohio 1994) (same).

61. 42 USC § 12182(b)(3).

62. *Kogan,* 964 F Supp at 271.

63. 29 USC § 2612(a)(1)(A)-(D) (1994).

64. 29 USC § 2611(2)(A).

65. 29 USC § 2611(11).

66. 29 CFR § 825.220(c) (1997).

67. 42 USC §2000e-3.

68. 42 USC § 12203(a) (ADA); 29 USC §623(d) (ADEA); 29 USC § 2615(a) & (b) (FMLA).

69. *See, eg, McNairn v Sullivan,* 929 F2d 974, 980 (4th Cir 1991), *citing Ross v Communications Satellite Corp,* 759 F2d 355, 365 (4th Cir 1985), *abrogated in part on other grounds by Price Waterhouse v Hopkins,* 490 US 228 (1989).

70. *See Hartsell v Duplex Products,* 123 F3d 766, 775 (4th Cir 1997) (noting that termination is an adverse employment action).

71. 42 USCA § 2000e-3(a); *Laughlin v Metropolitan Washington Airports Authority,* 149 F3d 253, 259 (4th Cir 1998).

72. *Id; see also Laughlin,* 149 F3d at 259 (court's refusal to analyze retaliation claim under participation clause was proper where there was no ongoing "investigation, proceeding or hearing" at time employee was terminated for covertly copying documents relevant to an EEOC charge and suit filed later by another employee).

73. *Id, citing Armstrong v Index Journal Co,* 647 F2d 441, 448 (4th Cir 1981).

74. *Hopkins v Baltimore Gas & Elec Co,* 77 F3d 745, 754 (4th Cir 1996); *Armstrong,* 647 F2d at 448.

75. *See, eg, EEOC v C & D Sportswear Corp,* 398 F Supp 300, 306 (MD Ga 1975) ("[W]here accusations are made outside the procedures set forth by Congress that accusation is made at the accuser's peril."); *Bray v Tenax,* 905 F Supp 324, 328 (EDNC 1995) ("While employees should be encouraged to work out problems without resorting to federal process, careless and uncounseled accusations

of discrimination are not necessarily protected by Title VII's opposition clause. Congress established Title VII procedures for a reason, and complaints made outside that system necessarily carry some additional risk.").

76. *Childress v City of Richmond,* 907 F Supp 934, 940 (ED Va 1995), *aff'd* 134 F3d 1205 (4th Cir 1998) (en banc), *cert denied,* 118 S Ct 2322, 76 Fair Empl Prac Cas (BNA) 1888; *Mayo v Kiwest Corp,* 898 F Supp 335, 337, (ED Va 1995).

77. 42 USC S 2000e(b) (Title VII); 42 USC § 12111(5) (1998) (ADA); 29 USC § 630(b) (ADEA); 29 USC § 2611(4)(A)(i) (FMLA) (1998).

78. *See* 42 USC § 2000e-5(e); *NAACP Labor Committee of Front Royal v Laborers' International Union of North America,* 902 F Supp 688, 699 (WD Va 1993). *Cf Price v Litton Business Sys,* 694 F2d 963, 965 (4th Cir 1982)(180-day limitations period under ADEA), and *Felty v Graves-Humphreys Co,* 785 F2d 516, 518-19 (4th Cir 1986)(same). *See also* 42 USC § 12117(a) (1998) (incorporating into the ADA the administrative charge and investigation procedures found in Title VII, including 42 USC § 2000e-5(e)-(f)).

79. *NAACP Labor Committee of Front Royal,* 902 F Supp at 699, *citing Kilgo v Bowman Transp,* 789 F2d 859, 876-77 (11th Cir 1986).

80. See statistics available at <www.eeoc.gov/stats/all.html> (last visited May 17, 1999).

81. *See, eg, Beall v Abbott Laboratories,* 130 F3d 614, 620 (4th Cir 1997), *citing Jenkins v Home Ins Co,* 635 F2d 310, 312 (4th Cir 1980) *(per curiam); Hill v AT&T Technologies,* 731 F2d 175, 180 (4th Cir 1984); *Woodard v Lehman,* 717 F2d 909, 915 (4th Cir 1983) (continuing violation theory available "only where an actual violation has occurred within that requisite time period").

82. *See, eg, Williams v Enterprise Leasing Company of Norfolk/Richmond,* 911 F Supp 988, 996–97 (ED Va 1995).

83. *See, eg, Evans v Technology Applications & Service Co,* 80 F3d 954, 963 (4th Cir 1996). *See also Dennis v County of Fairfax,* 55 F3d

151, 156 (4th Cir 1995) (Title VII claims that "exceed the scope of the EEOC charge and any charges that would naturally have arisen from an investigation thereof . . . are procedurally barred").

84. 42 USC § 1981a.

85. *Id.*

86. 42 USC § 1981a(b)(3)(A).

87. 29 USC § 2617(a)(1).

88. Michael D. Moberly, "A Better ADEA?: Using State Wage Payment Laws to Enhance Remedies For Age Discrimination," 32 Tulsa Law Journal 21, 21 (1996).

89. *Hazen Paper Co v Biggins,* 507 US 604, 614-17 (1993).

90. *See, eg, Christiansburg Garment Co v EEOC,* 434 US 412, 421 (1978)("a district court may in its discretion award attorney's fees to a prevailing defendant in a Title VII case upon a finding that the Plaintiff's action was frivolous, unreasonable, or without foundation, even though not brought in subjective bad faith").

91. For example, the North Carolina Equal Employment Practices Act, NC Gen Stat § 143–422.2 (NCEEPA), provides that "It is the public policy of this State to protect and safeguard the right and opportunity of all persons to seek, obtain and hold employment without discrimination or abridgement on account of race, religion, color, national origin, age, sex or handicap by employers which regularly employ 15 or more employees." This statute has been held to permit an action for wrongful discharge in violation of public policy in gender-discrimination cases. *See, eg, Hughes v Bedsole,* 48 F3d 1376, 1383-84 (4th Cir 1995). *See also North Carolina Dep't of Correction v Gibson,* 308 NC 131, 301 SE2d 78, 82 (1983) (holding that claims of discharge in violation of North Carolina public policy are analyzed under the same evidentiary patterns and standards of law as federal Title VII claims).

92. *Meritor Savings Bank v Vinson,* 477 US 57, 72–73 (1986).

93. *Burlington Indus v Ellerth,* 524 US at ___, 118 S Ct 2257, 2270 (1998); *Farragher v City of Boca Raton,* 524 US at ___, 118 S Ct 2275, 2292–93 (1998).

Chapter 10

Physicians' unions:

Developing strength in numbers*

One of the hottest topics of discussion among physicians today is the formation of labor unions. That this debate is even occurring would have stunned many of their predecessors only a generation ago, when the profession was an autonomous, self-regulating guild at the apex of its institutional power. What has catalyzed this debate?

A number of developments beginning in the latter part of 1996 spurred interest among physicians in union formation. The first was the August 1996 announcement of the American Podiatric Medical Association that it was working with the Office Professionals Employees International Union (OPEIU) to form a union for podiatrists. This was covered by the *New York Times* and received widespread attention. Another development, also reported in the general press, was the November 8, 1996,

ruling of the regional director of the National Labor Relations Board that physicians employed by the Thomas-Davis Medical Centers, P.C., in Tucson, Arizona, could form a bargaining unit and engage in collective negotiations with their employer.[1] In March 1999, the Service Employees International Union announced its intention to actively recruit physicians as members of its union. Last, lawmakers in Texas introduced legislation that would give self-employed physicians in that state the right to bargain collectively.

Needless to say, these developments attracted considerable attention among physicians. Union formation quickly became a topic of discussion at many state and county medical societies and other groups of physicians. As a result, the AMA and other professional organizations received and handled many inquiries about the law of union formation, what activities unions are allowed to engage in on behalf of physicians, the activities of existing physician unions, whether medical societies can organize unions, and

* Parts of this chapter are adapted from a manuscript titled "Physicians, Unions, and Antitrust," by the late Edward B. Hirshfeld. Originally copyrighted 1999 American Health Lawyers Association, Washington, DC. Used with permission.

what activities medical societies can engage in to assist physicians other than starting a union. Many state, county, and specialty medical societies have heard presentations from the main physicians' unions advocating that medical societies affiliate with a union. Some of these societies are considering such an affiliation.[2]

This debate culminated in the June 23, 1999, vote by the AMA to develop an affiliated national labor organization to represent employed physicians and, where allowed by law, residents. Further, the AMA's House of Delegates vowed to seek antitrust relief for physicians and medical groups and the creation of a national organization to support development and operation of local negotiating units. These units would provide an option for self-employed physicians and medical groups. Finally, the organization acted to expand its advocacy programs by initiating litigation and stepping up lobbying efforts in order to augment physician bargaining power with payers.

Why Are Physicians Interested in Union Formation?

Physicians who are attracted to unions usually fall into three categories, the self-employed; employees of group practices, hospitals, or another entity; and resident physicians. The self-employed are solo practitioners or partners or shareholders in group practices. Those who are shareholders may technically be employees of the medical corporation involved, but they are also owners of the group practice and are generally considered to be self-employed. Differences among these groups are significant. Each therefore warrants separate discussion.

Self-Employed Physicians

The primary interest in union formation has come from independent, self-employed physicians in solo practice or small groups. Self-employed physicians are interested in unions because managed care health plans have obtained an overwhelming amount of economic leverage over physicians. Their leverage arises from the ability to deliver (or withhold) large numbers of patients to physicians. The health plans direct patient volume to those physicians who will accept reductions in payment and cooperate with the health plan in its cost-reduction efforts, particularly in reducing the use of health care services. This power has enabled health plans to assume substantial control over medical decision making for patients, to drive down the incomes of many physicians, and to threaten the viability of physician practices that refuse to cooperate.

Physicians have felt unable to respond to the raw exertion of this power by health plans. Federal and state antitrust laws bar any collective action, such as boycotts, that would allow physicians to force health plans out of the market by refusing to participate on their panels. Federal and state policy has enabled health plans to obtain and exert economic power over physicians for the purpose of reducing the cost of health care.

Some health plans have not stopped at the use of leverage to drive down costs. They have engaged in conduct that has been arbitrary, unfair, and often cavalier toward the medical profession. These health plans believe, often correctly, that given the oversupply of many types of physicians (particularly specialists), they can get away with treating physicians badly. Self-employed physicians have felt unable to defend themselves from these abuses. Moreover, significant numbers of self-employed physicians have become

1998 Distribution of Patient Care Physicians by Employment Status

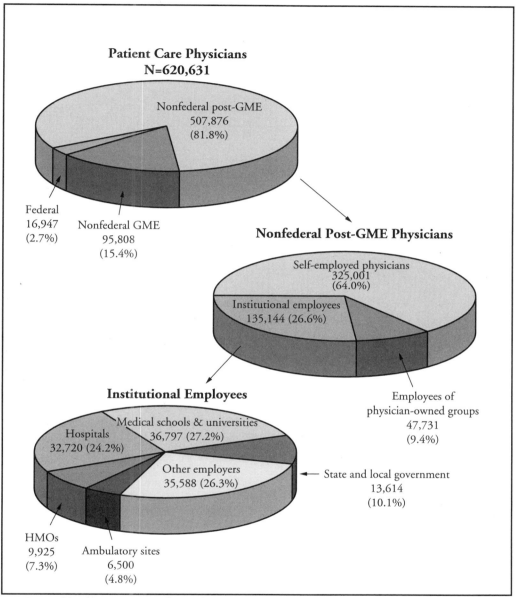

Prepared by the AMA Center for Health Policy Research.

concerned about what they see as the degradation of care as a consequence of utilization review and other management practices. A common refrain is, "I spent four years in medical school, and now, before I can put somebody in the hospital, I have to clear it with some clerk who spent a year in junior college."

Self-employed physicians have been exploring whether union formation will allow them to respond to the economic leverage of health plans with leverage of their own. Some are aware that the antitrust laws prevent them from engaging in collective negotiations as a group of independent physicians, but most have a mistaken belief that they could engage in collective bargaining if they joined a labor union authorized to represent individuals in collective bargaining. Generally, they lose interest in union formation when they find out that the antitrust laws do not allow them to engage in collective bargaining even if they are part of a union.

However, demand among self-employed physicians for legislative reform that would allow them to engage in collective bargaining is growing. Such physicians are lobbying their associations, including the AMA, and their federal representatives and senators to promote bills that would modify federal antitrust or labor laws (or both) to allow collective bargaining by self-employed physicians.

Traditionally Employed Physicians

Employed physicians often sought to become employees to escape the "permanent whitewater" of being self-employed in the current market environment. In so doing, they have attempted to achieve security of both position and income and protection from abusive practices by health plans. They are a large and diverse group. The number of employed physicians has increased greatly since 1980, with the largest increase among physicians employed by hospitals. The wide variation in employment settings poses challenges for traditional labor unions attempting to organize physicians. In the case of large groups and medical schools that employ significant numbers of physicians, those physicians have a tradition of professionalism that has rendered them less receptive to union organizing. However, the rapid changes in the market may alter that dynamic as some employers unilaterally change policies and procedures affecting physicians and their patients.

A recent AMA survey[3] indicates the following:

- The total percentage of patient-care physicians (excluding resident physicians and those employed by the federal government) who were employed in 1997 was 43 percent. The percentage employed in 1983 was 32.9 percent. However, this percentage has been stable since 1994. The major period of growth occurred between 1983 and 1994.

- The total percentage of patient-care physicians (excluding those employed by the federal government) in practice for five years or less who were employed in 1997 was 64.6 percent. The percentage employed in 1983 was 37.2 percent.

- The total percentage of patient-care physicians (excluding those employed by the federal government) who were employed by "institutional employers" (such as hospitals, state and local governments, and staff-model HMOs) in 1997 was 32.6 percent, compared to 21.3 percent in 1988.

- The total percentage of patient-care physicians (excluding those employed by the federal government) who are employed by physician-owned groups in 1997 was 10.6 percent, compared to 6.5 percent in 1988.

- The 32.6 percent of patient-care physicians who were employed by institutions in 1997 were distributed as follows (reported as a percentage of the total physicians employed by institutions):

Hospitals: 22.3 percent (compared to 15.8 percent in 1988)

Medical schools or universities: 21.2 percent (compared to 22.1 percent in 1988)

Independent contractors (this category includes physicians such as emergency room physicians and radiologists who resemble employees in that they contract out services to large organizations, typically hospitals, and for whom a case can be made that they are in fact employees): 14.2 percent (compared to 21.3 percent in 1988)

State and local governments: 8.6 percent (compared to 18.4 percent in 1988)

Staff-model HMOs: 8.3 percent (compared to 9.2 percent in 1988)

Ambulatory care, surgical care, emergency care centers: 4.1 percent (compared to 3.5 percent in 1988)

Other: 21.3 percent (compared with 9.7 percent in 1988). The AMA speculates that physicians employed by hospital affiliates, such as management services organizations (MSOs), may account for a significant part of the growth in this area. If that is the case, hospital employment, directly or indirectly, has accounted for a very substantial part of the increase in the employment of physicians.

Employed physicians are typically less concerned about the leverage exerted by managed care plans than are solo and small-group practitioners. They usually feel more comfortable with managed care and often believe that they are able to provide better quality care by working for an entity with the managerial capacity to apply principles of continuous quality improvement and other techniques designed to improve quality and reduce costs. But some employed physicians have become disenchanted with the practices of their employers. The most frequent reasons that employed physicians become interested in collective bargaining include one or more of the following events:

1. The employer sets goals for increased productivity without consulting the physicians about the likely impact of those goals on the quality of patient care.

2. The employer makes significant changes in the patient-care facilities, staffing of the facilities, or administrative procedures used in the facilities without consulting the physicians.

3. The employer demands reductions in physician income.

4. The employer breaks promises or uses heavy-handed techniques to force physicians to make concessions.

Employers frequently engage in such conduct in response to market pressures—mainly the need to reduce costs and improve efficiency. The physicians are usually aware of the market pressure the employer faces, are concerned about the viability of the employer, and are willing to work to achieve increased efficiency. However, physicians become upset when they feel that they have no influence or control over critical decisions that will affect them or their patients. The physicians are willing to face and deal with market pressures as a group, but they do not like the sense of vulnerability and lack of control that occur when the owner blindsides them on key decisions.

As a result, some employed physicians have become interested in forming unions to engage in collective bargaining with their employers. Since they usually are protected by the National Labor Relations Act or state labor laws, there have been many organizing efforts among employed physicians. In general, however, the interest among employed physicians in union formation is much less than it is among self-employed physicians.

Resident Physicians

Residents are employees of a hospital or another institution affiliated with a medical school. They are considered both employees (of the hospital or institution) and students. Because of their demanding work conditions and low pay, resident physicians have long been interested in unions. The largest physician unions (especially the Committee on Interns and Residents) specialize in representing residents. There has been increased interest in recent years in unions among residents, who allege that, because of cost-cutting efforts, hospitals are imposing more work demands on them unrelated to their education. Residents also claim that hospitals have reduced their nonprofessional staffs, particularly at night, and that they are demanding that residents perform many of the unskilled or menial tasks formerly handled by orderlies and other nonprofessional staff.

As discussed below, the National Labor Relations Board has had a long-standing policy that resident physicians are students, not employees, and therefore not entitled to protection by the National Labor Relations

Act. The Committee on Interns and Residents has filed a representation petition asking the NLRB to revisit that policy.

The Current Status of Physician Unions

While physician unions have drawn a substantial amount of attention during the past few years, the number of physicians who are union members is very small in comparison with the size of the profession. It is hard to obtain accurate information about the number of physicians enrolled in unions. Based on press reports, the AMA has estimated that between fourteen thousand and twenty thousand physicians are union members. Of that number, between six thousand and nine thousand are residents employed at hospitals.

Physicians' unions are not a new phenomenon. Indeed, they have existed for decades. For example, the Committee of Interns and Residents (CIR), which primarily represents residents employed by hospitals, was founded in 1957. Of the two largest unions that represent practicing physicians, one, the Union of American Physicians and Dentists (UPD), was founded in 1972, and the other, the Federation of Physicians and Dentists (FPD), was founded in 1981. In fact, the 1970s were, like today, a period of discontent in which there was substantial interest among physicians in unionization.[4] At that time, regulations developed by the Medicare program to reduce costs were beginning to have a substantial impact for the first time. Medicare used hospitals as a vehicle for implementing regulations, and hospitals had to make demands on physicians in order to comply. Physicians were unenthusiastic, to put it mildly, about the intrusion of hospital management into their practices.

Further, in some parts of the country, particularly California, managed care began to become a significant factor in the market. After a few years of intense interest and dialogue, however, interest in unions waned.

Recently, there has been a resurgence of interest in physicians' unions because managed care plans are now the dominant form of health care in most states, and large numbers of physicians are feeling the effects. Moreover, sensing physician dissatisfaction with managed care, certain larger unions have begun to focus their organizing efforts on physicians, especially self-employed physicians in independent practice. These unions include the Office Professional Employees International Union (OPEIU), the Service Employees International Union (SEIU), and the American Federation of State, County and Municipal Employees (AFSCME). Each of these unions is affiliated with the AFL-CIO, is very large and well financed, and is willing to spend substantial amounts in its organizing campaigns. AFSCME has been successful in affiliating with UPD and FPD, while SEIU has affiliated with CIR.

These unions are aware that antitrust laws prevent them from engaging in collective bargaining on behalf of self-employed physicians. With some exceptions, the unions do not attempt to mislead the physicians into believing that they can bargain for them. Instead, they emphasize that they are aggressive advocates that can help physicians at the local level. In addition, they highlight their affiliation with the AFL-CIO and the lobbying clout in the state capitals and Washington that the AFL-CIO has amassed. They also emphasize that AFL-CIO–affiliated unions control many self-funded health plans organized under ERISA and that AFL-CIO–affiliated unions negoti-

ate collective bargaining agreements with employers that control many other ERISA plans. They state or imply that this influence over self-funded plans can benefit physicians. Finally, they contend that they will work to obtain an exemption from federal antitrust laws to allow self-employed physicians to bargain.

Unions representing residents were among the first to organize physicians for collective bargaining.[5] In 1976, the National Labor Relations Board found that residents are students, not employees, and therefore were not entitled to the protection of the National Labor Relations Act.[6] However, in 1986, the Supreme Court of California found that residents are employees under California's Higher Education Employer-Employee Relations Act and could form a union.[7] The legal climate in New York State is also favorable to resident unions formed at publicly owned hospitals. Many other states allow residents to form unions under state labor laws applicable to employees of state and local units of government. In addition to the resident unions organized under state laws, a number of institutions with resident programs have voluntarily recognized resident organizations as the bargaining agents of residents.[8]

Current AMA policy supports the right of physicians to engage in collective bargaining. It is AMA policy to work for expansion of the numbers of physicians eligible for that right under federal law.[9] It is against the policy of the AMA, however, for physicians to withhold care from patients for purposes of gaining leverage in collective bargaining.[10] Other types of job actions designed to give the physicians leverage are permissible provided that they do not endanger patient care. The AMA also opposes requirements that mandate physicians to join a union when they do not want to participate.

The AMA takes the position that resident physicians are both students and employees and that they qualify as employees for purposes of the labor exemption to federal antitrust laws and the National Labor Relations Act. However, it has expressed concern about the potential for residency programs created for the education of a resident to become mandatory subjects of collective bargaining. Consequently, the AMA is attempting to persuade the Accreditation Council for Graduate Medical Education, a not-for-profit association that accredits almost all residency programs in the United States, to adopt a requirement that residency programs allow residents to form organizations for their mutual benefit and protection and engage in good-faith negotiations with those organizations. Such organizations would be barred from engaging in strikes and would not force any resident to participate who did not want to do so.

The Law of Union Formation

To understand the issues regarding the formation of physician unions, the prudent physician ought to be familiar with a few basic principles of the applicable law. There is an inherent conflict between the goals of antitrust laws—which were intended to promote competition among providers of goods and services as a way to enhance consumer welfare—and laws regulating labor unions.[11] The antitrust laws are designed to promote competition, which in turn leads to greater diversity among products and services, better quality, and lower prices. Therefore, the antitrust laws bar combinations and other collective actions among buyers or sellers of goods and services to raise prices or otherwise set the terms of dealing.

The purpose of the labor laws is to keep human labor from being treated as a commodity and to permit collective agreements and action among laborers to raise and standardize wages and improve their working conditions. Strikes, boycotts, and other collective activity to raise wages are permitted and even favored by the labor laws to protect and enhance the dignity of the worker.

The antitrust laws are broad enough to cover human labor, thus bringing the two sets of laws into conflict. Early in the twentieth century, federal courts found that labor was in fact subject to the antitrust laws, and collective activities among laborers designed to raise or standardize wages or otherwise affect the terms of dealing between workers and management were illegal. To resolve this conflict, labor activities were eventually expressly exempted from the antitrust laws, by both statutory and nonstatutory means.

The Statutory Exemption

The statutory exemption of labor from the antitrust laws is the product of three sets of statutes. After the antitrust laws were passed, they were considered applicable to labor organizing and were used to enjoin strikes.[12] Congress later passed the Clayton Act which, among other things, exempted labor-organizing activities from federal antitrust laws. Section 6 says: "the labor of a human being is not a commodity or an article of commerce" and that "nothing contained in the antitrust laws shall be construed to forbid the existence and operation of labor . . . organizations." In addition, Section 20 of the Clayton Act was included to identify certain activities, such as strikes, picketing, and boycotts, which, when done as part of "a dispute concerning the terms of conditions of employment," cannot be prohibited by a federal court.

Additionally, several other laws, though not antitrust statutes, are referred to when considering the scope of the exemption. This came about because federal courts were slow to recognize the full scope of the labor exemption in the Clayton Act, and the Supreme Court interpreted it very narrowly. In response, Congress in 1932 passed the Norris-Laguardia Act, which declared a national policy in favor of labor unions and stated that collective bargaining and union organization are protected activities. In 1935, Congress went even further, enacting the National Labor Relations Act, also known as the Wagner Act. This act created the National Labor Relations Board and is the basis for today's comprehensive labor code that regulates labor relations. The act does not contain an express exemption from antitrust laws. Instead, it is designed to protect the activities of labor organizations and the persons who participate in them. The act created a legally enforceable right for employees to organize, required employers to bargain with employees through employee-elected representatives, and gave employees the right to engage in concerted activities for collective bargaining purposes or other mutual aid or protection.

In 1947, Congress passed the Labor Management Relations Act (also known as the Taft-Hartley Act). It built on the National Labor Relations Act and corrected problems and inequities that had developed in the enforcement of that act. In 1959, Congress passed the Labor Management Reporting and Disclosure Act (also known as the Landrum-Griffin Act). Neither of these statutes has an express antitrust exemption.

However, they are used to define the scope of the exemption of the Clayton Act.

The Nonstatutory Exemption

Finally, federal courts have decided cases that interpret the scope of the exemption when the labor-relations statutes do not provide enough guidance or when they do not apply to the workers who want to engage in collective bargaining. The rules of law developed by the courts in these cases are known as "nonstatutory" exemptions. These exemptions were developed because the statutory-labor exemption covers the unilateral acts of labor organizations. However, some labor organizations began making agreements with employers that could be classified as restraint of trade. The nonstatutory exemption was developed by federal courts to define when these agreements were exempt from the antitrust laws.[13]

In summary, the labor exemption is the product of several sets of statutes and case law that declare the exemption and define the scope of activities covered by the exemption.

When the Labor Exemption May Apply to Physicians

To fall within the labor exemption, the activities in question must meet the following characteristics:

- The conduct must arise out of a labor dispute and must be the conduct of a labor organization.

- The labor organization must be acting in its own self-interest; that is, it should be acting to further its goals as a labor organization as opposed to the goals of another entity.

- The activities must involve the unilateral conduct of the labor organization. Collective action carried on with other entities, especially if those entities are not labor organizations, may violate the antitrust laws.

Traditionally employed physicians clearly fall within the labor exemption to the antitrust laws and may engage in collective bargaining with their employers. However, physician-employees who have attempted to form unions have not always had an easy path. Some courts have found that physicians are supervisory employees because their decisions direct other members of the health care team, such as nurses and technicians. When physicians are found to be supervisory employees as opposed to nonsupervisory employees, then they do not qualify for the protection of the National Labor Relations Act.

Loss of the protection of the National Labor Relations Act is a significant handicap. That act is designed to protect and enhance the ability of employees to engage in collective bargaining by restricting the tactics that an employer can use to prevent the formation and operation of a union. For example, the act requires employers to recognize a union and to bargain with it. When physicians are classified as supervisory employees, their employer does not have to recognize their union and does not have to bargain with it. The employer is not restrained by the regulations of the National Labor Relations Act in how it can attempt to break up the physician bargaining group.

A 1997 example of the successful organization of a union involves employed physicians of Medical West Associates, a clinic in Springfield, Massachusetts, that was owned by the Blue Cross and Blue Shield organization operating in Massachusetts. This group of about seventy physicians became interested in organizing when Blue Cross decided to sell the clinic without involving the physicians in the selection of a purchaser. The physicians organized themselves without the assistance of a major trade union.[14]

Self-Employed Physicians

Before physicians can engage in collective bargaining under the labor exemption, the bargaining process must be part of a labor dispute. For there to be a labor dispute, the collective bargaining must concern the terms and conditions of employment. Therefore, the physicians must be employees. There is no labor dispute for purposes of the labor exemption if the physicians are independent contractors, entrepreneurs, or independent businesses.

Self-employed physicians are not in an employment relationship. Instead, they are in independent practice. Courts usually consider them to be independent contractors, entrepreneurs, or independent businesses who do not qualify for the labor exemption. However, in recent years, physicians in independent practice have lost authority to health plans and hospitals. Both kinds of organization exert control over medical decision making. In addition, health plans have enough leverage that physicians often feel compelled to accept their terms of dealing.

Some commentators contend that physicians who are not employees of a hospital or a health plan but who are subject to a high degree of control by the hospital or health plan should qualify for the labor exemption because they are not truly independent. This is a legitimate issue. The fact that persons who seek to engage in collective bargaining are not in a formal employment relationship does not conclusively disqualify them from the labor exemption. Courts will look to the true nature of the relationship to determine whether the persons are employees in substance even though they do not have a formal employment relationship. Employers cannot escape the labor exemption and the protection extended to employees by the National Labor Relations Act and its successor statutes by calling their workers independent contractors instead of employees.

While courts are willing to look at the substance of the relationship to determine whether a person is an employee for purposes of the antitrust and labor laws, the concept of an employee is largely restricted to the traditional salaried or hourly employee who works during designated times at a designated place. There was a time when the definition of employee seemed to be more expansive. In *NLRB v Hearst*,[15] the US Supreme Court determined that protection of the National Labor Relations Act is "not confined exclusively to 'employees' within the traditional legal distinctions separating them from 'independent contractors'. . . ." The court went on to say that inequalities in bargaining power in controversies over wages, hours, and working conditions may as well characterize the status of independent contractors as employees and that the National Labor Relations Act may protect persons who, under traditional concepts and common-law definitions, are technically independent contractors.

However, not long after the *Hearst* case, Congress amended the National Labor Relations Act with the Labor Management Relations Act (also known as the Taft-Hartley Act). Those amendments made clear that the National Labor Relations Act was restricted to the traditional concept of an employee and that independent contractors do not

qualify for its protection. Since that time, the courts have held that common-law principles of agency law control the distinction between an independent contractor and an employee. The courts scrutinize certain particular factors to determine whether workers are employees or independent contractors. Typically, when the relationship between an independent physician and a hospital or health plan is compared to these criteria, it is generally determined that the physician is an independent contractor, not an employee. The criteria and how they are interpreted with respect to physicians are as follows.

- The extent of control that the alleged employer may exercise over the worker under the agreement between them. The greater the amount of control, such as the hours of work required and the time and place of work, the more likely it is that the individual is an employee. Independent physicians that contract with a health plan are almost never subjected to the same kind of controls that an employer places on employees, such as hours of work, vacation time, work rules, and many others.

- Whether the worker is engaged in a distinct occupation or business. If so, that is more indicative of independent contractor than employee status. Physicians are viewed by the courts (and themselves) as engaged in a distinct occupation.

- The kind of occupation and whether the work involved is usually done under the direction of an employer. If the occupation is normally done by self-employed individuals, that indicates independent contractor status. Historically, most physicians have been self-employed, although that is changing. According to AMA surveys, about 45 percent of physicians are now employed.

- The skill required for the work involved. The higher the degree of skill, the more likely it is that the individual is an independent contractor. There are few occupations that require a higher degree of skill than that of the physician.

- Whether the alleged employer supplies the instruments, tools, and place of work. If so, that indicates employed status. However, physicians in independent practice normally own or rent their own office space and equipment and employ their own staff.

- The length of time for which the worker is hired. Indefinite and long-term relationships are more indicative of employed status. Physicians' contracts with health plans are usually yearly.

- Whether the pay is by time period or by the job. Physicians in independent practice are normally not paid a salary by health plans. They receive a fee for each service, capitation, or some blend of the two.

- Whether the work is part of the regular business of the employer. If so, the person is more likely to be an employee. There was a time when health care delivery was not part of the business of an insurer, but that is changing. Delivery is becoming an increasingly important aspect of the business of a health plan.

- Whether the alleged employer and the worker believe that they have created an employment relationship. Normally health plans and physicians do not believe that they have an employment relationship.

In summary, self-employed physicians in independent practice do not qualify for the labor exemption from the antitrust laws and do not qualify for the protection of the National Labor Relations Act. They are classified as independent contractors, not employees. Therefore, they may not engage in collective bargaining with health plans.

Exception to the Independent Contractor Rule

There are some occupations, however, in which members who do not have an employment relationship with an employer have been allowed to engage in collective bargaining. Examples include owner-driver truckers, musicians, and film directors. These occupations are not generally comparable to independent physicians. They involve workers who are frequently in an employment relationship but where some portion of the workers in the occupation operate as independent contractors. The independent contractor relationship is generally closer to an employment relationship than physicians are accustomed to. Because of a higher degree of control, independent contractors tend to come to the place of the party that hires them, and they tend to work for one person at a time. The courts have allowed unions to engage in collective bargaining on behalf of both the employed members of the occupational group and the independent contractors.

The courts have crafted this exception to preserve the integrity of collective bargaining on behalf of the employed workers. If independent contractors, who are in competition with the employed workers, were excluded from the collective-bargaining process, they could undermine the bargaining agreements reached about pay and terms of employment. In other words, the courts allow this bargaining on behalf of independent contractors not to protect the independent contractors but to protect the members of the occupation who are in fact employees. These kinds of conditions generally do not occur in physician relationships with health plans and hospitals.

At some point in the future, there may be large numbers of physicians who are employees, and it may be possible to show that a union must negotiate on behalf of both employed and independent physicians to protect the employed physicians. However, neither Congress nor the courts have taken any action in this direction.

To summarize, employed physicians generally fall within the labor exemption from the antitrust laws and may engage in collective bargaining with employers. Whether or not employed physicians have the protection of the National Labor Relations Act when they attempt to engage in collective bargaining depends on whether they are classified as supervisory or non-supervisory employees. Self-employed physicians in independent practice do not fall within the labor exemption from the antitrust laws and are not entitled to the protection of the National Labor Relations Act. They may not engage in collective bargaining with health plans.

Can Unions Engage in Collective Bargaining on Behalf of Physicians?

Some physicians believe that a union affiliated with the AFL-CIO that has been certified to represent an occupation in labor disputes can engage in collective bargaining on behalf of self-employed physicians in independent practice. That is not the case. The ability of any group of individuals to fit within the labor exemption and

thereby gain the protection of the National Labor Relations Act depends on the status of the individuals, not on the status of the organization that seeks to represent them. An AFL-CIO–affiliated union that has been certified to engage in collective bargaining on behalf of a defined group of employees is not permitted to engage in collective bargaining on behalf of any individuals outside the defined group, regardless of whether they are employees or not. Since self-employed physicians in independent practice are independent contractors, not employees, no person or entity can engage in collective bargaining on their behalf.

A union can engage in collective bargaining on behalf of employed physicians under the protection of the National Labor Relations Act, provided that the union has complied with the procedures required by the act for representation of employed physicians.

The Cost of Organizing a Union

The cost of organizing and maintaining a union can be substantial. Organizing the union generally means recruiting membership and petitioning for certification as the exclusive bargaining agent of physicians in the face of intense opposition from the employer. The costs of waging a recruitment drive and an election campaign can be high. The employer is likely to use all of the tactics it can (legal and otherwise) to persuade physicians not to join a union. It is common for the employer to use courtroom tactics to slow down and frustrate the organization process. Countering these tactics takes substantial personnel time and costs for publishing and distributing literature and may result in substantial attorney's fees. Litigation may occur over allegations of unfair labor practices, the configuration of the proposed bargaining unit, and other issues. It is important to bear in mind, though, that as larger unions increasingly target physicians for membership, those unions will also be increasingly willing to pour their own substantial financial and legal resources into these organizing efforts.

Once organized, the union needs to select and maintain a staff; work with attorneys, economists, and accountants to prepare negotiating positions; hold meetings; and communicate with members regularly. These activities all result in costs. As an example, a group of Virginia physicians considered organizing a union and discussed the matter with persons associated with the AFL-CIO. They were told that the physicians should have fifty charter members contributing $1,000 each and committing to pay $100 per month to the union for a year.

Union Formation by Medical Associations

Nothing in the antitrust laws prevents a medical association from acting as a labor organization and engaging in collective bargaining on behalf of employed physicians who qualify for the labor exemption. To qualify for the ability to represent physicians in collective bargaining under the protection of the National Labor Relations Act, the association must qualify as a labor organization as defined by that act and be certified by the National Labor Relations Board. Under the National Labor Relations Act, a labor organization is defined as any group, agency, committee, panel, or plan in which employees, as defined by the National Labor Relations Act, participate and that is established at least partially for the purpose of

dealing with the employer concerning grievances, conflicts, wages, rates of pay, hours, or other conditions of work. An entity does not have to have a formal internal structure to constitute a labor organization under the act.

Therefore, it should be possible for a medical society to act as a labor organization under the National Labor Relations Act. However, conflicts of interest could arise that might disqualify the society. For example, if some members of the board of trustees of the association are owners of HMOs or other health plans that the society wants to engage in collective bargaining, that conflict of interest may disqualify it.

Further, acting as a labor organization may compromise the tax-exempt status of a medical society. For example, to maintain tax-exempt status under Section 501(c)(6) of the Internal Revenue Code, the association must engage in activities that benefit all physicians, as opposed to a subset or a segment of physicians. Conferring a benefit on a narrow subset of physicians may disqualify the society's exemption. Therefore, if a medical society wishes to form a union, it may be appropriate to form a separate organization to act as the union.

What Can Self-Employed Physicians Do to Advocate the Right to Form Unions?

While self-employed physicians in independent practice do not fall within the labor exemption and, consequently, may not engage in collective bargaining, there are activities that either a medical society or a union may perform on their behalf. These activities are directed at resolving or preventing the abusive treatment of physicians by health plans (not including reducing fees) and expressing the opinions of physicians about economic and regulatory issues. The forums for these activities include legislatures, government regulatory agencies, the courts, and dialogues with health plans. Examples of activities that are permissible include the following.

Legislative and Judicial Advocacy

First, medical societies can reinforce their traditional function of forceful advocacy on behalf of physicians and patients before legislatures and courts. Government advocacy has resulted in significant victories for physicians. These efforts should be continued and must be communicated to members effectively. Medical societies are the only entities that represent physicians exclusively.

Advocacy before Health Plans on Medical Policy

Second, the antitrust laws allow medical societies to advocate medical policy before health plans. In the event that practicing physicians believe that a health plan is following a medical policy that harms patients, they may collectively demonstrate the error to the health plan and advocate an alternative policy. In fact, the antitrust guidelines issued by the Federal Trade Commission and the US Department of Justice in August 1996 create an antitrust safety zone for medical societies (and other physician groups) to provide medical information to health plans for the purpose of improving the quality of care or the efficiency with which care is rendered. Therefore, when practicing physicians disagree with a health plan's medical policy, a medical society can marshal information in support of the physicians' views, confront the health plan, and advocate that the health plan change its medical policies. The medical society can-

not, however, threaten or lead a boycott of a health plan that does not change its policies. In addition, the advocacy carried on by the medical society cannot be coercive in nature, as this conduct may be interpreted as a threat to boycott by the health plan. But a medical society can take the issue to the media, to legislatures, and to the courts if an abusive practice is not corrected.

Advocacy about the "Hassle Factor"

Third, the antitrust laws allow medical societies to advocate the resolution of nonfee-related logistical issues with health plans on behalf of members, such as inefficient administrative processes that raise physicians' costs, undue delays in preauthorization of services, delays in paying claims, poor grievance procedures, and others. When practicing physicians or their patients are adversely affected by one of these problems, a medical society may marshal information about the problem, confront the health plan about the issue, and advocate a resolution. This kind of representation can be carried on with an individual health plan, with a group of plans, or with a health plan association. Some state and county medical societies already effectively engage in this kind of advocacy with payers. As with medical information, the medical society cannot threaten or lead a boycott of a health plan that does not change its policies. However, a medical society can take an issue to the media, legislatures, and the courts if an abusive practice is not corrected by health plans.

Assistance to Individual Members

A medical society can advocate on behalf of individual members who have a grievance or a problem with a health plan. For example, a physician may have been terminated from a health plan's provider panel for reasons that the physician believes to be unfair. The physician may have violated a gag policy or have challenged medical policy decisions of the health plan. The health plan may have been arbitrary in its treatment of the physician. A medical society can aggressively advocate on behalf of the physician with the health plan. A medical society cannot threaten or lead a boycott if a health plan does not resolve the issue satisfactorily. Once again the issue can be taken to other forums, such as courts, if a health plan does not correct arbitrary, unfair, or abusive treatment.

Development and Dissemination of Strategies for Succeeding in the Evolving Health Care System

For physicians to preserve their autonomy and to thrive in the evolving health care system, it is essential that they receive information about market developments and strategies and options for adapting to change. Medical societies can be trusted and credible sources of this information.

Forming a Management Services Organization or Health Plan

A number of state societies have formed management services organizations to assist physicians who want to organize networks. The services handled by management services organizations include consultation and administrative functions that require expensive computer software, hardware, and personnel, such as claims administration, eligibility, and data gathering for utilization review and medical management. Startup physician networks can get the benefit of sophisticated services without making major investments by relying on medical society management services organizations. Some

states have formed health plans such as HMOs or PPOs. Some county societies have formed their own health plans.

An Overview of Specific Unions

The following are brief profiles of the currently existing unions involved in some form of advocacy on behalf of physicians.

Union of American Physicians and Dentists

The Union of American Physicians and Dentists (UPD) is currently the largest union representing physicians, with about five thousand members. According to its staff, about 55 percent of the members are employed physicians and about 45 percent are self-employed in independent practice. Dues are $700 a year for employed physicians and $420 for self-employed physicians. The disparity is attributed to the fact that the union can engage in collective bargaining for the employed physicians but is barred by federal antitrust laws from bargaining on behalf of self-employed physicians.

UPD is affiliated with the American Federation of State, County, and Municipal Employees (AFSCME), a large union affiliated with the AFL-CIO. AFSCME became interested in representing physicians because it has organized unions at hospitals owned by state or local units of government and has included employed physicians. Rules of the National Labor Relations Board allow physicians to form separate bargaining units at hospitals.

Federation of Physicians and Dentists

With about twenty-five hundred members, the Federation of Physicians and Dentists (FPD) is the second largest union representing practicing physicians. It is affiliated with the National Union of Hospital and Health Care Employees, AFSCME, and the AFL-CIO. The union is based in Tallahassee, Florida, and represents about 33 percent of the physicians in Brevard County, Florida.

According to a 1998 article in *Medical Economics,* the leaders of this union are seeking avenues to challenge established labor laws.[16] The union claims to have plans to appeal to the Federal Trade Commission and the National Labor Relations Board for an interpretation of federal antitrust and labor laws that would allow independent physicians to engage in collective bargaining. It plans to argue that self-employed physicians are so highly controlled by health plans that they are, in reality, employees. To date, however, no actions have been taken by the FPD in this regard.

In fact, another union beat the FPD to the punch on this issue. In October 1997, Local 56 of the United Food and Commercial Workers filed a petition with the National Labor Relations Board (NLRB) to recognize it as the exclusive bargaining agent of a group of self-employed physicians who contracted to participate in an HMO. The NLRB denied the petition in January 1998.

Doctors Council of New York

The third largest union is the Doctors Council of New York (DCNY), which represents thirty-four hundred attending physicians, dentists, podiatrists, and veterinarians employed by New York City agencies, hospitals, and clinics. In 1991, this union led a strike at New York's Woodhull Medical Center to prevent layoffs of hospital personnel and to restore certain serv-

ices. The strike led to a settlement. At one time, DCNY represented ten thousand physicians in six states, but it halted activities outside New York when the Federal Trade Commission warned of possible antitrust violations.

Office Professionals and Employees International Union

Of the three substantial nonphysician unions that have entered the market for representing physicians, the Office Professionals and Employees International Union (OPEIU) has had the most reported success to date. It has affiliated with the American Podiatric Medical Association and has formed the First National Guild for Providers of the Lower Extremities. State chapters of the guild have been formed in Pennsylvania, California, Michigan, and New Hampshire. Others are being formed in at least three more states. OPEIU expects to enroll ten thousand of the nation's fourteen thousand podiatrists. However, there have been no reports of unions of allopathic physicians formed by the OPEIU.

OPEIU does not plan to engage in collective bargaining on behalf of self-employed podiatrists. To attract members, it emphasizes its relationship with the AFL-CIO and the influence of that organization in the Democratic Party. It contends that it will be an effective lobbyist. It also emphasizes its relationship with union-sponsored and Taft-Hartley health plans through the AFL-CIO and its influence over the health benefits of large, self-funded employers through collective-bargaining agreements negotiated by other AFL-CIO unions. OPEIU hopes to ensure coverage for podiatry services through those relationships.

Service Employees International Union

Another major union that hopes to expand the number of physicians that it represents is the Service Employees International Union. The fastest-growing union in the AFL-CIO, it has 1.3 million members nationwide, among whom about six hundred thousand are health care workers, including nurses, medical technicians, and other hospital employees. Following an eleven-year struggle, the SEIU in February 1999 won a vote to represent seventy-four thousand Los Angeles home care workers, organized labor's biggest victory in sixty years. The following month, the union's president, Andrew Stern, announced a major push to unionize physicians around the country.[17]

American Federation of State, County and Municipal Employees

The American Federation of State, Country, and Municipal Employees is a large and aggressive union affiliated with the AFL-CIO. Its interest in representing physicians derives from its work with hospitals owned by state or local units of government that have physicians as employees. It has affiliated with the UPD and the FPD.

Committee on Interns and Residents

The largest union of residents is the Committee on Interns and Residents (CIR). It is based in New York City and represents almost ten thousand residents in about fifty hospitals. It has led strikes, has engaged in collective bargaining, and has grown by nearly 40 percent in 1996–1997. In 1975, CIR led a strike of New York City interns and residents that resulted in the elimination of every-other-night call. In 1996, CIR

voted to affiliate with the Service Employees International Union of the AFL-CIO.

California Association of Interns and Residents

The California Association of Interns and Residents is the other major union of residents and has one thousand to two thousand members. It is affiliated with the Hospital and Health Care Workers Union 250 based in Oakland, California.

Conclusion

If managed care organizations and HMOs continue to grow in size, in presence, and especially in their power to dictate the terms and conditions of participation in their health care provider networks, physicians will continue to feel pressure to be part of some sort of entity—be it a large multispecialty practice or a hospital—to gain some bargaining power. Those physicians who would like to maintain the autonomy or other advantages of solo practice or small groups will be looking for alternative means by which to voice their concerns and wield some meaningful leverage in their service contracts. Therefore, the formation of physicians' unions and advocacy for changes in the labor and antitrust laws are likely to be hot topics for physicians in the next several years. Wisdom dictates that concerned physicians stay informed about these issues, pay attention to the surrounding debates, and get involved in advocating needed reforms. If physicians' voices are not heard on these issues, it is likely that both they and their patients will bear the consequences.

1. *See Thomas Davis Medical Centers v Federation of Physicians and Dentists.* Case No 28-RC-5449, National Labor Relations

Board Region 28 (Nov 8, 1996). This decision was affirmed by the National Labor Relations Board under the name *FPA Medical Management, Inc, and United Health Care Employees, NUHHCE, AFSCME, AFL-CIO,* 324 NLRB 128 (Oct 22, 1997).

2. Parts of this chapter were adapted with permission from an April 1998 seminar paper presented by the late Edward B. Hirshfeld, former associate general counsel of the American Medical Association, to the Physicians, Physician Organizations and PPMCs Law Institute held in Nashville, Tenn, by the American Health Lawyers Association.

3. These statistics are reported in Hirshfeld, *supra* note 2.

4. *See generally* Grace Budrys, *When Doctors Join Unions* (Ithaca: Cornell University Press, 1997).

5. T.A. Barocci, "Bargaining Strategies Among Physicians, USA," in *Industrial Relations and Health Services* 238 (Amarit Singh Sethi and Stuart J. Dimmock, eds, 1982).

6. *Cedars-Sinai Medical Center and Cedars Sinai Housestaff Ass'n,* 223 NLRB 251 (1976).

7. *University of California v Public Employment Relations Board,* 715 P2d 590 (1986).

8. Daniel W. Srsic, "Collective Bargaining by Physicians in the United States and Canada," 15 Comparative Labor Law 89, 105–107 (1993).

9. American Medical Association, Policy Compendium (1997), §§ H-385.971, H-385.973, H-385.976, H-385.983.

10. *Id* at H-405.998.

11. *See* Daniel J. Gifford, "Redefining the Antitrust Labor Exemption," 72 Minnesota Law Review 1379 (1988) for a discussion of the conflict between the purposes of the federal antitrust laws and the federal labor laws.

12. *Loewe v Lawlor,* 208 US 274 (1908); *Gompers v Bucks Stove & Range Co* 221 US 418 (1911).

13. *See generally* Earl W. Kintner & Joseph P. Bauer, *Federal Antitrust Laws,* vol IX § 72.7 pp 311–324 (Cincinnati, Ohio: Anderson Publishing Co, 1989).

14. Mary Chris Jaklevic, "Physicians Find Power in Unions," Modern Health Care 99 (Oct 6, 1997).

15. 322 US 111 (1944).

16. Robert L. Lowes, "Strength in Numbers: Could Doctor Unions Really Be the Answer?" 75 Medical Economics 115 (June 29, 1998).

17. "The Labor Movement's Eager Risk-Taker Hits Another Jackpot," *New York Times* page A10 (national edition, Feb 27, 1999).

Glossary

Abandonment: Physician's unilateral termination of a patient-physician relationship without the patient's consent at a time when the patient requires medical attention, without making adequate arrangements for continued care.

Abuse: A manner of operation that results in excessive or unreasonable costs to the Medicare or Medicaid programs.

Abuse of process: Use of legal mechanisms in a manner or for a purpose not supported by law. For example, pursuit of litigation based on little or no legal grounds, intended to harass and cause expense to a defendant. Damages may be recovered for expenses or loss caused a defendant by abuse of process.

Accrete: Term used by Medicare to describe the process of adding new enrollees to a health plan. *See also* **Delete**.

Action: Legal action; lawsuit.

Administrative law judge (ALJ): An employee of an agency, in particular the Department of Health and Human Services, who presides over civil fraud and abuse administrative hearings brought by the Office of Inspector General. The ALJ's decision is final and binding thirty days after it is served on the parties unless the decision is appealed to the Department Appeals Board (DAB) or the DAB grants an extension of time to file an appeal.

Admissibility of evidence: Refers to the issue of whether a court, applying the rules of evidence, is bound to receive or permit introduction of a particular piece of proof.

Advance directive: Written instructions expressing an individuals' health care wishes in the event they become incapacitated and unable to make them.

Affidavit: Sworn statement for use in trial or other legal process.

Affirmative defense: An answer to a lawsuit that does not deny the alleged conduct or failure but asserts a legal basis to excuse or foreclose liability. Examples include a statute of limitations defense or Good-Samaritan immunity.

Agency: A relationship between parties in which one party authorizes the other party to act for or to represent him or her.

Agent: A person authorized by another, known as the principal, to act for or represent the principal.

Allegation: Asserted fact or circumstance expected to be proved at trial.

Ambulatory patient group (APG): A reimbursement methodology developed by 3M Health Information Systems for the HCFA. APGs are to outpatient procedures what DRGs are to inpatient days. APGs provide for a fixed reimbursement to an institution for outpatient procedures or visits and incorporate data regarding the reason for the visit and patient data. APGs prevent unbundling of ancillary services.

Ambulatory surgical center: A freestanding, self-contained facility providing outpatient surgical services to patients who do not require inpatient hospitalization.

American Association of Health Plans (AAHP): The trade association that represents all forms of managed care organizations. Created in 1996 by the merger of the GHAA and the AMCRA. Based in Washington, DC, the AAHP has a heavy focus on lobbying, educational activities, and service to member plans.

American Managed Care and Review Association (AMCRA): A trade association that represented managed indemnity plans, PPOs, MCOs, and HMOs. Merged with GHAA in 1995 to become the AAHP in 1996.

Americans with Disabilities Act (ADA): Federal act that bars employers from discrimination against disabled persons in hiring, promotion, or other provisions of employment.

Anti-kickback statute: A provision of the Social Security Act that forbids any knowing and willful conduct involving the solicitation, receipt, offer, or payment of any kind of remuneration in return for referring an individual for any Medicaid- or Medicare-covered item or service or for recommending or arranging the purchase, lease, or order of an item or service that may be wholly or partially paid for through the Medicare or Medicaid programs. Violation of the anti-kickback provisions can result in a fine of up to $25,000 and up to five years' imprisonment.

Antisupplementation Provision: A provision of the Social Security Act that makes it a criminal offense to charge a higher amount than the Medicaid rate for a covered service provided to a Medicaid beneficiary. Violation of this provision can subject an individual to a fine of up to $25,000 and up to five years' imprisonment.

Apparent agency doctrine (APG): Doctrine which holds that a principal who represents to a third party that another is her agent is liable for harm caused to the third party by the apparent agent if the third party justifiably relied on the principal's representation. As an example, a health care organization can be held liable for the negligence of an independent private practicing physician if it can be shown that the organization failed properly to monitor the physician.

Appeal: A claim to a superior court of error in process or law by a lower court, asking the superior court to correct or reverse a judgment or decision. An appeals court has the power to review the decisions made in the trial court or a lower appellate court. An appellate court does not make a new determination of the facts, but examines the law and legal process as applied to the case.

Appellant: Party who appeals the decision of a lower court to a court of higher jurisdiction.

Arbitration: The reference of a dispute to an impartial third person chosen by the parties to the dispute who agree in advance to abide by the arbitrator's award issued after a hearing at which both parties have an opportunity to be heard.

Assault: Intentional act designed to make the victim fearful and produce reasonable apprehension of harm.

Assignment: Transfer of rights, responsibilities, or property from one party to another.

Assignment of benefits: The payment of medical benefits directly to a provider of care rather than to a member. Generally requires either a contract between the health plan and the provider or a written release from the subscriber to the provider allowing the provider to bill the health plan.

Attachment: A prejudgment remedy where a court orders seizure of a property by a sheriff who retains custody pending judgment.

Automatic stay: An order that, upon the filing of a bankruptcy petition, provides immediate, automatic protection to a debtor from virtually all creditors and from virtually all creditor activity. Among other things, it restrains creditors from collecting debts or other obligations that arose before bankruptcy and from continuing or commencing lawsuits against the debtor. If a creditor wants to pursue, for example, a lawsuit or collect a debt after a bankruptcy is filed, it must seek and obtain an order from the bankruptcy court granting it relief from the automatic stay.

Battery: Intentional and unauthorized physical contact with a person, without consent. An example would be a surgical procedure performed without express or implied consent. Victims of medical battery may obtain compensation for this contact, even if no negligence occurred.

Borrowed servant doctrine: Refers to a situation in which an employee is temporarily under the control of someone other than his or her primary employer. It may involve a situation in which an employee is carrying out the specific instructions of a physician. The traditional example is that of a nurse employed by a hospital who is "borrowed" and under the control of the attending surgeon during a procedure in the operating room. The temporary employer of the borrowed servant can be held responsible for the negligent acts of the borrowed servant under the doctrine of *respondeat superior* (see definition below).

Breach of contract: Failure to perform any requirement of a contract. If a legally enforceable contract is created, performance of promises contained in that contract may be compelled or the injured party may obtain compensation for damages from a court.

Burden of proof: Responsibility of proving certain facts necessary to support a lawsuit. If this burden is not met, the opposing side prevails on that issue, even without raising a defense or filing a response.

Capitation: Under standard capitation arrangements for specialists, the plan or provider group makes a set payment each month for each member. In return, the specialists must give these members any medically necessary covered services, as defined by the contract.

Captain of the ship doctrine: A particular doctrine making the physician responsible for the negligent acts of other professionals because he had the right to control and oversee the totality of care provided to the patient. Under this doctrine, the surgeon may be vicariously liable for the negligent act of any member of the surgical team. This doctrine is the law in some states but not in others.

Case in chief: That part of a trial in which the party with the initial burden of proof presents his evidence after which he rests.

Case law: Legal principles applied to specific fact situations. Case law is drawn from written court decisions in similar cases in a state or other jurisdiction. Case law is used to make decisions that are based on precedent, the judicial principle which requires that similar cases be treated alike. The entire body of case law principles is known as the common law.

Cause: A reasonable connection between an act or failure to act alleged as negligence and an injury sustained by the plaintiff. In a lawsuit for negligence, the issue of causation usually requires proof that the negligence of the defendant directly resulted in or was a substantial factor in the plaintiff's injury.

Cause of action: Facts or circumstances that support a legal right to seek corrective action or compensation.

Certificate of need (CON): The requirement that a health care organization obtain permission from an oversight agency before making changes. Generally applies only to facilities, capital equipment, and facilities-based services.

Chapter 7 case: A case filed under Chapter 7 of the Bankruptcy Code requires a debtor to relinquish ownership of his, her, or its assets, except certain exempt property, to a trustee who liquidates the assets and distributes the proceeds to creditors according to the priority scheme set forth in the code. For the individual, the notion of the fresh start discharging him or her from pre-petition debts is at the heart of this type of bankruptcy.

Chapter 11 case: A case filed under Chapter 11 of the Bankruptcy Code allows the debtor (which can be a business or an individual) to reorganize its financial affairs or orderly liquidate its assets pursuant to a plan of reorganization or liquidation. Under Chapter 11, a debtor usually remains in possession of its assets; the court, in certain circumstances, can appoint a Chapter 11 trustee to administer the estate.

Chapter 13 case: A case filed under Chapter 13 of the Bankruptcy Code allows an individual, meeting certain qualifications, including the maintenance of a steady income and debt not exceeding certain dollar amounts, to pay a portion of his or her debts over a period not to exceed five years.

Charitable immunity: Legal doctrine that developed out of the English court system and held charitable institutions blameless for their negligent acts. This immunity has been abolished in most states in recent years because of the widespread availability of commercial insurance.

Children's Health Insurance Program (CHIP): Federal initiative allocating funds to the states to expand health insurance to children whose families earn too much for traditional Medicaid yet not enough to afford private health insurance. Congress enacted the legislation creating this program in 1997.

Civil action: Legal proceeding by a party seeking correction or compensation, as distinguished from a criminal action, which is brought by the state to punish breaches of public order.

Civilian Health and Medical Program of the Uniform Services (CHAMPUS): The federal program providing health care coverage to families of military personnel, military retirees, certain spouses and dependents of such personnel, and certain others.

Civil investigative demand: The attorney general has the authority to serve a civil investigative demand on a person who may be in possession of any documents or information relating to a false claims investigation. A demand imposes a broader range of requests than an Office of Inspector General subpoena, including producing documents, providing responses to written interrogatories, or giving oral testimony concerning documentary material.

Civil liability: Legal responsibility to compensate for losses or injuries caused by acts or failures to act. Compensation is awarded as money damages paid by the defendant to the plaintiff. Civil liability is limited to monetary damages. A single act, however, may be both a criminal act and a civil wrong, also known as a tort.

Civil Monetary Penalty Law (CMPL): Under this law, the Office of Inspector General may bring administrative actions against providers who submit false or fraudulent claims to the United States or its agent for a medical item or service. The OIG need only demonstrate that the person knew or should have known that the claim was false or fraudulent. The penalty for violation of this law can be a fine of up to $2,000 for each item or service that is submitted, or a fine of $50,000 for violations regarding patient stabilization and appropriate transfers. In addition, the provider can be terminated from Medicare, Medicaid, and other state health programs.

Claim fraud: Use of various means (material misrepresentation, exaggeration of an injury, alteration of medical bills, and so on) to obtain benefits to which an insured or a physician is not entitled.

Clear and convincing evidence: A level of persuasion required to support certain non-criminal legal actions.

Clinical privileges: On qualification, the diagnostic and therapeutic procedures an institution allows a physician to perform on a specified patient population. Qualification includes a review of a physician's credentials, such as medical school diploma, state licensure, and residency training.

Clinical Laboratory Improvement Amendments of 1988 (CLIA): A federal law subjecting nearly all clinical laboratories operating in the United States—whether they are located in hospitals, physicians' offices, or freestanding facilities—to comprehensive federal quality regulation.

Code: Collection of laws in a state or on a particular topic. Examples include the Official Code of Georgia, the US Bankruptcy Code, and the Internal Revenue Code. These are constantly updated as a state legislature or Congress enacts new legislation.

Coinsurance: A provision in a member's coverage that limits the amount of coverage by the plan to a certain percentage, commonly 80 percent. Any additional costs are paid by the member out of pocket.

Common law: Body of principles that has evolved and continues to evolve from court decisions. Many of the legal principles and rules applied by courts in the United States had their origins in English common law.

Community rating: The rating methodology required of federally qualified HMOs, HMOs under the laws of many states, and occasionally indemnity plans under certain circumstances. The HMO must obtain the same amount of money per member for all members in the plan. Community rating does allow for variability by allowing the HMO to factor in differences in age, sex, mix (average contract size), and industry factors. Not all factors are necessarily allowed under state law. *See also* **Experience rating.**

Competitive medical plan (CMP): A federal designation that allows a health plan to contract for a Medicare risk contract without becoming a federally qualified health maintenance organization (HMO). Like an HMO, a CMP provides health care prepaid. However, a CMP differs from a federally qualified HMO because services must be provided primarily through the CMP, a CMP may be able to limit the scope of some of the services it is required to offer, and a CMP can require higher copayments and deductibles.

Complaint: A lawsuit; the initial document that a plaintiff files that commences a civil action. The complaint is intended to give the defendant notice of the basic facts alleged in the cause of action upon which the plaintiff demands compensation from her or corrective action by her.

Concurrent review: Refers to utilization management that takes place during the provision of services. Almost exclusively applies to inpatient hospital stays.

Consent: Agreement to accept the outcome of an action, such as to permit another person to perform some act or take part in some activity.

Consolidated Omnibus Budget Reconciliation Act (COBRA): Federal statute requiring employers with more than twenty employees to make group health coverage available for eighteen months, at employee expense, to employees who leave the employer for any reason other than gross misconduct.

Continuing care retirement community (CCRC): Self-sufficient life-care community in which residents, for a substantial entry fee along with a monthly maintenance fee, enter into a contractual relationship with the community that can last until the end of the resident's life.

Contract capitation: As in standard forms of capitation, the plan or provider organization makes capitation payments to specialists based on the number of members they are responsible for treating. However, in this form of capitation, a specialist does not get capitation credit for a member until the first appointment the member has with the specialist.

Corporate compliance program: A program designed, implemented, and enforced by a corporation to detect and prevent violations of fraud and abuse laws.

Corporate death sentence: A penalty that may be imposed under the federal *Guidelines on Sentencing of Organizations* on a corporation that does not take effective measures to prevent wrongdoing among its employees. If a death sentence is imposed on a corporation, the corporation will be fined an amount sufficient to divest it of all net assets.

Corporate practice of medicine acts or statutes: State laws that prohibit a physician from working for a corporation. In other words, a physician can only work for himself, herself, or another physician. Often asserted by certain members of the medical community to prevent doctors from working directly for managed care plans or hospitals.

Cost sharing: Any form of insurance coverage in which the member pays some portion of the cost of providing services. Typical types of cost sharing include deductibles, coinsurance, and copayments.

Cost shifting: When a provider cannot cover the cost of providing services under the reimbursement received, the provider raises prices to other payers to cover that portion of the cost. Some of the costs are shifted to and absorbed by private health insurance.

Counterclaim: Defendant's claim in opposition to a claim of the plaintiff.

Credentialing: The most common use of the term refers to obtaining and reviewing the documentation of professional providers. Such documentation includes licensure, certifications, insurance, evidence of malpractice insurance, malpractice history, and so forth. Generally includes both reviewing information provided by the provider and verification that the information is correct and complete. A less common use of the term applies to closed panels and medical groups and refers to obtaining hospital privileges and other privileges to practice medicine.

Crime: Act against society in violation of the law. Crimes are prosecuted by and in the name of the state.

Criminal negligence: Reckless disregard for the safety of others. It is the willfull indifference to an injury which could follow an act.

Damages: Money that a person receives by a court's order to redress harm or loss. There are a number of kinds of damages. *Compensatory damages* reimburse a person for lost income and medical expenses. *Nominal damages* are sometimes awarded even where no actual economic or noneconomic damages are suffered in order for the court to convey that a legally recognized error has been committed. Courts sometimes award *hedonic damages* for the loss of life's enjoyment. *Punitive damages* are those awarded to inflict economic punishment on defendants whom the court finds acted maliciously or in reckless disregard of the rights of others.

Death spiral: An insurance term that refers to a spiral of high premium rates and adverse selection, generally in a free-choice environment (typically, an insurance company or health plan in an account with multiple other plans or a plan offering coverage to potential members who have alternative choices, such as through an association). One plan, often the indemnity plan competing with managed care plans, ends up having continually higher premium rates such that the only members who stay with the plan are those whose medical costs are so high (and who cannot change because of provider loyalty or benefits restrictions, such as preexisting conditions) that they far exceed any possible premium revenue. Called the *death spiral* because the losses from underwriting mount faster than the premiums can ever recover, the account eventually terminates coverage, leaving the carrier in a permanent loss position.

Decedent: Legal term for a dead person.

Declarations page: The portion of an insurance policy that sets forth a general statement of the areas covered by the policy, policy limits, any applicable deductibles, and other basic information such as what individuals are specifically covered under the policy.

Deductible: The portion of a subscriber's (or member's) health care expenses that must be paid out of pocket before any insurance coverage applies, commonly $100 to $500. Common in insurance plans and PPOs, but uncommon in HMOs. May apply only to the out-of-network portion of a point-of-service plan. May also apply only to one portion of the plan coverage (for example, there may be a deductible for

pharmacy services but not for any other services).

Defamation: Intentional communication of false personal or business information that injures the reputation or prospects of another. Written defamation is known as libel. Spoken defamation is known as slander.

Defensive medicine: Physician use of extensive laboratory tests, increased hospital admissions, and extended hospital stays for the principal purpose of reducing the likelihood of malpractice suits by patients or providing a good legal defense in the event of such lawsuits.

Delete: The term used by the HCFA for the process of removing Medicare enrollees from a plan. *See also* **Accrete**.

Departmental Appeals Board (DAB): In a civil action brought by the Office of Inspector General, a party may appeal an ALJ's decision to the DAB. The DAB's decision is final and binding sixty days after the parties are notified of the decision. Any petition for review of the DAB's decision must be filed with the appropriate US Court of Appeals before the sixty-day period has expired.

Department of Health and Human Services (HHS): This cabinet-level department, through the Health Care Financing Administration, administers the Medicare and Medicaid programs and is the federal agency primarily concerned with health care fraud.

Department of Justice: Cabinet department responsible for the enforcement of health care fraud and abuse at the federal level. Health care fraud may be prosecuted by the antitrust, civil, and/or criminal divisions.

Deposition: Part of the pretrial discovery process in which a statement is taken under oath in the presence of a court reporter. The statement may be admitted into evidence if the witness is to attend in person. Deposition testimony may also be used to cross-examine a witness at trial.

Diagnosis-related group (DRG): A statistical system of classifying any inpatient stay into groups for the purpose of payment. The DRG classification system divides possible diagnoses into more than twenty major body systems and subdivides them into almost five hundred groups for purpose of Medicare reimbursement. Factors used to determine the DRG payment amount include the diagnosis involved as well as the hospital resources necessary to treat the condition. Also used by a few states for all payers and by many private health plans (usually non-HMO) for contracting purposes. Hospitals are paid a fixed rate for inpatient services corresponding to the DRG group assigned to a given patient.

Disclaimer: Repudiation of a claim vested in a person.

Discovery: Pretrial activities in the litigation process to determine the central questions and issues in dispute and evidence each side will present at trial. Discovery is intended to narrow trial questions to a minimum and to allow fair presentation of opposing evidence without surprise at trial. The discovery process also discloses information to the various parties that may ease out-of-court settlement.

Disenrollment: The process of termination of health-insurance coverage. Voluntary termination would include a member quitting because he or she simply wants out.

Involuntary termination would include a member leaving a plan because of changing employment. Another form of involuntary disenrollment is when the plan terminates a member's coverage against the member's will. This is usually permissible under state and federal laws for gross offenses such as fraud, abuse, nonpayment of premium or copayments, or a demonstrated inability to comply with recommended treatment plans.

DRG creep: The placement of patients in a higher-value DRG than is warranted by the patient's condition to receive higher Medicare reimbursement.

DRG payment window: The window of time before a patient's admission to a hospital when the services provided to the patient are eligible for Medicare reimbursement. Between the advent of a prospective payment system in 1983 and 1990, hospitals were eligible for reimbursement for outpatient services provided in the twenty-four hours before admission. In 1990, Congress expanded the DRG payment window to include services provided during the three days before admission and expanded services to include not only outpatient services but services furnished by any entity wholly owned or operated by the hospital.

Due care: Level of reasonable and ordinary observation and awareness owed by one person to another in specific relationships or circumstances. An example is the physician's duty of due care in attending to a patient. Due care anticipates and appropriately manages known, expected, or foreseeable events and complications of the patient's disease or treatment.

Due process: Level of fair method required by the US Constitution in execution of government activities. Due process in legal proceedings must reflect both fairness in substance (ie, the activity is appropriate and constitutional) and fairness in procedure (ie, a method of proceeding that affords persons involved in the proceeding with notice and opportunity to present evidence and advocate on their own behalf).

Durable medical equipment (DME): Medical equipment that is not disposable and is only related to care for a medical condition. Examples include wheelchairs, home hospital beds, and so forth. An area of increasing expense, particularly in conjunction with case management. DME is covered by Medicare Part B.

Durable power of attorney: Legal instrument enabling an individual to act on another's behalf. In the health care setting, it includes the authority to make medical decisions for another.

Early and Periodic Screening, Diagnostic and Treatment mandate of the Medicaid Act (EPSDT): This federal law requires states to provide any service that Medicaid offers and a physician has deemed "medically necessary."

Employee Retirement Income Security Act of 1974 (ERISA): This law establishes minimal participation, funding, and termination standards for employer-sponsored pension plans and health-insurance plans.

Endorsement: A provision added, often for an additional premium, to an insurance policy to add a particular form or type of coverage that the policy does not expressly provide—or even one that it excludes—in its remaining sections.

Equity model: A term applied to a form of for-profit, vertically integrated health care delivery systems in which the physicians are owners.

Ethics in Patient Referrals Act: Official name for the federal laws that have become known as the Stark Laws or Stark I and Stark II. *See* **Stark I** and **Stark II**.

Euthanasia: Act conducted for the purpose of causing the death of a person suffering from a medical condition.

Evidence: Proof of a fact, which is legally presented in a manner prescribed by law, at trial.

Evidence of insurability: The form that documents whether an individual is eligible for health plan coverage when the individual does not enroll through an open enrollment period. For example, if an employee wants to change health plans in the middle of a contract year, the new health plan may require evidence of insurability, often both a questionnaire and a medical examination, to ensure that it will not be accepting adverse risk.

Exclusion: An insurance policy provision that expressly disclaims coverage or otherwise withdraws coverage that might otherwise be included under the policy language.

Experience rating: The method of setting premium rates based on the actual health care costs of a group or groups.

Expert witness: Person invited to testify at a hearing or trial who brings special knowledge, skill, or training to the proceeding where matters in dispute are beyond the average person's knowledge. Unlike a fact witness, who testifies because of her involvement in the facts of the dispute, an expert witness may be asked for an opinion about specific issues in the case. Experts educate the court about the scientific, engineering, medical, or other specialized circumstances involved in the dispute. Unlike fact witnesses, expert witnesses are typically compensated for their time in court.

Extracontractual benefits: Health care benefits beyond the scope of the member's actual policy. These benefits are provided by a plan to reduce utilization. For example, a plan may not provide coverage for a hospital bed at home, but it is more cost effective for the plan to provide such a benefit than to continue admitting a member to a hospital.

False Claims Act (FCA): The criminal False Claims Act makes it illegal to present a claim upon or against the US government that the claimant knows to be false, fictitious, or fraudulent. The civil False Claims Act provides that any person who knowingly presents, or causes to be presented, to the US government a false or fraudulent claim for payment or approval; knowingly makes, uses, or causes to be made or used a false record or statement to get a false or fraudulent claim paid or approved by the government; or conspires to defraud the government by getting a false or fraudulent claim allowed or paid violates the act. The act also has *qui tam* provisions. (*See **Qui tam,*** below.) Under the civil provisions of the FCA, a defendant can be assessed a penalty of at least $5,000 and as much as $10,000 per claim, plus three times the damages incurred by the federal government in its prosecution and investigation of the case. The criminal provisions provide for a fine of $25,000 and up to five years' imprisonment upon conviction.

False statements statutes: Any law that prohibits any false, fictitious, or fraudulent statement to the United States or any government agency. Such laws are often used to prosecute health care providers who make false Medicare or Medicaid claims.

Favored nation discount: A contractual provision between a provider and a payer stating that the provider will automatically provide the payer the best discount it provides anyone else.

Federal acquisitions regulations (FAR): The regulations applied to the federal government's acquisition of services, including health care services.

Federal Bureau of Investigation (FBI): As the federal government's law enforcement agency, the FBI investigates federal crimes, including health care fraud.

Federal Employees Health Benefits Program (FEHBP): The health insurance program for federal employees and their families. The FEHBP is administered by the US Office of Personnel Management.

Federally qualified health center (FQHC): An entity that has entered into an agreement with the Health Care Financing Administration (HCFA) to meet Medicare program requirements and is receiving a grant under Sections 329, 330, or 340 of the Public Health Service Act.

Federal qualification: Applies to HMOs. It means that the HMO meets federal standards regarding benefits, financial solvency, rating methods, marketing, member services, health care delivery systems, and other standards. An HMO must apply for federal qualification and be examined by the Office of Managed Care, including an on-site review.

Federal qualification does place some restrictions on how a plan operates but also allows it to enter Medicare and FEHBP markets in an expedited way. Federal qualification is voluntary and not required to enter the market.

Felony: Serious crime usually punishable by imprisonment for a period of longer than one year or by death.

Fiduciary: A person in a position of trust or confidence who undertakes a particular duty to act for the benefit of another who must trust the good intention and performance of the fiduciary. Because of the disparity in power and knowledge between the fiduciary and the beneficiary, the law places unusually high standards of behavior on fiduciaries. Examples of fiduciary relationships include parent and child, doctor and patient, guardian and ward, attorney and client, estate trustee and beneficiary.

Finder of fact: In a trial, the jury, or the judge in trials conducted without juries.

Foundation: A not-for-profit form of integrated health care delivery system. The foundation model is usually formed in response to tax laws that affect not-for-profit hospitals or in response to state laws prohibiting the corporate practice of medicine. The foundation purchases both the tangible and intangible assets of a physician's practice, but the physicians then form a medical group that contracts with the foundation exclusively for services to patients seen through the foundation.

Fragmented claims: Billing separately for procedures rather than using a global billing code covering all of these services, when billing separately produces a higher payment rate.

Fraud: Intentional misinformation, misdirection, or misrepresentation to another person that causes legal injury or loss to that person. Fraud is an intentional wrong. Examples of fraud in medical practice would be to mislead patients about indicated procedures or therapies, to misstate diagnoses or treatment codes to falsely maximize reimbursement, or to conspire with patients to misrepresent injuries to obtain undeserved benefits.

Fraud alerts: During the past few years, the Office of the Inspector General has issued fraud alerts as a way of informing the health care industry about prohibited practices.

Full capitation: Term used to refer to a physician group organization receiving capitation for all professional expenses, not just for the services it provides itself. It does not include capitation for institutional services. The group is then responsible for subcapitating or otherwise reimbursing other physicians for services to its members.

Gatekeeper: An informal, although widely used, term that refers to a model for a primary care case-management health plan. In this model, all care from providers other than the primary care physician, except for true emergencies, must be authorized by the primary care physician before being rendered. This is a predominant feature of almost all HMOs.

Global capitation: A capitation payment that covers all medical expenses, including professional and institutional expenses, and may not necessarily cover optional benefits (for example, pharmacy). Often called total capitation.

Good-Samaritan statute: Law enacted by a state legislature to encourage physicians and others to stop and assist emergency victims. Good-Samaritan laws grant immunity from liability for negligence to a person who responds and administers care to a person in an emergency situation. Statutes vary from state to state in their specifics.

Grand jury: Jury called to determine whether there is sufficient evidence that a crime has been committed to justify bringing a case to trial. It is not the jury before which the case is tried to determine guilt or innocence.

Group model HMO: An HMO that contracts with a medical group for the provision of health care services. The relationship between the HMO and the medical group is generally close, although there are wide variations in the relative independence of the group from the HMO.

Group practice: The AMA defines group practice as three or more physicians who deliver patient care, make joint use of equipment and personnel, and divide income by a prearranged formula.

Group practice without walls (GPWW): A group practice in which the members of the group come together legally but continue to practice in private offices scattered throughout the service area. Sometimes called a clinic without walls (CWW).

Group purchasing organization: An entity authorized to act as a purchasing agent for a group of individuals or entities who are furnishing services payable by Medicare or a state health care program, and who are neither wholly owned by the GPO nor subsidiaries of a parent corporation that wholly owns the GPO (either directly or through another wholly owned entity).

Guardian: Person appointed by a court to manage the affairs and to protect the interests of a person who is declared incompetent to manage personal affairs. Incompetence may be due to physical or mental status; courts appoint guardians to manage economic or personal matters, including medical treatment choices.

HCFA Common Procedural Coding System (HCPCS): A set of codes used by Medicare and generally used by private insurance companies and managed care plans.

Health Care Financing Administration (HCFA): A branch of the Department of Health and Human Services that is responsible for administering the Medicare and Medicaid programs.

Health care quality improvement program (HCQIP): In 1992, HCFA established this program, which promotes partnerships between PROs and hospitals, health plans and physicians. These partnerships profile patterns of medical care, identify areas in which treatment could be improved, assist in the development of quality improvement efforts, and measure improvements.

Health Insurance Portability and Accountability Act of 1996 (HIPAA): This statute, often known as Kennedy-Kassebaum after its sponsors in the US Senate, attempts to make available private insurance to persons with preexisting medical conditions, among other topics. Critics contend that insurers have skirted the law's intent by setting premiums at such a high level that they are unaffordable.

Health maintenance organization: A system of health care delivery that not only pays for the care but also arranges for the provision of services. For the HMO to pay for the cost of health care, members must receive care from a participating provider who has contracted with the HMO. In most HMOs, members choose a primary care physician from a panel of physicians affiliated with the HMO. The primary care physician serves as a gatekeeper, authorizing all visits to specialists.

Healthplan Employer Data Information Set (HEDIS): Developed by the NCQA with considerable input from the employer community and the managed care community, it is an ever-evolving set of data-reporting standards. It is designed to provide some standardization in performance reporting for financial, utilization, membership, and clinical data so that employers and others can compare performance among plans and across occupational structures. HEDIS is designed to provide some standardization in performance reporting standards. It is a voluntary system that uses primarily process measures but also includes some outcome and structural measures. It covers preventive care, acute care, and chronic care.

Hearsay rule: Rule of evidence restricting the admissibility of evidence that is not the personal knowledge of the witness. Hearsay evidence is admissible only under strict rules.

Holding: A specific conclusion made by a court in a case, used to support the final judgment of the court in the case. A holding may be used to persuade later courts on the same point of law in similar cases.

Illegal drug distribution statute: A federal law that is applicable when a health care scheme is accompanied by narcotics distribution not in the proper course of medical treatment by a licensed professional.

Illegal remuneration statute: Another term for the anti-kickback statute.

Immunity: Protection given certain individuals that shields them from liability for certain acts. An example is immunity for physician peer-review comment and activities.

Incompetence: Legal status of dependence on a natural or appointed guardian to make decisions and manage business or personal affairs. Incompetent persons cannot bind themselves by contract, cannot consent to or refuse medical treatment, cannot be held to assume consequences of choices they make. Medically, incompetence is the inability of a person to understand and manage personal affairs or take responsibility for personal choices. Once this status or condition is legally recognized, a guardian is appointed to act in that person's place.

Indemnity: Obligation to reimburse for losses. A person may indemnify another under the terms of an agreement that requires payment of specific losses under specified conditions. Insurance contracts are examples of indemnity agreements, as are hospital agreements to indemnify employed physicians in specific conditions of liability or defense.

Independent contractor: Person who agrees to perform tasks that are completed without control or direct supervision by the party employing the contractor. Ordinarily, this arrangement and relationship shield the employer from liability for negligent acts of the independent contractor that occurred during the performance of the work contracted to be performed. Independent contractors are legally distinguished from employees, whose performance is supervised, directed, and controlled by the employer and for whose work the employer is vicariously responsible. Depending on the circumstances, a physician may be either an independent contractor or an employee in practice.

Independent practice association (IPA): An organization that has a contract with a managed care plan to deliver services in return for a single capitation rate. The IPA in turn contracts with individual providers to supply the services either on a capitation basis or on a fee-for-service basis. The typical IPA encompasses all specialties, but an IPA can be solely for primary care or it may be a single specialty.

Informed consent: A patient's agreement to permit diagnosis or treatment of an illness or injury based on the patient's knowledge of the facts needed to choose whether or not to submit to the medical process considered. Informed consent is a patient's agreement to undergo a medical procedure after risks, benefits, alternatives, and consequences have been discussed and weighed.

Injunction: Court order requiring a person to perform or refrain from performing a certain act. Failure to abide by an injunction may result in a citation for contempt of court and imprisonment. The person directed is said to be enjoined by the court order.

Integrated delivery system (IDS): A local or regional health care network that provides a full range of services for all aspects of health care for patients in a defined geographic area. Such services may include wellness programs, preventive care, ambulatory clinics, outpatient diagnostic and laboratory services, emergency care, general hospital services, rehabilitation, long-term care, congregate living, psychiatric care, home health care, and hospice care.

Interrogatories: Part of pretrial discovery; these are written questions submitted to an opposing party to be answered before and in preparation for a trial. The written answers are signed and affirmed as true by the party or witness to the suit.

Invasion of privacy: Violation of an individual's right to be free from unwarranted publicity and intrusions. Disclosure of a medical condition without legal justification or release could represent such a violation. Invasion of privacy is a tort, for which civil liability damages are awarded to compensate for mental suffering or humiliation or other losses of the person whose privacy was violated.

Joint and several liability: Responsibility shared by a number of persons who are found to have contributed to a patient's injuries. Establishment of joint and several liability means that each or any one of those liable can be made to satisfy the whole loss to the patient and must sue the other liable parties for contribution to the payment.

Joint Commission on Accreditation of Healthcare Organizations (JCAHO): A nonprofit independent organization dedicated to improving the quality of health care in organized health care settings. The primary functions of the JCAHO include the development of organizational standards, awarding accreditation decisions, and providing education and consultation to health care organizations. An organization accredited by the JCAHO generally is deemed to be eligible for Medicare and Medicaid reimbursement.

Judge: Person who guides court proceedings to ensure impartiality and enforces rules of evidence. The trial court determines the applicable law and states it to the jury. An appellate judge, by contrast, hears appeals and renders decisions constituting the correctness of the actions of the trial judge, the law of the case, and the sufficiency of the evidence.

Judgment: Official decision of a court about the respective rights and claims of the parties to a suit litigated.

Judicial notice: Act by which a court, in conducting a trial or forming a decision, will of its own motion and without evidence recognize the existence and truth of certain facts bearing on the controversy (eg, serious falls require x-rays).

Jurisdiction: Subject or geographic limits to power and authority of courts and other government agencies and officers.

Leading case: Court decision in a particular jurisdiction pertaining to specific facts and circumstances that have decided the same issues involved in a later case. A leading case is determinative of the same issues in subsequent cases unless distinctions from the leading case are established.

Legal reserve: The minimum amount of money that an insurer must keep in reserve to meet future claims and obligations. The amount of legal reserve is determined by state law.

Liability: As it relates to damages, an obligation one has incurred or might incur through a negligent act.

Liability insurance: Contract to have someone else pay for any liability or loss thereby in return for the payment of premiums.

Libel: Written defamation, by any kind of communications, including pictures.

Litigation: Trial in court to determine legal issues, rights, and duties among the parties to the suit.

Living will: Document in which an individual expresses in advance his wishes regarding the application of life-sustaining treatment in the event he or she is incapable of doing so at some future time.

Mail fraud statute: Federal law prohibiting anyone who has devised a scheme to defraud from using the mails to further the scheme.

Malfeasance: Execution of an unlawful or improper act.

Malice: The performance of a wrongful act without excuse, with apparent intent to inflict an injury. Under some circumstances of conduct, the law will infer malicious intent from the evidence of defendant's actions.

Malpractice: Professional misconduct or failure to properly discharge professional duties by failing to meet the standard of care required of a professional.

Managed care: A broad term used to describe the integration of the financing and delivery of health care. The term *managed care* includes within its ambit a variety of health care organizations, including HMOs, preferred-provider organizations, and physician-hospital organizations.

Management-service organization (MSO): A form of integrated delivery system. Sometimes similar to a service bureau, the MSO often actually purchases certain hard assets of a physician's practice and then provides services to that physician at fair market rates. MSOs are usually formed as a means to contract more effectively with managed care organizations, although their creation does not guarantee success.

Mandated benefits: Benefits that a health plan is required to provide by law. This is generally used to refer to benefits above and beyond routine insurance benefits, and it generally applies at the state level, where there is a high level of variability from state to state. Examples include defined days of inpatient substance abuse or mental health treatment and other special condition treatments. Self-funded plans are exempt from mandated benefits under ERISA. *See* **Employee Retirement Income Security Act of 1974 (ERISA).**

Master group contract: Also known as a master policy, this is the actual contract between a health plan and a group that purchases coverage. The master group contract provides specific terms of coverage, rights, and responsibilities of both parties.

Material misrepresentation: A false or misleading statement on an application for an insurance policy that influences the insurer's decision as to the prospective insured's insurability. These statements may create the basis for rescinding the policy.

McCarran-Ferguson Act: Legislation stipulating that federal law would apply to the insurance business only to the extent it is not regulated by state law.

Medicaid: A federal and state-funded program administered by participating states that finances health care for the poor. States receive federal matching funds and are free to design their programs as long as they cover certain federally mandated services

and run their programs within federal parameters. Demonstration projects, especially for managed care, may get waivers from certain requirements imposed by the federal government. Most individuals are eligible for Medicaid because they receive cash assistance through federal or federally assisted welfare programs, such as Aid to Families with Dependent Children or Supplementary Security Income (SSI). Medicaid also covers some low-income children and pregnant women without regard to their eligibility for cash-assistance programs.

Medicaid fraud control units (MFCUs): Entities located in forty-two states and funded jointly by states and federal money that are charged with investigating and pursuing convictions against health care providers who defraud the Medicaid program. These units are usually affiliated with the state attorney general's office and directed by an assistant attorney general. An MFCU's authority is concurrent with the OIG at HHS.

Medical-loss ratio: The ratio between the cost to deliver medical care and the amount of money that was taken in by a plan. Insurance companies often have a medical loss ratio of 92 percent or more; tightly managed HMOs may have medical loss ratios of 75 percent to 85 percent, although the overhead (or administrative-cost ratio) is concomitantly higher. The medical-loss ratio is dependent on the amount of money brought in as well as on the cost of delivering care. Thus, if the rates are too low, the ratio may be high even though the actual cost of delivering care is not really out of line.

Medicare: The federal health-insurance program covering most Americans over age sixty-five, the permanently disabled, and people with end-stage renal disease. Medicare is divided into two parts, Part A and Part B, coverage. Part A, the Hospital Insurance Program, covers hospital and other institutional health services. Part B, Supplemental Medical Insurance, covers outpatient hospital visits, physician services, and other types of outpatient services, DME, and diagnostic tests. Part A is compulsory coverage and is financed by a payroll tax on employers and employees. Part B is optional coverage, and most individuals who elect this coverage must pay a monthly premium. State Medicaid programs pay Part B premiums for persons who are entitled to Medicaid in addition to Medicare.

Medicare and Medicaid Patient and Program Protection Act (MMPPA): A 1987 federal law that broadened the grounds for excluding health care providers from participation in Medicare and Medicaid programs. This statute also granted the Office of the Inspector General (OIG) the authority to exclude from Medicare and state health care program participation individuals or entities who violate the law, even if there has been no criminal conviction.

Medicare-Medicaid Antifraud and Anti-abuse laws: Federal laws designed to control and punish fraud and abuse in connection with claims for payment under the Medicare and Medicaid programs.

Medicare + Choice: Federal program that seeks to broaden the types of health plans available to the elderly and disabled beyond the traditional fee-for-service program or Medicare HMOs. The new plans envisioned by the government include private, fee-for-service insurance plans, PPOs, provider-sponsored organizations, and medical savings accounts.

Medicare secondary-payer statute: A federal law providing that when payment sources in addition to Medicare are available, those sources are primary payers and Medicare is the secondary payer.

Medicare SELECT: A fifty-state Medicare demonstration project that permits Medicare supplemental insurance companies (ie, Medigap insurers) to offer a preferred provider organization policy to Medicare recipients. Medicare SELECT policies may waive or reduce deductibile and coinsurance payments if the plan participant uses a network provider. Plan participants are free to choose a non-network provider, but the Medicare SELECT policies may restrict or eliminate payment of deductibles and coinsurance that the policy would otherwise cover.

Medigap: Private insurance designed to supplement Medicare coverage by paying for medical costs that Medicare does not pay, such as deductibles and coinsurance.

Minor: A person who has not yet reached the age determined by law for transactional capacity, that is, a legally incompetent person. Minors cannot usually be held responsible for their contracts or other civil actions. Minors, therefore, cannot ordinarily consent to their own medical treatment.

Misdemeanor: Unlawful act of a less serious nature than a felony, usually punishable by a jail sentence for a term of less than one year or a fine.

Misfeasance: Improper performance of an act.

Misrepresentation: Words or conduct that amount to an assertion not in accordance with the existing facts or circumstances. An "innocent misrepresentation" is made by a person who has reasonable grounds for believing that the representation is true. A "negligent misrepresentation" is made when a person has no reasonable grounds for believing that the representation is true, even if the speaker believes it to be true. A "fraudulent misrepresentation" is made by a person who is aware of the falsity of the representation that causes the other party to enter an arrangement or an agreement, or to rely to her detriment on the false representation.

Money-laundering statute: A federal statute that prohibits any monetary transaction in excess of $10,000 where the money was obtained from certain specified unlawful activities, including theft of federal funds or mail or wire fraud.

Motion: Request to a judge for an order or ruling.

National Association of Insurance Commissioners: National organization of state officials charged with regulating insurance. It has no official power but wields tremendous influence. The association was formed to promote national uniformity in insurance regulation.

Negligence: Failure to exercise the degree of diligence and care that a reasonably prudent person would be expected to exercise under the same or similar circumstances. Failure that approximately causes an injury is recognized as a basis for compensation owed to the injured party.

Network Model HMO: A health plan that contracts with multiple physician groups to deliver health care to members. Generally limited to large single-specialty or multispecialty groups. Distinguished from group

model plans that contract with a single medical group, IPAs that contract through an intermediary, and direct contract model plans that contract with individual physicians in the community.

Nonfeasance: Failure to act, when there is a duty to act, as a reasonably prudent person would in similar circumstances.

Office of Audit: The branch of Office of Inspector General (OIG) that performs audits of large health care entities to ensure that they are filing accurate cost reports. The Office of Audit also identifies areas of waste or abuse in HCFA's administration of these programs.

Office of Evaluations and Inspections: The branch of the Office of Inspector General (OIG) that analyzes particular reimbursement or systems issues and produces reports on various topics.

Office of Inspector General: Every federal agency has an inspector general who is responsible for ferreting out waste, fraud, and abuse in that agency's programs. The HHS OIG is responsible for enforcing most fraud and abuse civil penalties and program exclusions. The OIG's office is divided into three sections: (1) the Office of Audit, (2) the Office of Evaluations and Inspections, and (3) the Office of Investigations.

OIG subpoena: One of the primary ways that investigators and prosecutors obtain information in health care fraud and abuse cases. The OIG subpoena power permits the OIG to compel only documentary information and not testimonial information. The OIG subpoena may request documents for use in civil, criminal, or administrative investigations. The OIG may also serve a subpoena on parties that have no immediate connection with the HHS. *See also* **Civil investigative fraud**.

Omnibus Budget Reconciliation Act (OBRA): What Congress calls the annual tax and budget reconciliation acts. Most of these acts contain language significant to managed care, generally in the Medicare market segment.

Operation Restore Trust: A two-year health care fraud demonstration project instituted by the OIG on May 3, 1995, targeting nursing home, home health, and durable medical equipment (DME) providers in California, Florida, Illinois, New York, and Texas. Under this program the OIG issued special fraud alerts to let the public know about health fraud schemes; established a new fraud and waste hotline; and created a voluntary disclosure program for providers targeted by the initiative.

Ordinance: A rule established by the authority of the state. Generally, this is an enactment by the legislative branch of a municipality such as a city council.

Original source: In *qui tam* actions, the term refers to an individual who has direct and independent knowledge of the information on which the allegations are based and has voluntarily provided the information to the government before filing an action.

Party: A legal person or entity. *Party* is a more general term than person and is useful since it can refer to organizations, groups, and legal persons such as corporations and partnerships.

Peer review: Evaluation of the quality and effectiveness of a health care professional's services, performed by physicians or other professionals who have training similar to those being reviewed.

Peer-review organization (PRO): An independent, private organization generally operating at the state level that reviews medical necessity, as well as quality and cost of care for Medicare and Medicaid programs. PROs conduct reviews primarily in connection with inpatient hospital care. Established under TEFRA.

Perjury: Willful false testimony under oath, punishable as a crime.

Physician-hospital organization (PHO): Legal (or sometimes) informal organizations that bond hospitals and their attending medical staff. Frequently developed for the purpose of contracting with managed care plans. A PHO may be open to any member of the staff who applies, or it may be closed to staff members who fail to qualify (or who are part of an already overrepresented specialty).

Physician practice management company (PPM): An organization that manages physicians' practices and in most cases either owns the practices outright or has the rights to purchase them at some point in the future. PPMs concentrate on physicians, not hospitals, although some PPMs have also branched into joint ventures with hospitals and insurers.

Preferred provider organization (PPO): A plan that contracts with independent providers at a discount for services. The panel is limited in size and usually has some type of utilization review system associated with it. A PPO may be risk bearing, similar to an insurance company, or nonrisk bearing like a physician-sponsored PPO that markets itself to insurance companies or self-insured companies via an access fee.

Preponderance of evidence: A level of persuasion required to award judgment in civil lawsuits for damages. Another way of stating this is that preponderance is a standard of better-than-equal evidence.

Presumption: An initial rational position of law that can be challenged by evidence presented in legal proceedings. Examples include presumption of innocence of the accused in a criminal matter or the presumption of legitimacy of a child born to a married couple.

Private inurement: What happens when a not-for-profit business operates in such a way as to provide more than incremental financial gain to a private individual, for example, if a not-for-profit hospital pays too much money for a physician's practice or fails to charge fair market rates for services provided to a physician. Can result in IRS penalties.

Privilege: Immunity or exemption resulting from a particular legal situation. As an example, the patient-physician privilege is a rule of evidence by which communications made to a physician by a patient in the course of treatment may not be used, absent consent, as evidence in court. It is the patient's privilege to keep such information from disclosure; it is the physician's duty to resist attempts to compel disclosure. The patient-physician privilege of confidentiality is recognized by statute in most states.

Professional Standards Review Organization (PSRO): Organization responsible for determining whether care and services provided were medically necessary and meet professional standards regarding eligibility for reimbursement under the Medicare and Medicaid programs.

***Qui tam* action:** Abbreviation of the Latin phrase *qui tam pro domino rege quam pro si ipso in hac parte sequitur,* which means, "He who brings the action for the king as well as for himself." *Qui tam* provisions of a statute permit a private person to bring a lawsuit on behalf not only of himself but also of the US government. The individual bringing the *qui tam* action can receive between 15 percent and 25 percent of whatever is recovered from the lawsuit, with the remainder going to the government.

***Qui tam* relator:** The private person who may bring a lawsuit on behalf of the US government as well as himself or herself, based on his or her knowledge of wrongdoing. A relator is often a current or former employee or an employee of a competitor or subcontractor of the organization accused of wrongdoing.

Racketeer-Influenced and Corrupt Organization Act (RICO): A federal statute that prohibits the receipt of any income from a pattern of racketeering activity. To prove a RICO case, the US government must show that the activity has an effect on interstate commerce, an association of the defendant with the enterprise and participation in its activities, and the commission of a predicate act (for example, wire or mail fraud) at least twice in the past ten years.

Rating: Determining the cost of a given unit of insurance for a given year.

Reasonable person: Hypothetical person used as an objective test or standard against which a defendant's conduct in a negligence suit can be judged. The reasonable person is the figurative standard of care. For example, a standard of care in medical practice could be established by the answer to the question, "What would a reasonably knowledgeable and skilled physician be expected to have done under the circumstances described?"

Reciprocity: Agreement by which two states recognize the licensing procedures of each other, consider them valid, and grant licenses to practice based on the other's licensure.

Regulation: A rule or order prescribed for the management of specific activities subject to government control. Regulations can be rules or orders issued by executive authority or by an administrative agency of the government.

Release: An agreement to relinquish a right or claim against another person or persons, usually exchanged for a payment or a promise, called consideration. A signed release agreement indicates that a claimed injury has been compensated.

Rescission: Voiding of a contract (such as an insurance policy) from its date of issue by the insurer because of material misrepresentations on the application for insurance. The act of rescission must take place within the contestable period or the time limit on certain defenses. The policy is treated as never having been issued, and the sum of all premiums paid plus interest, less claims paid, is refunded.

Reserves: The amount of money that a health plan puts aside to cover health care costs. It may apply to anticipated costs or to money that the plan does not expect to have to use to pay for current medical claims but keeps as a cushion against future adverse health care costs.

Res ipsa loquitur: Latin for "The thing speaks for itself." It is a legal doctrine sometimes applied in a negligence action when the plaintiff has no direct evidence of negligence but where the nature of the injury under the particular circumstances indicates to reasonable persons that such injuries do not occur in the absence of negligence. The doctrine is applicable to cases where the defendant had exclusive control of what caused the harm to the plaintiff and where the plaintiff could not have contributed to the injury. Use of the doctrine does not, however, assure the plaintiff a judgment. After the proof of the elements of *res ipsa loquitur,* the doctrine shifts to the defendant the burden to prove that conduct was reasonable and appropriate or that other mechanisms caused the plaintiff's injury.

Res judicata: Latin for "The thing is decided." What has been decided on or decided by the courts.

Resource-based relative value scale (RBRVS): A fee schedule that uses a complex formula to determine the payment due a physician for patient services. Factors that are considered in determining the payment due include the resources used, practice expenses, malpractice expenses, geographic location, and whether the services were provided on an inpatient or an outpatient basis. Medicare began phasing this in in 1992. The practical effect has been to diminish reimbursement for procedures such as cardiac surgery and raise reimbursement for primary care office visits.

Respondeat superior: Latin for "Let the master answer." It is the legal doctrine that imposes vicarious liability on an employer for breaches of duties by employees. The duty is the employer's, imposed if the employer engages others to perform tasks on the employer's behalf, which is work within the scope of employment. For example, a hospital is liable for the negligent acts of a nurse it employs if the acts occurred while the nurse was performing tasks within a nursing job description.

Responsible corporate officer doctrine: A doctrine holding that an officer, even without criminal intent or actual knowledge of an offense, can be convicted for the criminal acts of lower-level company employees merely because of his or her responsible share in overseeing the company's business activities and failure to correct or prevent the criminal violations.

Retrospective rating: Method of experience rating that adjusts the final premium of a risk in accordance with the experience of that risk during the term of that policy for which the premium is paid.

Retrospective reimbursement: Method of payment to providers by a third party after costs or charges have actually been incurred by insureds.

Retrospective review: Reviewing health care costs after they have been rendered. There are several forms of retrospective review. One form looks at individual claims for medical necessity.

Risk contract: Also known as a Medicare risk contract. A contract between an HMO and the HFCA to provide services to Medicare beneficiaries under which the health plan receives a fixed monthly payment for enrolled Medicare members and

then must provide all services on an at-risk basis.

Risk management: Management activities aimed at lowering an organization's financial and legal exposures, particularly to lawsuits.

Safe harbor: Regulatory or statutory provisions that shield certain designated payment arrangements from criminal prosecution or program exclusion. Safe harbor provisions are contained in the Stark Laws and the anti-kickback statute.

Section 125 plan: Refers to a type of flexible benefit plan. The term derives from the section of the Internal Revenue Code that defines such plans (known as cafeteria plans) and stipulates that employee contributions to Section 125 plans may be made with pretax dollars.

Self-insured or self-funded plan: A health plan in which the risk for medical cost is assumed by the company rather than an insurance company or managed care plan. Under ERISA, self-funded plans are exempt from state laws and regulations such as premium taxes and mandatory benefits. Self-funded plans often contract with insurance companies or third-party administrators to administer the benefits.

Sentinel effect: The phenomenon that when it is known that behavior is being observed, the particular behavior changes, often in the direction that the observer is looking for. As an example, utilization management and profiling systems often lead to reductions in utilization before much intervention even takes place simply because providers know someone is watching.

Service plan: A health-insurance plan that has direct contacts with providers but is not necessarily a managed care plan. The archetypical service plans are Blue Cross and Blue Shield plans. The contract applies to direct billing of the plan by providers (instead of billing the member directly), a provision for direct payment of the provider (instead of reimbursement of the member), a requirement that the provider accept the plan's determination of "usual, customary or reasonable" charges and not balance bill the member in excess of that amount, and a plethora of other terms. Such plans may or may not address issues of utilization or quality.

Slander: Spoken defamation about one person in the presence of another person that harms the slandered person's income, reputation, or character.

Social Security Act: Federal law under which the federal government administers the Old Age, Survivors, Disability, and Health Insurance Program (OASDHI). Includes Medicare and Medicaid.

Spending down: Gradual depletion of assets until indigent, thus qualifying for Medicaid benefits. Generally associated with nursing home or other long-term care.

Staff-model HMO: An HMO that employs providers directly and whose providers see members in the HMO's own facilities. A form of closed-panel HMO.

Standard of care: The measure of assessment applied to a defendant's conduct for liability determination, comparing what occurred with what an ordinary, reasonable, and prudent person would have done or not done.

Standards of quality: Authoritative statements of minimum levels of acceptable performance or results, excellent levels of performance or results, and the range of acceptable performance or results.

Stare decisis: Latin for "Let the decision stand." This is the principle of case law that requires courts to apply the approach and rationale of previously decided cases to subsequent cases involving similar facts and legal questions. When a point of law has been settled by decision, it forms a precedent that is binding for lower courts. Later decisions may distinguish their facts or circumstances to come to different results but must otherwise adhere to the rule of precedent.

Stark I: Shortened name for the physician self-referral prohibitions introduced to Congress in 1988 by California representative Fortney "Pete" Stark. The initial law became effective January 1, 1992, and provides that a physician or an immediate family member who has a financial relationship with an entity may not refer a Medicare patient to that entity for clinical laboratory services unless an applicable exception exists. In addition, the law prevents an entity with which a physician has a financial relationship from billing Medicare or a beneficiary for clinical laboratory services pursuant to a prohibited referral.

Stark II: Colloquial name for the 1993 amendments to Stark I that extend the physician self-referral restrictions to Medicaid services and beneficiaries and expand the referral and billing prohibitions to ten additional designated health services reimbursable by Medicare and Medicaid. Those services are: (1) physical therapy; (2) occupational therapy; (3) radiology services, including magnetic resonance imaging, computerized axial tomography scans, and ultrasound services; (4) radiation therapy and services; (5) durable medical equipment and supplies; (6) parenteral and enteral nutrients, equipment, and supplies; (7) prosthetics, orthotics, and prosthetic devices; (8) home health services and supplies; (9) outpatient prescription drugs; and (10) inpatient and outpatient hospital services. Stark II became effective on January 1, 1995.

Statute: A written law enacted by the legislature to achieve a specific legislative objective.

Statute of limitations: Laws that specify the permissible time interval between an occurrence giving rise to a civil cause of action and the filing of a lawsuit. Failure to file suit within the prescribed time is an affirmative defense. These time limits for filing suit vary from state to state. Most statutes of limitation have exceptions to stop the time from elapsing. In malpractice suits, the time allowed to bring suit is stopped or does not begin to run until the party claiming injury by the defendant first discovers or should reasonably have discovered the injury.

Stipulation: Acknowledgment by a party of a specific fact or circumstance that will not be disputed in a case. One party may stipulate that a witness is qualified to testify or that a physician had been an employee of a facility at the time of disputed care. Stipulations save time and expense by removing certain issues from trial proceedings.

Stockholder derivative lawsuit: Also known as a shareholder derivative lawsuit, this is an action brought by a shareholder on behalf of a corporation because the corporation was caused to suffer damage but redress the act causing the damage.

Stop-loss insurance: A form of reinsurance that provides protection for medical expenses above a certain limit, generally on a year to year basis. It may apply to an entire health plan or to any single component. As an example, a health plan may have stop-loss reinsurance for cases that exceed $100,000. After a case hits $100,000, the plan receives 80 percent of expenses in excess of $100,000 back from the reinsurance company for the rest of the year.

Strict liability: Responsibility for harm caused by special activities or circumstances. This is liability without the need to prove a negligent act or failure. The proof of damages sustained by the plaintiff in connection with the situation and the involvement of the defendant support the finding of strict liability. Examples could be management by the defendant of inherently dangerous activities, placing a defective and dangerous product into commerce, or assembling hazardous substances or mechanisms.

Subpoena: Latin for a court order requiring a person to appear in court to give testimony or be punished for not appearing.

Subpoena *duces tecum*: Subpoena that requires a person to personally present to the court a specified document or property possessed or under the person's control.

Subrogation: The contractual right of a health plan to recover payments made to a member for health care costs after that member has received such payment for damages in a legal action.

Subscriber: The individual or member who has health plan coverage by virtue of being eligible on his or her behalf rather than as a dependent.

Summons: Court order, directed to the sheriff or other appropriate official, to notify the defendant in a civil suit that a suit has been filed and when and where to appear.

Supplemental medical insurance: Another term for Medicare Part B coverage.

Tax Equity and Fiscal Responsibility Act (TEFRA): One key provision of this 1982 act prohibits employers and health plans from requiring full-time employees between the ages of sixty-five and sixty-nine to use Medicare rather than the group health care plan.

Telemedicine: Long-distance practice of medicine through the use of electronic communications.

Third-party administrator: Method by which an outside person or firm, not a party to a contract, maintains all records regarding the persons covered under the insurance plan.

Third-party payer: Any organization, private or public, that insures or pays health or medical expenses on behalf of beneficiaries or recipients, such as Blue Cross and Blue Shield, commercial insurance companies, Medicare, and Medicaid. An individual usually pays a premium for coverage in all such private and some public programs. The organization then pays bills on the insured's behalf. These payments, called third-party payments, are distinguished by the separation between the individual receiving the service (the first party), the institution or individual supplying it (the second party), and the organization paying for it (the third party).

Tort: Civil wrong in which a person has breached a legal duty with harm caused to another. To establish liability for a tort, an injured party must establish that a legal duty was owed to the plaintiff by the defendant, that the defendant breached that duty, and that the plaintiff suffered damage caused by the breach. Torts can be negligent or intentional.

Unbundling: The practice of provider billing for multiple components of service that were previously included in a single fee. For example, if dressings and instruments were included in a fee for a minor procedure, the fee for the procedure remains the same, but there are now additional charges for the dressings and instruments.

Underwriting: Under one definition, this refers to bearing the risk for something (for example, a policy is underwritten by an insurance company). Under another definition, this refers to the analysis of a group that is done to determine rates and benefits or to determine whether the group should be offered coverage at all.

Uniform Policy Provisions Law (UPPL): Statutory policy provisions of health-insurance policies that specify some of the rights and obligations of the insured and the insurer. These provisions, with some modifications, are part of the insurance laws of all fifty states and the District of Columbia.

Upcoding: Using improper billing codes to charge Medicare or Medicaid for an item or service to receive higher payments than would ordinarily be due for the care of a patient.

Utilization review: Program designed to reduce unnecessary hospital admissions and to control the length of stay for inpatients through the use of preliminary evaluations, concurrent inpatient evaluations, or discharge preplanning.

Venue: Geographic district in which a lawsuit is or may be brought.

Vicarious liability: Derivative responsibility for an agent's or employee's failures based on the defendant's employer-employee or principal-agent relationship. The responsibility is imposed because the ability to supervise, direct, and control employees to safeguard others lies with the employer.

Waiver: Intentional and voluntary agreement to forgo a known claim or right. For example, a patient could waive the privilege of confidential communication, or a defendant could waive the right to challenge certain testimony. Sometimes, a right may be unintentionally waived if it is not exercised in time.

Wanton act: Grossly negligent, malicious, or reckless conduct that implies a disregard for the consequences or for the rights and safety of others.

Warranty: Express or implied commitment or promise undertaken as part of a contract but aside from the central contract purpose. It is to be distinguished from a representation. A warranty is given contemporaneously with the contract agreement as part of the contract. A representation precedes and may be seen as an inducement to enter the contract.

Whistleblower: An employee who reports the illegal or wrongful actions of his or her coworkers.

Wholesale HMO: A term sometimes used when a licensed HMO does not market itself directly but rather contracts with another HMO and accepts capitation in return. This most commonly occurs when an IDS wants to accept global capitation from an HMO, and in return capitate other providers, since many states will only allow an HMO to capitate providers. Therefore, an IDS obtains an HMO license, but does not go directly to market to the public, and thus does not disrupt existing relationships with other managed care organizations.

Wire fraud statute: A federal statute that prohibits the use of wire, radio, or television communication in interstate or foreign commerce for the purpose of executing a scheme to defraud.

Workers' compensation: A form of social insurance provided through property-casualty insurers. Workers' compensation provides medical benefits and replacement of lost wages that result from injuries or illnesses that arise in the workplace; in return, the worker cannot normally sue the employer unless true negligence exists. Workers' compensation has undergone dramatic increases in cost as group health has shifted to managed care, resulting in workers' compensation carriers adopting managed care approaches. Workers' compensation is often heavily regulated under state laws that are significantly different from those used for group health insurance and is often the subject of intense negotiation between management and organized labor.

Appendix

Computer databases and Internet sites

Computer databases

Bioethicsline
Georgetown University, Kennedy Institute of Ethics.

Health
Based on Hospital Literature Abstracts.

Healthlawyer (American Health Lawyers Association)

Healthonline
This on-line service is the result of a collaborative effort between the Healthcare Forum and Kaiser and Associates. This new tool uses a colorful, user-friendly graphic interface. For information call Susan Klein at 415 421-8810, x376.

Hospital And Health Administration Index, Health Planning and Administration Index

LEXIS Health Law Library and MEDIS

MEDLINE
Based on Index Medicus. The National Library of Medicine (NLM), a division of the National Institutes of Health, now provides access to MEDLINE free of charge over the World Wide Web at www.nlm.nih.gov. Free MEDLINE is limited to Web-based searching on the Internet because of great savings to NLM in telecommunications and software costs.

An index to the world's most extensive collection of published medical information, MEDLINE provides access to 8.8 million references of articles published in 3,800 biomedical journals. It covers the fields of medicine, nursing, dentistry, veterinary medicine, the health care system, and preclinical sciences, and it contains records back to 1966.

Two Web-based products, Internet Grateful Med and PubMed, provide the points of access between user and database: Internet Grateful Med provides free access to MEDLINE, AIDSLINE, HEALTH-STAR, AIDSDRUGS, AIDSTRIALS, HISTLINE, OLDMEDLINE, and other databases. This Web application helps users create and refine searches and submits them to the NLM's retrieval engines. Internet Grateful Med also offers an order feature called Loansome Doc, a document delivery service set up between registered searchers and medical libraries to provide full-text copies of medical articles.

PubMed provides free access to MEDLINE, simple and advanced search features, links to some publishers' sites for full-text journal articles, and links to molecular biology databases of DNA/protein sequences and 3-D structure data. Twenty-four full-text journals are currently available, some by subscription only.

Silver Platter Information

Westlaw
Health services database.

Internet sites

The expansion in Internet access promises to generate vast new computer resources for health law research. New Web sites are proliferating at such a rate that any catalog of them will be quickly outdated, but at present these are a sampling of sites relevant to health law and policy.

Aetna Health Plans, www.aetna.com/aeindex.htm
Describes the company's health insurance products and services.

Agency for Health Care Policy and Research (US Department of Health and Human Services) www.ahcpr.gov
This site has both a keyword search function and a browse function that allows the researcher to locate selected information on thirty-seven topics, including children's health, evidence-based medicine, health insurance, access to care, managed care, mar-

ket forces, outcomes research, quality of care, and women's health. The site features findings from AHCPR-supported research, information on funding, opportunities, and on-line access to *Research Activities,* an official publication of AHCPR. A site map explains navigational tools and lists offerings in major categories.

AIDS Education Global Information System (AEGIS) www.aegis.com
This Web site offers news reports from the Centers for Disease Control and Prevention, wire services, and major newspapers; an on-line library of HIV-related journals; and a database engine that allows users to search scientific abstracts from the National Library of Medicine, among other AIDS-related documents. A total of approximately 300,000 files are available. The nonprofit service is operated by the Sisters of St Elizabeth of Hungary in San Juan Capistrano, California.

Alcoholics Anonymous, www.aa.org

Alpha Center, www.ac.org
Established in 1976, this nonprofit, nonpartisan health policy center, based in Washington, DC, helps public- and private-sector clients obtain necessary information on health care issues.

American Academy of Pediatrics, www.aap.org
Contains articles on the state Children's Health Insurance Program, among other matters.

American Accreditation Healthcare Commission, URAC, www.urac.org
This nonprofit organization was founded in 1990 to establish accreditation standards for managed health care. Its membership

represents a range of health care constituencies: industry, providers, purchasers, consumers, and regulators. Policy-makers in sixteen states and the District of Columbia have incorporated the organization into the regulatory process.

American Association of Blood Banks, www.aabb.org
Includes information on education and training of medical professions concerning blood banking.

American Association of Health Plans, www.aahp.org
This organization represents more than a thousand HMOs, PPOs, and other managed care plans. Its Web site includes reports on such topics as women's health and chronic care.

American Association of Managed Care Nurses, www.aamcn.org

American Association of Retired Persons, www.aarp.org

American Bar Association, www.abanet.org
This site includes excerpts from BNA's *Health Care Daily* to members of its Health Law Section.

American Board of Medical Specialties, www.abms.org
This is an umbrella organization for the twenty-four approved medical specialty boards in the United States. Established in 1933, the ABMS coordinates the activities of its member boards and provides information to the public, the government, the profession, and its members concerning issues involving specialization and certification in medicine.

American Civil Liberties Union, www.aclu.org
This site includes resources on HIV/AIDS law.

American College of Health Care Executives, www.ache.org
Provides information on helpful books, periodicals, and research materials.

American College of Integrated Delivery Systems, www.acids.org.
This organization was formed to answer the need to educate health care executives, physicians, nurses, office managers, pharmaceutical professionals, and other allied health professionals on the future of integrated delivery systems.

American College of Physicians, www.acop.org

American College of Surgeons, www.facs.org
This site includes a list of the organization's recently published articles on health policy.

American Federation of State, County, and Municipal Employees, www.afscme.org

American Health Care Association, www.ahca.org
This is a federation of fifty state health organizations, representing nearly 12,000 non-profit and for-profit assisted living and nursing facilities and subacute care providers for elderly and disabled individuals.

American Health Information Management Association, www.ahima.org
With 38,000 members, this organization classifies and analyzes health information, transitioning from paper to computer-based

medical records, while maintaining patient confidentiality.

American Health Lawyers Association, www/healthlawyers.org

This enormous site is a cornucopia of health care legal information.

American Hospital Association, www.aha.org

This site provides helpful information about, among other things, the AHA's extensive resource center.

American Medical Association, www.ama-assn.org

This extensive Web site includes a number of subfiles on policy and advocacy issues, including access to insurance coverage, Medicare, utilization management, HIV/AIDS, and end-of-life care, among many others. It also includes an on-line version of *JAMA*, the *Archives of Internal Medicine*, and nine other specialty journals. In addition, it includes the full text of the AMA's congressional testimony on everything from Medicaid to gag clauses and summaries and analyses of state and federal health insurance reforms.

The American Medical Women's Association, www.amwa-doc.org

Essentially a billboard for abortion advocacy.

American Nurses Association, www.nursingworld.org

Includes an on-line journal of nursing issues.

American Public Health Association, www.apha.org

Includes information on legislative affairs and advocacy, news, and publications.

American Public Welfare Association, www.apwa.org

This is a nonprofit, bipartisan organization of individuals and agencies concerned with human services, including health care reform. This site includes specific budget proposals from the Clinton Administration regarding various health care items.

American Sociological Association, www.asanet.org

American Telemedicine Association, www.atmeda.org

This site supplies abstracts of articles and a range of valuable links.

Americans for Free Choice in Medicine, www.afcm.org

This organization promotes a philosophy of individual rights, personal responsibility, and free-market economics in health care. It advocates medical savings accounts, among other goals.

Association for Healthcare Philanthropy, www.go-ahp.org

Association of American Medical Colleges, www.aamc.org

Association of State and Territorial Health Officials, www.astho.org

This association represents the public-health agencies of the United States and US territories.

Association of University Programs in Health Administration, www.aupha.com

Contains a helpful list of publications concerning health-administration education.

Avicenna Health, www.avicenna.com

Named after the tenth-century Persian philosopher and physician, this site seeks to provide physicians with a reliable common pool of professional information.

Blue Cross and Blue Shield Association, www.bluecares.com

California Association of Health Facilities, www.cahf.org
CAHF is a professional association for long-term care in California. Founded in 1950 and originally representing only nursing homes, CAHF represents for-profit and nonprofit facilities.

California Medical Association, www.cmanet.org

California Telehealth and Telemedicine, http://telemed.calhealth.org
Provides information on relevant California statutes, newsletters, resource guides, and links.

CalLaw, www.callaw.com
This site is a source for recent California case law. It offers news, analysis, classified ads, local court rules, state and federal appellate opinions, and information on all cases before the state supreme court.

Caregiving Online, www.caregiving.com

Catholic Health Association of the United States, www.chausa.org
This is the national leadership organization of more than 1,200 Catholic health care sponsors, systems, facilities, and related organizations and services. This site includes daily news, directories, and copious amounts of information regarding long-term care and a wide range of other public policy issues. It also provides a large number of hypertext links to other pertinent sites.

Center for Budget and Policy Priorities, www.cbpp.org

Center for Evaluative Clinical Sciences, Dartmouth Medical School, www.dartmouth.edu/dms/cecs

Center for Health Care Strategies, www.chcs.org
Established in 1995, the center is a nonpartisan policy center affiliated with the Woodrow Wilson School of Public and International Affairs at Princeton University.

Centers for Disease Control and Prevention-Scientific Data, Surveillance, Health Statistics and Laboratory Information, www.cdc.gov

CNN Interactive: Health, www.cnn.com/HEALTH/index.html

Coalition for Patient Rights, www.nationalcpr.org
This Lexington, Massachusetts–based organization advocates the protection of patient privacy, including the privacy of medical records.

Columbia/HCA, www.columbia.net

Committee on Interns and Residents, www.cirdocs.org

Computer-Based Patient Record Institute, www.cpri.org

Consumers for Quality Care, www.consumerwatchdog.org/ public_hts/medical

Cost and Quality Quarterly Journal, www.cost-quality.com

Critical Path AIDS Project,
www.critpath.org

Cyberspace Telemedical Office,
www.telemedical.com

The Dartmouth Atlas of Healthcare,
www.dartmouth.edu/dms/atlas
Contains a list of publications, tables of
contents, and a limited number of graphics.

Data Interchange Standards Association,
www.disa.org

**Department of Health and Human
Services,** www.hhs.gov

**Department of Health and Human
Services, Office of the Inspector General
(DHHS/OIG),** www.hhs.gov/progorg/oig
This site provides advisory opinion letters in
which the government interprets proposed activities and determines whether they constitute a legitimate means of doing business or a
violation of the federal Medicare/Medicaid
anti-kickback prohibitions.

Disease Management Forum,
www.sapien.net/dm/index.htm

Doctor's Guide to the Internet,
www.docguide.com

Duke Health Policy Cyberexchange,
www.hpolicy.duke.edu
Provides information on policy research organizations, universities, foundations, and
relevant government agencies.

**Duke University-Health Data Standards
Database,** www.mcis.duke.edu/standards

EDI InfoNet, www.wpc-edi.com

Electronic Policy Network,
www.epn.org/
This superb Web site, produced by the
American Prospect journal, provides information on a wide range of health policy such
as Medicaid for children, Medicare HMOs,
and recent legislation.

Emory University Library-HealthWeb,
www.gen.emory.edu/medweb/
medweb.comsumer.html

Employee Benefit Research Institute,
www.ebri.org

**Employers' Managed Health Care
Association,** www.lmrc.org/mhca.htm

**EPA Office of Air Quality Planning and
Standards,** www.epa.gov

Evidence Based Medicine,
hiru.mcmaster.ca/ebm/default.htm

Families USA, www.familiesusa.org
This is a nonprofit, nonpartisan organization focused on the achievement of high-
quality affordable health care and long-term
care for all Americans.

Federal Register, fr-cos.com

Federal Telemedicine Gateway,
www.tmgateway.org
Provides information on federally funded
telemedicine projects.

Federal Web Locator,
www.law.vill.edu/Fed-Agency
The US government has announced its intention to shift from print to electronic
publishing, including via the Internet.
Many government Web sites are already
widely known for their excellence in content
and presentation. Therefore, it is important

to have access to a reliable site to track government developments on the Internet. The Federal Web Locator, compiled by the Villanova Center for Information Law and Policy, is just such a site. This searchable index to US government resources is well organized and comprehensive and begins helpfully with a list of recently added sites. Sites are organized by branch of government or federal agency.

Federation of American Health Systems, www.fahs.com
This trade group represents investor-owned health systems.

Federation of State Medical Boards of the United States, www.fsmb.org
The federation is composed of sixty-nine member boards whose primary responsibilities and obligations are to protect the public through the regulation of physicians and other health care providers.

Fed World, www.fedworld.gov
This is an enormous resource for technical, scientific, and other information provided by the federal government. Fed World is taxpayer supported through the National Technical Information Service.

First to Know Medical Bulletin, www.ivanhoe.com

Food and Drug Law Institute, www.fdli.org
This is a membership organization of providers of products and services to the food, drug, medical device, and cosmetics industries, including major food and drug companies and attorneys working in food and drug law.

Future Health Care, www.futurehealthcare.com

GAO Reports, www.gao.gov/reports.htm
Each day, the Governmental Accounting Office issues a list of newly available reports and testimony, available via the Internet. It includes a specific subfile on reports addressing allegations of fraud, waste, abuse, or mismanagement of federal funds.

Galen II, www.library.ucsf.edu/journals
Named after the ancient Greek anatomist, physiologist, and physician, this is the Web page of the library of the University of California at San Francisco. It provides access to more than 100 academic medical journals.

General Accounting Office, www.gao.gov
This site offers reports from the GAO on budget issues and health care matters, among other topics.

General Services Administration (Fedlaw), www.legal.gsa.gov
This site provides links to the federal judiciary and Congress. It also provides access to state and territorial law, arbitration and mediation, general research and reference, and professional associations and organizations. There are links to the *United States Code,* the *Code of Federal Regulations,* the *Federal Register,* and executive orders.

Geo Health Web, www.pharmulary.com
This is an interdisciplinary Web site offering a full range of health care information and networking, established as a nonprofit service by the National Center for Computer Education and Research in Healthcare at the St Louis College of Pharmacy.

GPO Gate, www.gpo.ucop.edu
The US Government Printing Office publishes a collection of databases known as GPO Access: www.access.upo.gov/su_docs/aces/aacesOO2.html. This service offers the searchable and retrievable full text of numerous government publications, including the Federal Register, Congressional Record, congressional bills, *United States Code, Economic Indicators,* and *GAO Reports.* GPO Access is offered at several alternative sites, including the GPO Gate site at the University of California at San Diego, a good search interface with helpful options. Databases may be selected by title or subject, and database descriptions are available to help the user make a choice. The Quick Search interface offers Boolean operators and the option to limit searches by title words. (At the time this book went to press, the FullFeature Searching option was not available.) A search may also be conducted on the document headline, that is, usually the title, across a selected number of databases simultaneously. Search help is available at the site.

**HCAA-Home Care Association of America Home Page,
www.hcaa-homecare.com**

Health Access, www.healthaccess.net

Health Administration Responsibility Project (HARP), www.harp.org
This site is a resource for physicians and patients seeking to establish the tort liability of managed care organizations. It provides practical information on how to fight denial of coverage by managed care plans.

Health Association of New York State, www.hanys.org

Health Care Financing Administration, www.hcfa.gov

Healthcare Integrity and Protection Data Bank, www.npdb.com/HIPDB/h
This is a national fraud and abuse data collection program for reporting and disclosing certain final adverse actions taken against health care providers, suppliers, or practitioners.

**Health Care Law Research on the Internet-University of Maryland Law School,
www.law.ab.umd.edu/marshall/ health/**
A vast range of health care resources are collected, indexed, and linked from this site.

Health Care Quality Resources Directory, www.quality.org/html/hc-res.html

**Health Care Without Harm,
www.noharm.org**
This Washington, DC–based environmental health organization is made up of health care professionals, hospitals, environmental advocates, religious organizations, and individuals. Its goal is to transform the health care industry so it no longer is a source of environmental harm by eliminating the pollution in health care practices without compromising safety or care.

Health Decisions, Inc, www.hdi.com
This Golden, Colorado–based organization contracts with health plans to assist patients assess their own treatment plans and to develop patients' knowledge of their options. The company makes use of on-line computer databases and its own library resources, along with a staff of researchers and nurses.

HealthFinder, www.healthfinder.gov

HealthGate, www.healthgate.com

Health Hero Networks, www.hhn.com

Health Hippo, www.hippl.findlaw.com
Health Hippo is a collection of policy and regulatory materials related to health care. Its whimsical name notwithstanding, this is an extensive compendium of materials and hypertext links on such issues as advance directives, fraud and abuse, labs, long-term care, Medicare, Medicaid, mental health, public health, and rural health, along with such topics as "Hipponews" and "Hippotalk."

Health Industry Business Communications Council, www.hibcc.org

Health Insurance Association of America, www.hiaa.org

The Health Law Resource, www.netreach.net/~wmanning/ index.html
This site is intended as a resource for health care practitioners, professionals, or anyone interested in learning more about the dynamic field of health care law and, more specifically, the regulatory and transactional aspects of health care law practice.

HealthPages, www.thehealthpages.com

HealthPartners, www.healthpartners.com

Health Policy EPN's Recommended Links, epn.org/idea/hciclink.html

Health Privacy Project, www.healthprivacy.org
This organization seeks to raise public awareness of the importance of health pri-

vacy to improved health care, on both an individual and a community level. Founded in 1997, this project is part of Georgetown University Medical Center's Institute for Health Care Research and Policy.

Health Scope, www.healthscope.org

HealthWorld Online, www.healthy.net

Help for Health, www.helpforhealth.com

The Henry J. Kaiser Family Foundation, www.kff.org
This site offers information about the Foundation's publications on health policy and provides links to other pertinent sites.

Hieros Gamos Guide to Law and Government, www.hg.org
Hieros Gamos was established in 1994 by Lex Mundi, a global association of 133 independent law firms. *Hieros gamos* is a Greek term referring to the harmonization of similar opposites, in this case, of written and electronic information. This site has more than 20,000 original pages and more than 70,000 links. It is one of the more comprehensive sites for legal information. It includes information on over 6,000 legal organizations, including every government in the world. This site's more than 200 practice areas, more than 300 discussion groups, and 50 business guides provide free access to substantive information.

HIV/AIDS Treatment Information Service, www.hivatis.org

HIVLAWToday, www.HIVLawToday.com

The HMO Page, www.hmopage.org/index.html
This Web site is a jeremiad against managed care in general and includes such topics as

the Atrocity of the Month and the Hall of Shame, along with an entertaining humor column and cartoons.

Homecare in Cyberspace,
www.ptct.com/html/industry.html

Home Care Magazine,
www.homecaremag.com

Hospital Web, neuro-
www.mgh.harvard.edu/hospitalweb.nelk

How to Fight Your HMO,
www.bright.net/~ewp/
fight_your_hmo.html
Designed by an Ohio woman whose surgery for endometriosis was not covered by her managed care plan, this site provides practical, feisty advice, along with information on HMO reform.

Idea Central: Health Policy,
http://epn.org/idea/health.html
Bimonthly virtual journal on health policy issues.

Infomine, lib-www.ucr.edu/govpub/
This is a scholarly database of federal, state, and local government resources that can be searched by subject, keyword, or title. It is a service of the University of California.

Inside Health Care,
www.insidehealthcare.com
This supersite supplies links to more than 100 other sites relating to health care policy, news, search engines, publications, reference works, directories, government information, and vendors.

The Institute for Child Health,
www.ichp.ufl.edu

Integrated Health Care Organization,
www.iha.org

Internal Revenue Service,
www.irs.ustreas.gov

International Association of Defense Counsel, www.iadclaw.org
This Chicago-based organization publishes and disseminates information on the law, on its development and reform, and on the practice of law, particularly from the viewpoint of the litigator in the civil defense and insurance fields.

International Association of Physicians in AIDS Care, www.iapac.org

International Foundation of Employee Benefit Plans, www.ifebp.org

IPRO, www.ipro.org/Consumer/index.htm

Joint Commission on Accreditation of Healthcare Organizations,
www.jcaho.org
Accredits more than 19,000 health care organizations in the United States and abroad.

The Journal of Cost and Quality,
www.cost-quality.com

The Journal of the American Medical Association, www.jama.com

JournalWatch Online, www.jwatch.org

Kaiser Permanente,
www.kaiserpermanente.org

Law Journal Extra! Health Law,
www.ljx.com/practice/health/index.html
Contains health law and policy news in a magazine format.

Lippincott's Nursing Center-American Journal of Nursing Online, www.ajn.org

List of Excluded Individuals/Entities (LEIE), www.hhs.gov/progorg/oig/cumsan/index.htm
The Office of Inspector General's List of Excluded Individuals/Entities provides information to health care providers, patients, and others regarding over 15,000 persons and entities that are excluded from participation in Medicare, Medicaid, and other federal health care programs.

Loyola University Chicago Law School Institute for Health Law, www.health-law@luc.edu

Managed Care Information, www.managedcareinfo.com
This vast site is a managed care reference library, resource, and information center.

Managed Care Magazine, www.managedcaremag.com

Managed Care On Line, www.mcol.com

Massachusetts Association of HMOS, www.mahmo.org

Massachusetts Medical Society, www.massmed.org

Mayo Health Oasis, www.mayo.ivi.com

MedHelp, www.medhelp.org

Medical Malpractice Resource Page, http://webs.soltec.net/fish/medmal.htm
Contains a wide range of subfiles on the topic.

Medical Outcomes Trust, www.outcomes-trust.org

Medicare Information Website, www.medicare.gov
This is the Health Care Financing Administration's Web site with helpful Medicare advocacy information.

Medicine on the Net Quality Resources, www.mednet-i.com

Mediqual Quantitative Reports Data Base, www.mediqual.com

MedLine Public Access, www4.ncbi.nlm.nih.gov/PubMed/

MedScape, www.medscape.com

MedSite Navigator, www.medsitenavigator.com

Medsite Navigator's List of Electronic Medical Journals, www.medsitenavigator.com/med/Journals
Contains a comprehensive list of electronic medical journals, including some on policy issues.

Med Web, www.medweb.emory.edu/medweb/
This is one of the best and most easily accessible indexes to medical sites on the Internet. Its directory has only two levels and can be searched quickly. The first provides medical specialty; the next gives Web sites. It has access to a wide range of journals, including a number on AIDS.

MGMA Online, www.mgma.com
Prepared by the Medical Group Management Association, this comprehensive site provides information on how medical practice, governance, management, and delivery are being affected by managed care, health care reform, and integration.

Microsoft Industry-Healthcare,
www.microsoft.com/industry/healthcare

Minnesota Health Data Institute,
www.mhdi.org

National Academy for State Health
Policy, www.nashp.org
Formed in 1987, this organization is a non-profit, multidisciplinary forum of and for state health policy leaders from the executive and legislative branches. Based in Portland, Maine, it assists policy-makers in exchanging insights, information, and experience and in developing practical, innovative solutions to complex health policy issues confronting states. Steering committees of volunteers from various executive branch agencies, legislatures and their staffs, and state universities play a key role in identifying the organization's agenda and in developing innovative and effective strategies to improve the delivery and financing of health care.

National AIDS Clearinghouse,
www.cdc.gov
This site is designed to facilitate the sharing of HIV, AIDS, and STD resources, along with news and trends. It is a service of the Centers for Disease Control.

National AIDS Update Conference,
www.nauc.org

National Association for Home Care,
www.nahc.org

National Association of Health Data
Organizations Ambulatory Data
Collection Guide,
www.nahdo.org/amb.html

National Association of Health Data
Organizations-National Health

Information Resource Center,
www.nhirc.org

National Association of Insurance
Commissioners, www.naic.org

National Association of Managed Care
Physicians, www.namcp.com

National Automated Clearing House
Association, www.nacha.org

National Business Coalition on Health,
www.nbch.org/nbch

National Center for Health Statistics,
www.cdc.gov

National Coalition on Health Care,
www.nchc.org
The National Coalition on Health Care is a nonpartisan alliance of more than 100 groups that share the five following goals: (1) securing health insurance for all; (2) improving quality of care; (3) cost containment; (4) equitable financing; and (5) simplified administration. This Washington, DC–based group conducts surveys, commissions papers by leading researchers, holds public forums, and publishes position papers. These are aimed at the informed consumer, administrator, and health-insurance executive. This is not a large Internet site but is powerful in its content.

National Committee for Quality
Assurance (NCQA), www.ncqa.org
This is an independent, nonprofit Washington-based group that surveys and accredits managed care organizations to assess whether they meet agreed-upon standards of quality. NCQA sells detailed two-page reports on individual health plans that are geared toward providing consumers

with more detailed information about how their health plans have fared.

National Conference of State Legislators, www.ncsl.org

The goals of this organization are to improve the quality and effectiveness of state legislatures, to foster interstate communications and cooperation, and to ensure legislatures a strong, cohesive voice in the federal system. NCSL's health program serves as an information clearinghouse for policy-makers, writing and disseminating publications for legislators on such issues as AIDS, health access, cost containment, long-term care, maternal and child care, and adolescent health.

National Council on Aging, www.ncoa.org

National Federation for Independent Business, www.nfibonline.com

This organization represents small businesses and often takes policy positions on health care law and policy.

National Health Law Program, www.healthlaw.org

This is a Los Angeles-based nonprofit organization that represents the poor, minorities, and the aged in obtaining equity and nondiscrimination in federal, state, local, and private health care programs. Its primary role is to assist legal services attorneys, paralegals, and private attorneys representing eligible low-income clients nationwide by providing advice and technical assistance; acting as co-counsel in selected cases; collecting and disseminating information; maintaining a specialized library; and publishing training manuals, advocacy guides, and articles in legal periodicals.

National Institutes of Health, www.nih.gov

National Library of Medicine (Health and Human Services), www.nlm.nih.gov

This site offers medical library services to the public, health professionals, libraries in medical schools, hospitals, and research institutions.

National Patient Safety Foundation, www.ama-assn.org/med-sci/npsf/main.htm

This organization was founded by the AMA to "improve measurably patient safety in the delivery of health care" through the collection, sharing, and application of information regarding patient safety.

National Practitioner Data Bank, www.npdb.com

This is the central repository for information on physicians and dentists. It contains reports on medical malpractice payments, adverse licensure actions, adverse clinical privilege actions, and adverse professional society membership actions.

National Senior Citizens Law Center, www.nsclc.org

This is an advocacy group for low-income elderly persons.

NetWellness, www.netwellness.org

The New England Journal of Medicine, www.nejm.org

Newspage, www.newspage.com

New York Online Access to Health, www.oah.cuny.edu

Nobel Prize in Physiology or Medicine, www.almaz.com/nobel/medicine
This excellent site contains the names of all Nobel prize winners since the prize's creation in 1901 and the specific work for which they were honored. It also includes biographical information and hypertext links to other related sites.

Office Professionals and Employees International Union, www.opeiu.org

Oxford Health Plans, www.oxhp.com

Pharmaceutical Quality Group, www.pharmweb.net

Physician's Guide to Medical Liability Litigation, www.afss.com/medical/physguid.htm
This guide is intended as a reference for physicians practicing in Michigan. Some of the information it provides is Michigan-specific and does not apply in other states.

President's Advisory Commission on Consumer Protection and Quality in the Health Care Industry, www.hcqualitycommission.gov
This Final Report of the President's Advisory Commission, issued in March 1998, summarizes the Clinton Administration's assessment of the quality of health care in the United States. This report contains a snapshot of numerous statistics driving the national debate over health care reform, identifies areas that need improvement, and attempts to formulate policy goals for reform through a mixture of government regulation and encouragement of industry-led quality control and access-increasing efforts. It is a worthwhile read if only for the purpose of understanding how the federal government assesses the current state of health care in America.

Public Citizen, Health Research Group, www.citizen.org
This Washington, DC–based citizens interest group conducts policy-oriented research on health care issues. Its interests include hospital quality and costs, doctors' fees, physician discipline and malpractice, state administration of health programs, drugs, carcinogens, and medical devices. It favors a single-payer, Canadian-style comprehensive health program.

RAND Corporation, www.rand.org
This Santa Monica, California–based think tank has, over the past fifty years, developed into the largest nonprofit program in health policy in the United States and one of the largest in the world. Its mission is to advance knowledge about how cost, quality, and access to care can be altered to promote better health care systems. Researchers are currently focusing on health policy concerns in such diverse areas as quality and appropriateness of care, health care financing, access to care and health services delivery, HIV and AIDS, and mental health. Its work is carried out primarily through three centers: the Center for the Study of Employee Health Benefits, RAND/UCLA/Harvard Center for Health Care Financing Policy Research, and UCLA/RAND Research Center on Managed Care for Psychiatric Disorders.

Reuters Health Information, www.reutersheatlh.com
Contains regularly updated medical news and health information.

The Robert Wood Johnson Foundation, www.rwjf.org/main.html
This Web site includes text on such topics as state health reform, cost containment, chronic care, substance abuse, and dying in

America. It also describes existing foundation programs and procedures for applying for a grant.

Roswell and Alistair: Mismanaged Care (A Forum), www.roswellandalistair.com/mismanaged_care.htm
This absolutely hilarious site consists of a sustained attack on managed care and "bloodsucking insurance companies." A must-visit.

St Louis University School of Law Center for Health Law Studies, http://lawlib.slu.edu/healthcenter
One of the most heavily used features of the St Louis University Web site is "Selected Internet Resources in Health Law and Policy," an annotated guide to information sources on health law on the Internet. This continually updated guide provides a starting point for using the Internet to research health law and policy. It also supplies short reviews of Web sites providing health law and policy information. These reviews describe the contents of the site, its accessibility, and its usefulness. Visitors to the site are able to hyperlink to these sites and others.

Service Employees International Union, www.seiu.org

Social Security Administration, www.ssa.gov
This site includes the full text of the Social Security Act, recent legislation, testimony before Congress by social security officials, and complete social security rulings from 1960 through 1997.

SoftWatch, www.softwatch.com

State of New York, Department of Health-Consumer Section, www.health.state.ny.us

StatPath Group, www.statpath.com

Tax Analysts Home Page, www.tax.org
Tax Analysts operates twenty-one Internet sites on specified areas of taxation.

Telemedicine Information Exchange, www.telemed.org
This site was created and is maintained by the Telemedicine Research Center, with major support from the National Library of Medicine. It includes a subfile on legal issues, links, publications, and legislation.

THOMAS, http://thomas.loc.gov
Library of Congress legislative information via the Iternet.

US Agency for Health Care Policy and Research, www.ahcpr.gov

US Code Annotated, www.law.cornell.edu
This server offers recent and historic US Supreme Court opinions, a hypertext version of the full *United States Code,* US Constitution, *Federal Rules of Evidence* and *Federal Rules of Civil Procedure,* and recent opinions of the New York Court of Appeals.

US Department of Health and Human Services Policy Directory, www.dhhs.gov

US Food and Drug Administration, www.fda.gov

University HealthSystem Consortium (UHC), www.uhc.edu

University Law Review Project,
www.lawreview.org
This site attempts to collect links to law-review Web sites.

Vanderbilt Institute for Public Policy
Studies (VIPF), www.vanderbilt.edu
Under the direction of Professor James F. Blumstein, the Vanderbilt Institute for Public Policy Studies examines health care regulation and evolving roles in hospital management, how the legal system affects or constrains the evolution of the health care marketplace, and federal fraud and abuse laws. The center holds an annual seminar on medical malpractice for state supreme court justices.

Washburn University Law School,
www.washlaw.edu
Contains a wide spectrum of legal information.

WebTaxi, www.webtaxi.com
This is a navigational service designed to help Internet users conveniently search the Web. This free service was developed to offer efficient access to search engines, newsgroups, and thousands of hard-to-reach databases.

Webdoctor, www.gretmar.com/
webdoctor/journals.html
Contains on-line medical journal articles.

Women in Managed Care, Inc,
www.wimc.org

World Health Organization,
www.who.org

Yahoo! Health Directory,
www.dir.yahoo.com/health

Index

Equal Pay Act of 1963 (EPA), 143
ERISA plans, 179
Errors-and-omissions insurance coverage, 55
Estate planning, 25, 28–29
Ethics in Patient Referrals Act, 113
Evans v Technology Applications & Service Co, 171
Excess insurance coverage, 58, 59
Exclusion(s), 16–18
  in business property insurance policies, 65
  from federal health care programs in
    professional liability insurance policies, 58
  mandatory, 16–17
  permissive, 16–18
Exclusive contracting, 135
Expert testimony, 75, 76
Extended reporting endorsement, 57
Ezekwo v NYC Health & Hospitals Corp, 139

F

Fair Labor Standards Act (FLSA), 161
False Claims Act, 11, 13, 14–15, 19
False statements relating to health care matters
  (18 USC § 1035), 11, 13
Family and Medical Leave Act (FMLA) of 1993,
  155–156, 157, 160–161
Family trust, 29
Fanny v Berman, 105
Farragher v City of Boca Raton, 171
Fazen, Marianne F., 124
Federal health care offense, defined, 11
Federal Trade Commission (FTC), 187, 189
Federation of Physicians and Dentists (FPD), 178,
  188–189
Federation of State Physicians' Health
  Programs, 48
Felty v Graves-Humphreys Co, 171
First National Guild for Providers of the Lower
  Extremities, 189
Fisher, E. A., 124
Fitness-for-duty medical examinations,
  154, 170
Flynn, Michael, 92
Foundation-model integrated delivery system
  (IDS), 119–120
401(k) plans, 24
Fozovsky, Fay A., 105
Franklin, Benjamin, 29
Franklin, James C., 167–168
Front pay, 160

G

Gaba, David, 53
Gardner, Steven, 92
Gardner v Aetna Cas & Sur Co, 67
Garrow v Elizabeth Gen Hosp & Dispensary, 139
Gender discrimination, 143–147, 171
Gerner, C. J., 53
Gifford, Daniel J., 191
Gifts, 24–25, 26–27, 29
Githens, P. B., 53
Glassman, Myron, 53
Glassman, Nanci, 53
Gold, Joshua, 67
Goldberg v B. Green and Company, 168
Golin, Carol Brierly, 63
Gompers v Bucks Stove & Range Co, 191
Good faith consent, 100–101
Good Samaritan laws, 77–78
Gorab v Zook, 53
Grenier v Cynamid Plastics, 170
Grievance procedures, 156, 162–164
Griso, Thomas, 106
Group Practice without Walls (GPWW), 111–113,
  114
Guerrero v Burlington County Memorial Hospital, 139

H

Haas, Doni, RN, 50
Halperin v Abacers Technology Corp, 169
Hammer clause, 61
Hannon v Turnage, 139
Harassment, 142, 145–147, 161, 162–163, 166
Harding v Winn-Dixie Stores, 169
Harris v Forklift Sys, 168
Hartsell v Duplex Products, 170
Hazen Paper Co v Biggins, 168, 171
Healow v Anesthesia Partners, Inc, 139
Health and Human Services, US Department of,
  8, 132
Health care benefit program, defined, 11
Health care expenditures, 8
Health Care Financing Administration, 117
Health care fraud (18 USC § 1347), 12
Health care fraud and abuse, 7–29
  asset forfeiture, 9, 11, 15–16
  benefit program, defined, 11
  civil remedies, 13–14
  competent representation and, 10
  convictions for, 8

Professional liability insurance *continued*
  defense counsel, provision and selection of,
    59–60, 71
  extended reporting endorsement, 57
  failure to obtain/maintain, 129
  policy limits, 58–59
  punitive damages, coverage for, 61–62, 78
  retroactive dates, 57
  settlement, control of, 60–61
  staff coverage, 62
  tail coverage, 57
  type of policy, 56–57
Professional-practice standard of disclosure,
    96–97, 98–99
Property insurance, 64–65
Protected property interest, 127, 139
Proxy consent, 100–101
Punitive damages, 61–62, 78

Q

Quid pro quo harassment, 146
Qui tam provisions, 14

R

Racial discrimination, 143–147
Reasonable accommodation, 150, 151, 153, 160
Reasonable cause, 158–159
Record-keeping, 40 (*see also* Documentation)
Reduction-in-workforce discrimination cases, 148–149
Reed, Marie C., 53
Referrals, 44–45
Refusal of treatment, 38, 96, 99
Rehabilitation Act of 1973, 130, 149–150
Reisner, R., 106
Religious discrimination, 147–148
Reservation-of-rights letter, 71
Resident physicians, 176, 178
Respondeat superior doctrine, 41
Responsibility, acceptance of, 49
Restraint of trade, 181
Retaliation claims, 156–157, 164, 170
Retirement plans, 24
Risks, disclosure of, 36, 38, 53, 95
Robbins v United Parcel Service, 170
Ross, Lainie Friedman, 106
Ross v Communications Satellite Corp, 170
Rouwenhorst, Robert C., 91
Rozovsky, Fay A., 105, 138
Russell v Harwick, 105

Rustad, Michael, 67
Ryan, C. R., 53

S

St Mary's Honor Center v Hicks, 168
St. Peter, Robert, 53
Salis v United States, 105
*Sandcrest Outpatient Services v Cumberland
    County Hospital System, Inc.,* 139
Schapiro, Renie, 124
Schloendorff v Society of New York Hospital, 105
School Bd of Nassau County v Arline, 169
*Schreiber v Physicians Insurance Company of
    Wisconsin,* 53
Schroeder, Steven A., 124
Scripps Clinic, 115
Second opinions, 45
Self-employed physicians, 174–176, 182–184,
    186–188
Seniority, 149
Service Employees International Union, 173, 179,
    190
Sethi, Amarit Singh, 191
Sexual harassment, 142, 145–147, 161, 162–163, 166
Sexual misconduct, 41
Shahawy v Harrison, 139
Shapiro v Thompson, 138
Sharrow v Bailey, 170
Shortell, Stephen M., 138
Siegel v Mt Sinai Hospital of Cleveland, 105
Silver, Julie K., 123
Simkins v Moses H. Cone Mem Hosp, 139
Simon, R., 106
Single-specialty group practice, 114–115
Sloan, Frank A., 53, 92
Slobogin, C., 106
Social Services Block Grant Program, 16
Solo practice, 109–110
*Sosa v Board of Managers of Val Verde Memorial
    Hospital,* 128, 139
Southeastern Community College v Davis, 169
Srsic, Daniel W., 191
Staff, selection and training of, 41–43
Staff-model integrated delivery system (IDS),
    120–121
Standard of care, controlling, 45–47
Stark I Act, 113
Statutes of limitation, 40, 52, 57, 74
Statutes of repose, 74
Stern, Andrew, 190
Substance abuse, 47–48, 130

Substituted consent, 103–104
Substituted-judgment analysis, 103
Summary judgment, 85–86
Supervisory liability, 42–43
Sussman v Overlook Hospital Association, 129

T

Taft-Hartley Act (*see* Labor Management
     Relations Act)
Tail coverage, 57
Tax-deferred retirement plans, 24
Taxes, 23–29
  capital gains, 24
  charitable giving, 25–26
  decreasing taxable income, 24–25
  establishing domicile, 27–28
  estate planning, 25, 28–29
  federal income tax, 23–24
  gifts, 24–25, 26–27, 29
  increasing deductions, 25–27
Tax-exempt bonds, 25
Texas Medical Disclosure Panel, 102
Theft or embezzlement in connection with health
     care (18 USC § 669), 11, 12–13
Therapeutic privilege, 100
Third-party claims, 73, 78
*Thomas Davis Medical Centers v Federation of
     Physicians and Dentists,* 190
Title VII, Civil Rights Act of 1964, 143–148,
     156–157, 160, 161
Tomes, Jonathan P., 106
Training
  in crisis management, 49
  to heighten employee sensitivity, 166
  as part of a compliance plan, 19
  physician's own, 43–44
  as a way to prevent medical malpractice
     claims, 42
Trans World Airlines v Hardison, 168
Treatment review boards, 101
Truman v Thomas, 105
Turpen v Missouri-Kansas-Texas RR Co, 168

U

Umbrella insurance policies, 66
UM/UIM insurance coverage, 66
Unanticipated conditions during surgery, 99–100
Undue hardship concept, 147, 153, 160, 168
Union of American Physicians and Dentists
     (UPD), 178, 188

United States v Little Al, 21
United States v $95,945.18, 21
*United States v One Parcel at 7715 Betsy Bruce
     Lane,* 21
United States v Paccione, 67
United States v Rylander, 21
United States v A Single Family Residence, 21
United States v Thomas, 21
United States v Wollman, 21
Unitrust, 27
*University of California v Public Employment
     Relations Board,* 191

V

van der Vaart, Sandra Dillard, 139, 140

W

Wachter, Robert M., 124
Wagner Act (see National Labor Relations Act)
Waiver of explanation, 100
Wallen v Minnesota Dept of Corrections, 169
*Walton v Mental Health Association of Southeastern
     Pennsylvania,* 169
Ware, John E., 53
Waste disposal, 65
Watson v Worthy, 105
Wear, Stephen, 106
Whistleblowers, 14–15, 19
White, Becky Cox, 106
White v Rockingham Radiologists, Ltd, 139
Wigal, Grace J., 138
Wilkinson v Vesey, 97
Willful blindness, 14
*Williams v Enterprise Leasing Company of
     Norfolk/Richmond,* 171
Wire fraud, 11, 12
Woodard v Lehman, 171
Woodbury v McKinnon, 138
Woodhouse v Magnolia Hospital, 168
Wright, Calvin, 92
Wrightson v Pizza Hut of America, Inc, 168
Written discovery, 83–84
Wrongful discharge, 144, 150, 151, 171

Z

Zero-tolerance policy, 9
Zucker, Abigail, 124